TORONTO
TO 1918

The History of Canadian Cities

TORONTO
TO 1918
An Illustrated History

J.M.S. Careless

James Lorimer & Company, Publishers
and
National Museum of Man,
National Museums of Canada
Toronto 1984

To my wife, who listened,
encouraged, and always eased the way.

ISBN 0-88862-665-7 cloth

Cover design: Don Fernley
Maps: Assembly Dave Hunter

Canadian Cataloguing in Publication Data

Careless, J. M. S., 1919-
Toronto to 1918

(The History of Canadian cities series)
Co-published with the National Museum of Man, National Museums of Canada.
Bibliography: p. 212
Includes index.

1. Toronto (Ont.) — History. I. National Museum of Man (Canada). II. Title. III. Series: The History of Canadian Cities.

FC3097.4.C37 1983   971.3'541   C83-099128-X
F1059.5.T6857C37 1983

James Lorimer & Company, Publishers
Egerton Ryerson Memorial Building
35 Britain Street
Toronto, Ontario M5A 1R7

Printed and bound in Canada
6 5 4 3 2 1   84 85 86 87 88 89

Illustration Credits

City of Toronto Archives (CTA): 176 top, back flap. **CTA, James Collection**: front cover, 2, 148, 156, 159 bottom right, 160 bottom, 165, 167 top, 171, 177, 178, 184 upper left, 188 bottom, 191, 195, 196 upper left, 198, 199, backcover lower right. **CTA, Department of Public Works Collection**: 159 except bottom right, 168 bottom. **CTA Board of Education Collection**: 188 top. **Metropolitan Toronto Library Board**: 18, 20, 24, 28, 32, 34, 36, 37, 40, 44, 45 bottom, 49, 50, 53 top, 55, 61, 63, 65 top, 66 right, 67, 68, 72, 75, 79, 84, 88, 90 bottom left and upper right, 92, 93, 95, 99, 108, 110, 113 bottom right, 114, 116 left, 119, 121, 123, 127, 129, 131, 134, 135 bottom, 140 left, 142, 144, 164 top, 176 bottom, 180, 186, 189, back cover upper right. **Public Archives Canada**: 52, 53 bottom, 65 bottom, 82, 164 bottom, 167 bottom, 196 top right and bottom right. **PAC/Foreign and Commonwealth Office, United Kingdom**: 66 left, 85, 87, 90 upper left and bottom right. **Royal Ontario Museum**: 8, 12, 22, 23, 26, 42, 45 top, 47, 57, 70, 98, 106, back cover upper left. **Archives of Ontario**: 80, 103 left, 105, 135 upper right, 140 right, 160 top, 173, 182, 196 bottom left, 197. **Toronto Transit Commission**: 132, 146, 184 except upper right, 185, back cover bottom left. **Massey-Ferguson Limited**: 113 top and bottom left, 153. **Toronto Jewish Congress/Canadian Jewish Congress, Ontario Region Archives**: 158, 170. **Metropolitan Toronto Police Museum**: 145, 192. **Consumers' Gas Company Limited**: 168 top. **Art Gallery of Ontario, Toronto** (Gift of the CNE Association, 1965): 174. **Archives, Eaton's of Canada Ltd.**: 116 right. **Percy J. Robinson**, *Toronto During the French Regime* (Toronto, 1933): 10. **The Canada Newspaper Cartoonists' Association**, *Torontonians As We See 'Em* (Toronto, 1905): 151. **Freya Hahn Collection**: 135 upper left. **Mrs. Alfred A. Stanley Collection**: 162. **Ralph Greenhill Collection**: 103 right.

Table of Contents

Foreword: The History of Canadian Cities Series   6

Acknowledgements   7

Introduction: The Lakeland Site   9

Chapter One: The Government Village, 1793–1825   19

Chapter Two: The Commercial Port-Town, 1825–47   43

Chapter Three: The Railway and Regional Hub, 1847–71   71

Chapter Four: The Industrializing City, 1871–95   109

Chapter Five: The Nearly National Metropolis, 1895–1918   149

Appendix: Statistical Tables   200

Notes   204

Suggestions for Further Reading and Research   212

Index   217

Appendix
List of Tables

   I The Growth of Manufacturing in Toronto, 1871–1921
  II Males/Females in Toronto's Population, 1831–1921
 III Toronto as a Percentage of Ontario Population, 1831–1921
 IV Population Growth in Central Canadian Cities, 1851–1921
  V Population Growth in Toronto, 1801–1921
 VI Birthplace of Toronto's Population, 1851–1921
VII Major Religious Affiliations of Toronto's Population, 1841–1921
VIII Ethnic Origins of Toronto's Population, 1851–1921
 IX Age Composition of Toronto's Population, 1831–1921
  X Value of Building Permits Issued in City of Toronto, 1901–14
 XI Bank Clearings for Toronto, 1895–1918
XII City of Toronto Assessments, 1834–1921
XIII City of Toronto Mayors, 1834–1921

List of Maps

1. The Site of Toronto   14

2. The Location of Toronto   16

3. The Town to 1830   38

4. Toronto's Main Rail Links, 1851–86   78

5. The City to the 1860s   91

6. Toronto Annexations, 1834–1914   125

7. Municipal Divisions: 1834, 1880 and 1908   126

8. Toronto's Inner City to the 1900s   137

9. Toronto by 1915: Land Use   181

Foreword
The History of Canadian Cities Series

The History of Canadian Cities Series is a project of the History Division, National Museum of Man (National Museums of Canada). The project was begun in 1977 to respond to a growing demand for more popular publications to complement the already well-established scholarly publications programs of the Museum. The purpose of this series is to offer the general public a stimulating insight into Canada's urban past. Over the next several years, the Museum, in cooperation with James Lorimer and Company, plans to publish a number of volumes dealing with such varied communities as Montreal and Kingston, Halifax and Quebec City, Ottawa and Sherbrooke.

It is the hope of the National Museum of Man that the publication of these books will provide the public with information on Canadian cities in visually attractive and highly readable form. At the same time, the plan of the series is to have authors follow a similar format, and the result, it is anticipated, will be a systematic, interpretative and comprehensive account of the urban experience in many Canadian communities. Eventually, as new volumes are completed, *The History of Canadian Cities Series* will be a major step along the path to a general and comparative study of Canada's urban development.

The form for this series — the individual urban biography — is based on a desire to examine all aspects of community development and to relate the parts to a larger context. The series is also based on the belief that, while each city has a distinct personality that deserves to be discovered, the volumes must also provide analysis that will lift the narrative of a city's experience to the level where it will elucidate questions that are of concern to Canadians generally. These questions include such issues as ethnic relationships, regionalism, provincial-municipal interaction, social mobility, labour-management relationships, urban planning and general economic development.

In this volume, J. M. S. Careless details the exciting early history of Toronto from its origins through to the end of the Great War. The various steps in the city's evolution — fur-trade depot, village, port, commercial town, railway and regional hub, "nearly" national metropolis — are traced in the pleasing writing style that has graced Professor Careless's earlier works. For each period, Careless weaves together the city's economic, social and political history and describes and analyses the changing population and urban landscape.

This volume, which appears in time for Toronto's sesquicentennial celebrations, has been prepared by one of Canada's most eminent historians. Professor Careless, widely known for his many award-winning works on Canadian history, is also a well-known urban historian, and his work in this field is continued in this fine study. A companion volume to this book, *Toronto Since 1918: An Illustrated History*, by James T. Lemon, is scheduled for publication during 1984.

Professor Careless's text has been enhanced by well-selected paintings, engravings, maps and photographs. This illustrative material is not only visually enjoyable, it also plays an essential part in re-creating the past. While illustrations and maps cannot by themselves replace the written word, they can be used as a primary source in a way equivalent to more-traditional sources. The fine collection of illustrations in this volume captures images of a wide variety of situations in Toronto, allowing a later generation to better understand the forms, structures, fashions and group interactions of an earlier period.

Already published in this series:
Alan Artibise, *Winnipeg* (1977)
Max Foran, *Calgary* (1978)
Patricia Roy, *Vancouver* (1980)
John Weaver, *Hamilton* (1982)

Alan F. J. Artibise
General Editor

Acknowledgements

Virtually any scholarly work of history is a cooperative effort, even when it has nominally one author. I thus have to thank a number of individuals and the staffs of institutions who together shared sizeably in the making of this book. Taking the latter group first, I must especially acknowledge the constant aid received at the Public Archives of Canada, Archives of Ontario, City of Toronto Archives, Metropolitan Toronto Public Library, and Thomas Fisher Rare Book Library of the University of Toronto. Yet that list could be much enlarged, to include (among still more) the Library of Congress in Washington, the libraries and museums of McGill University in Montreal, those of Harvard University in Cambridge, the Royal Ontario Museum, the United Church of Canada Archives, and the Library of the Foreign and Commonwealth Office of the United Kingdom, which gave permission to use invaluable early photographs of Toronto in the 1850s.

Turning to individuals, I am grateful to my colleague at the University of Toronto, Professor James Lemon (whose study of Toronto in this series will follow on from mine), for making available to me research papers done in the Department of Geography on our common city of concern. I am no less grateful to Miss Edith Firth, a prime authority indeed on early Toronto, for her advice and expertise so cordially provided; to Mr. Stephen Otto, who kindly gave me the benefit of his inquiries into the architects of the nineteenth-century city; and to an old friend and former student, Professor Frederick Armstrong of the University of Western Ontario, himself a leading and well-published scholar on Toronto's history. In fact I owe him a particular debt, not only for generous aid throughout, but for reading and constructively criticizing my manuscript to very valuable effect. In Professor Alan Artibise of the University of Winnipeg I had an ideal series editor, fully knowledgeable and helpful, but judicious and guiding, as an editorial chief should be; and with Ted Mumford, as editor for the publisher, I had a happy and effective working partnership, which finally got the volume out.

I am also most appreciative of grants received from the National Museum of Man and of the University of Toronto's funds provided to holders of the rank of university professor, which went towards costs incurred in travel and research, typing and acquisition of illustrations.

Besides all this, I should express my thanks to my daughter Andrea Careless, now of Victoria, whose several previous years of research into economic data on the growth of Canadian cities were pursued towards my still-intended broader study of Canadian metropolitan development; yet the materials she amassed and organized that pertained to Toronto could be, and have been, applied to the present book. Here, however, I must above all acknowledge the key part played by Mrs. Gail Crawford, my research assistant, who over the past three years worked specifically on this Toronto volume. She efficiently investigated the local repositories, especially the city archives, filling in gaps in my earlier inquiries or updating them. She made initial sweeps for maps, illustrations and statistical sources, drafted the appendix tables, and typed the completed manuscript. Altogether, I could not have been more admirably assisted.

Finally, I should pay warm tribute to my graduate students at Toronto for their theses, studies and research work over two decades in seminars on Ontario regional and Canadian metropolitan history. From all they taught me, I might have made this a much fuller account of the rise of Toronto, were it not that the text space was strictly, though inevitably, confined by the requirements of an extensively illustrated study.

J. M. S. Careless
May 1984

The unsettled site of Toronto in 1793: the harbour looking west to the entrance, the main shoreline on the right, the protecting peninsula (later island) to the left.

Introduction
The Lakeland Site

A city is shaped by people, their wants and ideas, their organization and technology. Yet it is shaped as well by the location and nature of its site, the place where people gather. Thus it was with Toronto. Long before it became an urban community, long before incoming Europeans reached it, Toronto was a recognized location in wilderness America, frequented by native peoples of the surrounding Great Lakes country. For this lakeshore landing in the forests near the head of Lake Ontario gave access to an age-old Indian travel path that ran north to reach Georgian Bay on Lake Huron. In effect, this was a shortcut between the Lower and the Upper Great Lakes across the neck of the southern Ontario peninsula. And so the Toronto location had a specific significance of site: as a junction-point of land and water routes that transected the Great Lakes region. Other cities of Canada have their own distinctive site features; many similarly began as vantage points on some established course of travel. But in Toronto's case, its accessible lake harbour, low, easily traversed shoreline, and gate position on a passage through the midst of southern Ontario, were distinguishing aspects from prehistoric times — and destined to have repeated influence on its subsequent history.

"TORONTO" BEFORE URBAN OCCUPATION

The Indian way north from Toronto (which may originally have meant "Trees in the Water," though "Lake Opening" and "Place of Meeting" are other possibilities) could make use of several river entries around the landing area.[1] Mainly, however, the route ran up the valley of the Humber, across to the Holland, which flows into Lake Simcoe, and from there by other water links to Georgian Bay. The first stage of this route followed a trail some twenty-eight miles along the wooded banks of the Humber, evidently because that stream was much impeded by fallen timber and beaver dams.

The Toronto Trail or Carrying Place was thus a wearing portage. Still, in an age when long-distance travel moved by canoe, this direct path cut off many more hundreds of miles by the long way from the Lower to Upper Lakes. Even in far later days, this short land crossing would have enduring value, to be realized anew by roads and rails. But during Indian times it was a feasible way through a forest wilderness. Hence the Carrying Place at its start saw repeated transits, and shifting encampments or longer-lasting villages dotted about the landing-ground as this primitive traffic pattern went on through time without written record.

The Toronto route entered written history when French venturers probed up the St. Lawrence into the Great Lakes region from their trading base at Quebec. Étienne Brulé most probably travelled the "passage de Toronto," as the French came to call it, as early as 1615. The passage also figured in the warfare between the Huron Indians around Georgian Bay and the Iroquois Confederacy south of Lake Ontario, which saw the crushing of the Hurons by mid-century. Thereafter a sizeable Iroquois (Seneca) village, Teiaiagon, emerged by the Humber entry to the Toronto Trail. Here, in France's own expansion westward, explorers, fur traders and missionaries arrived to cross the passage, while French supply boats used the harbour. Moreover, fur dealers up from the English base at Albany on the Hudson visited Teiaiagon as well.[2]

In ensuing wars, which began with Indian conflict in the 1680s but became an Anglo-French imperial contest lasting to 1713, the Seneca abandoned the Teiaiagon site to the roving Mississauga; and these hunter-gatherers were not village-dwellers, although they maintained encampments and fisheries around the landing-place. Then in 1720 the French established their own post at Toronto, largely to intercept fur cargoes from north and west before they flowed on across Lake Ontario to English rivals in the expanding colony of New York. Here was a further indication of

Toronto's site significance, for that junction-point might assuredly feed trade either eastward to the St. Lawrence and Montreal, now the main French commercial base, or southward to the Mohawk-Hudson system and its British port, New York.

In any event, the first French post at Toronto, a modest storehouse closed by 1730, was merely an adjunct to a much more substantial fort at Niagara, France's bulwark against British penetration of its Great Lakes empire. Increasing British pressures, however, and by 1749 designs to strengthen the inland chain of French forts, led to the re-establishment of a post at Toronto. Fort Rouillé, or Fort Toronto, was erected there in 1751 on the shore some three miles east of the Humber (in the grounds of the present Canadian National Exhibition). It was truly a fort, with timber bastions linked by palisades, mounting four small cannons, and garrisoned by a few soldiers plus some labourers and batteaux transport men — Toronto's first little military embodiment.[3] And in 1754 imperial war returned again, although its battles took place elsewhere. In July 1759 Fort Niagara fell to British attack, whereupon the French force at Toronto burned their far weaker fort and withdrew. Two months later, the British capture of the key stronghold of Quebec spelled the end of French rule in Canada. It was already over at Toronto, leaving only blackened timber ruins in a clearing of some 300 acres.

Under British authority, fur trading revived in the Toronto area, and by the 1780s Jean Baptiste Rousseau had become the established local trader, maintaining a house and post near the Humber mouth well into the next decade. Moreover, partners in Montreal's powerful North West Company grew interested in the Toronto Passage, as potentially a less costly way to their far-flung western fur domain than via the many portages of the traditional Ottawa River route to the Upper Lakes. Nonetheless, the Toronto site still lay within the fur wilderness world — until the American Revolution loosed a transformation. While that struggle went on from 1775 to 1783, it is true that little altered. The major British inland strong points of Niagara and Detroit held firm, and the Toronto locale remained a quiet backwater. Yet the outcome of the Revolution was greatly to affect the site, which had thus stayed securely within the British Empire.

Above all, the peace of 1783 that recognized the United States drew an international boundary down the Great Lakes. Toronto again fronted on a vulnerable border, shielded only by some twenty

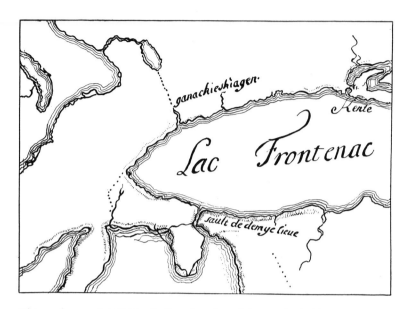

This crude map of 1674 by the French explorer Joliet marks the Toronto Passage between Lake Ontario ("Frontenac") and Georgian Bay via Lake Simcoe. An Indian village then on the route is named, as is "Kente" (Quinte), a French mission site. As well, an early reference is made to Niagara Falls: "A falls of half a league."

miles of lake. And with an unfriendly, increasingly powerful American republic opposite, that could be an uneasy position for years ahead. Yet the boundary also signified that Toronto would be part of a separate entity in America — the Canadian entity, as it evolved — and so would take shape within Canadian patterns of government and growth. The American water border might readily be crossed, certainly by the peaceful movement of goods, people and ideas; yet it could also be a dividing screen, behind which Toronto looked to British links and backing and secured its own realm to develop. Further, the political fact of the border soon led to political decisions to found a town at the Toronto site as an inland centre to sustain the British side of the lake line. In a real sense, the Revolution boundary impelled the rise of Toronto.

Beyond all this, the Revolution produced a movement of people to occupy the empty British inlands: loyal American colonials who turned northward from the vengeance of their republican foes. From 1784 these Loyalists settled on the upper St. Lawrence west to the foot of Lake Ontario where the town of Kingston now began to rise, and onward to the Bay of Quinte. Others cleared farms in the Niagara Peninsula; still others gathered near Detroit on Lake Erie shores. Their numbers grew yearly through continued influx and a vigorous birthrate. Accordingly, in 1791 the new British province of Upper Canada was erected for the 14,000 predominantly anglophone inhabitants of these areas beyond the French Canadian lands of the St. Lawrence valley — henceforth Lower Canada. And Upper Canada received a basic framework of English law and institutions, no less basic for Toronto at its core.

Settlement scarcely reached the Toronto locality until 1793. But well before, as it spread towards that site from both ends of Lake Ontario, the signs of change were plain. Several prominent figures in Montreal, including leading North West Company members, petitioned for land grants in the Toronto district, with settlement projects and trade monopolies in mind or plans to develop communications over the Toronto Passage. In response, Lord Dorchester, then British governor-in-chief at Quebec, moved to acquire Indian land rights in the vicinity. In 1787 the Toronto Purchase was effected, whereby for some £1,700 in cash and goods the Mississauga conveyed title to a fourteen-mile stretch along the lakefront, from present-day Scarborough westward past the Humber to the Etobicoke, and inland reaching back some twenty-eight miles: truly a bargain-basement deal.[4] In 1788 the Toronto Purchase was first surveyed, while Captain Gother Mann of the Royal Engineers drafted a plan for a Toronto townsite, featuring a one-mile square of city lots adjacent to the harbour entry, bordered by an open common with larger residential lots beyond. This was rather an artificial exercise in late eighteenth-century imperial town planning, yet indicated how actively Toronto was now being considered as a prime interior site for urban development. Moreover, Governor Dorchester further displayed his interest in developing Toronto when in 1791 he ordered grants there, totalling 2,400 acres, for three of his chief land petitioners.[5]

The grants were not to be completed. The creation of Upper Canada that very year produced a new government with authority over its provincial lands, and under a lieutenant-governor with ideas of his own, Colonel John Graves Simcoe. Simcoe's personal judgment that a town should be established at Toronto was not necessarily opposed to Dorchester's, but characteristically he came to it through his own strong opinions. He arrived in Upper Canada early in 1792, beginning government at Kingston, but he soon moved to Niagara, deeper in the province, to make it his provincial capital. Yet the colonel was not satisfied with "the contemptible Fortress of Niagara" under American guns across a narrow river.[6] He looked instead to more centrally located Toronto, behind the wider water reach of Lake Ontario, where a garrison and governance could be more safely based and where the Toronto Passage gave access to the whole Upper Lakes country beyond. In 1793 he arrived at that site to direct its occupation, his ship piloted into harbour by the resident fur trader, Rousseau. It was a symbolic juncture of old and new: between a fur depot enclosed in primal forests and the rise of a town in an emerging countryside.

SITE FEATURES AND TORONTO'S GROWTH

The pre-settlement era had already revealed vital geographic aspects of Toronto's site: its focal lake harbour with access to the passage inland, its location on through-traffic routes up the Great Lakes and outward via either the Hudson or the St. Lawrence, and its boundary position, set across from the mounting American presence in the continental interior. Yet other features of Toronto's physical setting became significant once the lakeland site became a town.

Clearly it had always mattered for a landing-ground at the

The Don Valley in the 1790s. Sketched probably from Governor Simcoe's homesite above the river, this view conveys the thick woods stretching inland from the shore.

Toronto site that its lakeside margin was low and fairly flat (Map 1). It was of much more consequence for a town, however, that here there was an outspread, gentle-sloping shore plain for occupation, with effective communication inward. And if there was a fairly sudden rise of fifty to seventy-five feet behind this plain (just below the present east-west artery of St. Clair Avenue, where the shoreline of long-vanished glacial Lake Iroquois sweeps up), this had still been negotiable along various stream channels by canoes in portage, and remained a problem rather than a barrier for later forms of transport. Moreover, ravines and creek beds cut deeply into the rise, in time affording easier gradients for roads or railways in the ascent from the shore level to higher plains. And from here again there were no great surface obstacles to moving on through the rolling hills that spread northward in order to reach Lake Simcoe, then Georgian Bay and the Upper Lakes.[7]

Still, the original home and continuing core of Toronto was the Shore or City Plain proper, the low waterside area that stretched some two to three miles inland and extended roughly from the Don River on the east to the Humber on the west. East of the Don, the shoreline began to rise to the Scarborough Bluffs, clay cliffs about 350 feet high, soon pinching out the plain to narrow beaches. West of the Humber, the shore similarly became less sheltered, if not as raised. But centred in between lay broad Toronto Bay or harbour, protected from the open lake and all but enclosed by a long, low, sandy peninsula cloaked with trees. Here there was plenty of room and depth of water for ships to berth by the shielded harbourside. The one drawback was that sailing vessels often had to beat out the bay's westerly facing entrance against prevailing winds. Yet the coming of steamboats in the 1820s subsequently met that difficulty, further to be solved when storms in the 1850s carved a new channel through the eastern end of the peninsula, the Eastern Gap that also created Toronto Island.

The sheltered bay and harbourfront, the low-lying expanse behind, and beyond that again, the rise to higher plains, these were the surface features that most basically affected the layout of urban Toronto, its streets and transport systems, land uses, and in due course the distribution of its business and residential districts. They also raised problems of their own. For one thing, the nearly flat Shore Plain imposed difficulties of drainage, and its churned-up masses of thick clay often made streets in the young town a succession of mud holes. For another, parts of this waterside plain initially were dank mosquito-ridden marshes, which also affected building, not to mention health, while the ground-rise behind it could block off some roads or make their development more expensive. Still further — if less material — Toronto had no particular power of natural setting, no mountain backdrop, no rugged seacoast walls or sweep of river, just a flat shore backed by low lines of inland hills. Nevertheless, in general it had a very accessible, highly usable site. And perhaps any attractiveness of setting would have to lie in the broad, shimmering lake before it, the wooded curve of Toronto Island, the spreading farm landscape that backed the town, and its rising buildings themselves.

The spread of farming was certainly vital to a young Toronto, not only to provide food supplies for the town-dwellers, but also markets for their wares in agricultural districts that emerged around it. Moreover, the fact that the whole locality lay in the midst of the generally fertile soils of future southern Ontario meant that it was excellently placed to grow with the trade of a rising agricultural community. In this regard, climate also was decidedly significant. The Great Lakes region receives ample, fairly regular rainfall, and its Lower Lakes area enjoys a longer, warmer growing season than most parts of Canada. Toronto's climate, moderate in general geographic terms, does have its own excesses: from oppressively hot and humid spells in summer to bitter, windy cold snaps in winter or too many raw, melt-and-freeze spring days. Still, it lies outside heavy-snow belts, does not face the cold extremes of northern Ontario or the prairies, and long, pleasant autumns help make up for the summertime invasions of steamy southern air, or springs that come all too reluctantly and waywardly. In short, an emerging Toronto and its surroundings not only had a sufficiently moderated, moist climate in which a considerable range of farming could flourish, but also had less-exacting needs for fuel and shelter than the great mass of Canada.

All the same, there were abundant resources for fuel and shelter in the thick forests of the area. Clearing the dense growth posed heavy tasks for incoming urban settlers of the 1790s, but felled trees provided town-building lumber from early water-driven mills on the Humber and Don, while burning the plentiful excess produced valuable potash for export. Good timber was also on hand for shipbuilding, wagons or furnishings. And quantities of wood from

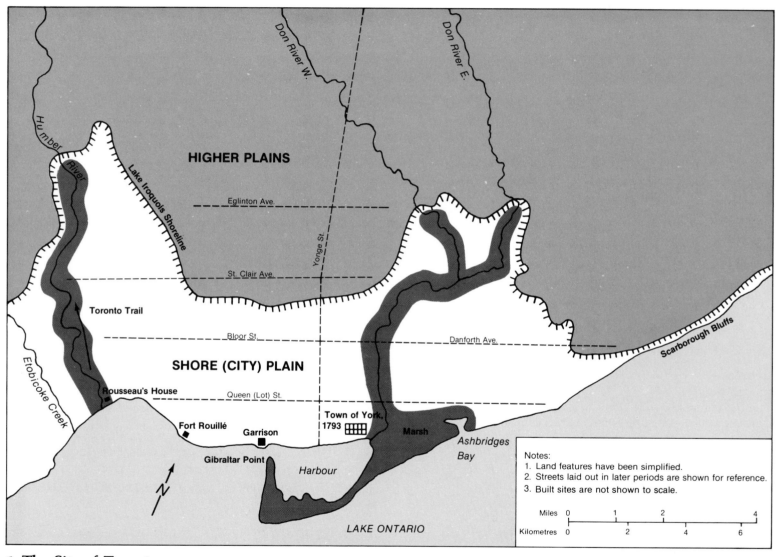

HIGHER PLAINS

Don River W.

Don River E.

Humber River

Lake Iroquois Shoreline

Eglinton Ave.

Yonge St.

St. Clair Ave.

Toronto Trail

Etobicoke Creek

Bloor St.

Danforth Ave.

Scarborough Bluffs

SHORE (CITY) PLAIN

Rousseau's House

Queen (Lot) St.

Town of York, 1793

Fort Rouillé

Garrison

Marsh

Ashbridges Bay

Gibraltar Point

Harbour

LAKE ONTARIO

N

Notes:
1. Land features have been simplified.
2. Streets laid out in later periods are shown for reference.
3. Built sites are not shown to scale.

Miles   0   1   2   4
Kilometres 0   2   4   6

1 The Site of Toronto

farther districts, gathered at the harbour, could be exported as well. Toronto, in fact, became an important lumber shipping point, though not in its early years.

Furthermore, as the pioneering phases passed away, other resources in or about the site entered into its development. Thus the sand and gravel of the vicinity, and good clay beds for brickmaking, began to furnish building materials for a rising brick-and-mortar town in the earlier nineteenth century, one no longer almost wholly shaped in wood. Not shaped in stone, however. Since bedrock here was mostly buried deep beneath clay and gravel plains, with few outcrops, building stone had largely to be shipped in; for instance, it had been brought in to adorn the aspiring Victorian city of the 1850s, by then booming with the railway age. So it was with coal, which became a growing need as local forest timber disappeared, as steamboats and locomotives switched from wood-burning in the later nineteenth century, and as steam-driven industry proliferated in Toronto around the same time. Yet water transport now brought it ample coal (and iron) via the Lakes. And in the early twentieth century, cheap hydroelectric power produced at Niagara Falls provided a whole new energy source for growth. During the same period, similarly, the opening of the Ontario mining and lumbering North made fresh raw materials available down transit routes that led to Toronto. Hence, emerging needs for energy or material supplies were largely met by the city's mounting ability to draw these to itself, thanks particularly to its position on main lines of communication.

Here we come back to location on traffic routes, conceivably the most enduring aspect of Toronto's site significance.[8] Set at the mid-front of what became heavily occupied southern Ontario, agriculturally rich and industrially powerful, the city rose to dominate this valuable heartland through a well-developed transport and communications system — that could not only deliver goods effectively by lake, road and rail, but also radiate the centre's influential press views, its political authority or financial power. Toronto was well placed, besides, to reach northward to more distant trade areas, from the time of the original Toronto Passage to that of twentieth-century mining booms. It could equally reach southward from its Ontario shore to the swelling metropolis of New York or to prosperous American states about the Great Lakes

— all to provide it with traffic, markets, and sources of investment or business expertise (Map 2). To the east, the Lake Ontario–St. Lawrence transport system opened on Montreal, and Toronto remained closely linked to this major Canadian outlet from earliest days, as well as to the power, people and wealth of Britain beyond the Atlantic. To the west, by the later nineteenth century, the city could use trunk routes that led either to American mid-western centres like Chicago or to rising settlements in the northwestern Canadian prairies. At least by the First World War, Toronto had realized manifold advantages from its intersecting position on lines of continental transit across the Great Lakes basin.

Still, everything said so far simply indicates that Toronto had many potentialities if human beings grasped them under suitable conditions in history, not that anything in geographic features predetermined its rise to a great city. Its pre-settlement prelude suggests as much. While the Toronto Carrying Place and Passage had figured repeatedly in the French fur trade, the main lines of that trade had continued to run via the Ottawa route to the northwest or via the Lower Lakes route through Niagara to the Ohio and Mississippi southwest. Thus, Toronto had remained a minor post in between, fairly late to be made a French fort, and by no means having the strategic importance of Montreal as the St. Lawrence gateway to the interior, or even that of other inland forts.[9] Similarly, after the British conquest, Toronto had remained just one of a number of local trading stations along the Lake Ontario shore, any of which well might have become a small settled port once the whole region was finally populated. But then came the running of a man-made British-American boundary across the physical environment of the Great Lakes, and the consequent decision to place a defending, controlling town upon it at Toronto's site. From this point on, the various potentials of that place could come into action, once human enterprise took them up.

In sum, site factors do not necessarily ordain the emergence of a city, but do enter deeply into shaping its growth. Yet that involves as well such human factors as interests, power and work, along with innovation, expectation, and what we consider luck. Out of this amalgam comes an urban community. Out of it came the evolution of a town at Toronto to a regional, then national, Canadian metropolis.

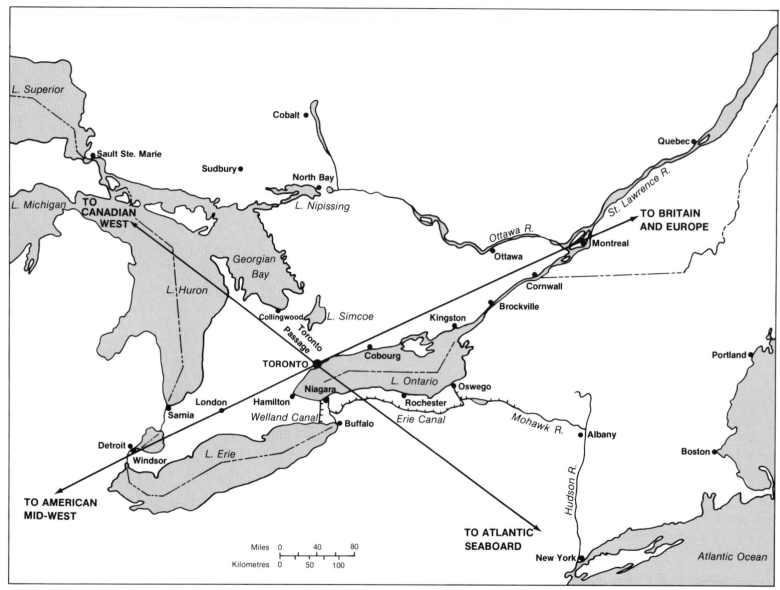

2 Location of Toronto

PATTERNS IN METROPOLITAN DEVELOPMENT

That evolution, which by the world war of 1914–18 had made Toronto second only Montreal in urban size and power in Canada, essentially comprised several main stages in metropolitan development: the process whereby a major city comes to dominate an extensive economic territory or hinterland by controlling its commerce, knitting the area into a transport network, centring many of its industrial activities, and organizing financial services for it. The hinterland territory may well contain many smaller cities and towns with their own lesser tributary districts, but all are linked to the overriding dominance of the master-city. And this metropolitan-hinterland pattern of development, equally evidenced by other leading cities in Canada or in the world beyond, is an integral feature of the whole urbanization of human society.[10]

In Toronto's case, the phases of economic metropolitan growth often overlapped or went on concurrently; but in broadest outline, they occurred most significantly in four successive stages. Firstly, in commerce, the urban community that began in 1793 built up a trading hinterland through providing its surrounding areas with marketing facilities. The initial village settlement acquired a merchant group that distributed goods to the adjacent population and received their products; as a growing port-town, it developed long-range wholesale commerce beyond merely local retail trade; and as a city by 1834 it beat rival nearby centres in thrusts for more hinterland business. Secondly, in transport, this enlarging city now linked its port and spreading commerce to a much wider regional hinterland by way of railways: beginning with the 1850s, long-distance, all-year rail routes vastly improved its land communications, far outclassing slow, seasonal early roads. Thirdly, from about the 1870s, sizeable factory industry arose in and around Toronto as a well-served transport centre, making it an increasing focus of wealth, technological headship and manufacturing supply in Ontario. And fourthly, out of capital derived in commerce, transport and industry emerged financial power, strongly displayed at least by the 1900s in big banking head offices and investment houses; a development which further tied hinterland areas, now reaching national bounds, to the credit-and-debit sway of the commanding metropolis of Toronto. By 1918 all this had taken place, even though new metropolitan growth and further hinterland extensions would scarcely cease for the city at that date.

Yet Toronto's rise did not only display these economic workings. Political factors were also highly important. The original town served as governing seat of Upper Canada; it became a capital again for some years during the union of Upper and Lower Canada in the mid-nineteenth century; and with the much broader Canadian federal union of 1867, it was made the capital of the newly created province of Ontario. The executive, parliamentary, judicial and administrative activities thus established at Toronto gave it special distinction and power even in its youngest village days. And in subsequent periods, political functions that centred in the city kept it dominant as a prime place of decision for the public and private concerns of areas well beyond it. Moreover, Toronto's role as home of prominent elite groups, as a concentration point of major ethnic and religious bodies, and in time as well as headquarters of popular movements or working-class organizations, also gave it widening social holds upon its hinterland. So did the city's influence on cultural developments, through its leading place in provincial education, publishing, professional and artistic life, and generally, over time, through its becoming a central source of information, cultivation and opinion. In evident ways, Toronto's rise to metropolitan status proceeded in much more than solely economic terms.

Accordingly, in tracing the city's growth from the beginnings in 1793 down to 1918, the basic theme can duly follow the development of the original village-capital to metropolitan existence through successive stages of major economic change; but into this there must be woven a series of other constantly related themes. These have to include political behaviour and social patterns among the urban elites and masses, population growth and ethnic composition, cultural activities, the shaping of Toronto's built environment, land uses, and its municipal life and services. Besides that, the urban community has its own internal structure of classes, families and generations. But above all, it remains externally linked with far broader realms, the complementing countryside, the region and the nation, and it responds to forces from beyond their limits also. This wider aspect, too, is bound up with the specific record of Toronto's development to be presented here: from the first settling of the tranquil lakeland site in the 1790s to the thriving Great Lakes metropolis of the young twentieth century.

Simcoe builds his base at Toronto, 1793. C. W. Jefferys's painting portrays the governor and officers supervising military construction by the Queen's Rangers.

Chapter One
The Government Village, 1793–1825

Urban places in North America did not necessarily derive from the settlement of their surrounding countrysides. Often the reverse occurred; a town was founded and frontier settlement spread about it. Notably in Canada, many major centres first began in nearly empty territory. And some came into being, as Toronto did, through specific action to establish an official base of power: to control or defend a territory and maintain government over it. It can well be noted that places as far spread as Halifax and Quebec, Toronto, Regina and Victoria, all initially took form as territorial bases of authority before significant settlement grew up outside them. Moreover, Quebec as the bastion of the seventeenth-century French Empire on the St. Lawrence, Halifax as the key to Britain's naval power in the northwestern Atlantic from the mid-eighteenth century, and Toronto as the late eighteenth-century seat of British garrison and government in the Great Lakes interior, had especially comparable roles to play. Even as raw villages in their earliest years, they shared the distinctive character of imperial bases — which from the start helped to promote their own development, and in due course that of neighbouring, supporting countrysides.

FOUNDING AN IMPERIAL BASE

On 30 July 1793, a bustling Lieutenant-Governor Simcoe landed at Toronto Bay to supervise the planting of a garrison and town. With him came his perceptive wife, Elizabeth, his staff and men of the Queen's Rangers, who were both an armed force and construction crew. Rangers sent in advance were already working on an encampment; Rousseau, the Humber River trader, and two Mississauga families were also on hand. The Simcoes chose a good spot for their portable canvas house, boated to the end of the harbour, then, as Mrs. Simcoe wrote in her diary, "walked through a grove

of fine Oaks where the Town is intended to be built." She noted that the low, wooded peninsula that sheltered the harbour broke the lake horizon and improved the view, "which indeed is very pleasing," while the waters of the bay were "beautifully clear and transparent."[1] So Toronto began, on a kind of agreeable summer outing.

Simcoe had made a preliminary visit to the site in May, and confirmed that here, assuredly, he should base control of his province of Upper Canada. Having been a distinguished British officer who had fought in the American Revolution at the head of the Loyalist Queen's Rangers, he was concerned with dangers of another American war and the need to make his colony militarily secure. The new governor combined the imperious outlook of an eighteenth-century aristocrat with the free-ranging visions of a natural optimist. He projected a whole series of towns besides Toronto for his province (all marked on a birchbark map drawn by his wife), including a future capital, London, located well inland in the southwestern reaches of Upper Canada.[2] Yet while he saw Toronto as only a temporary political headquarters, he also saw it as the essential military stronghold and naval base that would guard the border. He deemed it to be "the natural arsenal of Lake Ontario, and to afford an easy access over land to Lake Huron."[3] A fleet built in Toronto's excellent harbour could command the lake; a fort at the harbour entrance would keep off any attack. It might all be made "very strong at slight expence, and in the progress of the Country impragnable."[4] A dockyard, a sawmill to make lumber, and the town plot, these too were embraced in Simcoe's enthusiastic scheme.

But his superior, Governor-in-Chief Dorchester in Lower Canada, though he had already planned for a town at Toronto, did not agree that a place so remote from British power on the St. Lawrence could make an acceptable naval base, and for that purpose

Elizabeth Simcoe's diary and sketches vividly record Toronto's founding years. In her late twenties then, and of Welsh origin, she appears above in Welsh dress. At left is her sketch of Castle Frank, the Simcoe's Don retreat. Its namesake, Francis Simcoe (who at age four here had his own goat-drawn sleigh), died at twenty-one in war in Spain. Above at left the Garrison erected at the harbour entry, as depicted by Mrs. Simcoe in 1796. Its powder magazine stands below the slope.

fixed on Kingston. Simcoe thought Kingston "absolutely indefensible," open each winter to American attack across the frozen upper St. Lawrence.[5] Yet Dorchester controlled military expenditures, and refused them for Toronto. The Upper Canadian governor still did what he could there with the Queen's Rangers under his own command. He had them build a log-hut garrison by the harbour entry, beside what henceforth was to be Garrison Creek, and also constructed storehouses that might be fortified on a sandy tip of the low peninsula opposite, now grandly named Gibraltar Point. No doubt the disapproval of higher authority left Toronto's military position lamentably weak. But while its harbour might support a sizeable war fleet, the surrounding terrain was too low and too lacking in strong natural defences to provide really good protection. Nonetheless, Simcoe's own assurance, or wishful thinking, had profound consequences. Thanks to him, Toronto was launched as a garrison point, and soon as seat of government; and so could gradually become a functioning urban community, as others gathered to supply and serve its paid soldiery and officials.

The townsite itself was located further east within the harbour towards the Don River: a compact, ten-block rectangle enclosed by the present Front, George, Duke and Berkeley streets, set just below the baseline of a broader grid of concessions surveyed for farming settlement to northward. Subsequent extensions of the townsite would generally conform to the basic right-angled grid pattern thus imposed upon the landscape, of utilitarian, straight-run streets, showing small concern for any natural lies of land. At the eastern end of the town plot, near the Don, a reserve was created for government buildings; on the west, towards the Garrison, a much more extensive military reserve. And behind the town, a series of one-hundred-acre "park lots" were laid out, strips running north across the Shore Plain from the concession base line (later Queen Street, but first called Lot Street) to presently existing Bloor. These estates were intended as grants to mollify government officials unhappy at having to move from properties at Niagara to a wilderness post. Furthermore, Simcoe renamed Toronto, York, celebrated to the boom of cannon on 27 August 1793, in honour of the high-born if unspectacular British commanding-general, the Duke of York.[6]

In the next two years, a town settlement gradually took form, to become known as "Little York" in distinction from older, greater Yorks. Officials quickly sought town and park lots, though were slower to occupy them. A few more farms were opened in the vicinity, particularly up the Don. A government wharf was built, and a government sawmill on the Humber; while Isaiah Skinner, a New Jersey Loyalist, put up his own saw and grist mill on the Don. The Simcoes, too, had a house erected above the latter stream: Castle Frank, named for their small son and built of squared timbers with columned porticos of pine logs. But town-raising went on only slowly, given the dearth of actual settlers yet, and while the Rangers were busy enough on military projects. In 1794, however, William Berczy arrived, the leader of some sixty families of German emigrants who had turned from a settlement venture in New York State to Simcoe's promise of large land grants.

Berczy, a well-educated, gifted artist, now became land developer, road contractor and town builder, too. He received grants in Markham township northeast of York for his "German Company," but also employed himself and his followers for some time at the York townsite. There they cleared roadways, built Berczy's own residence and company warehouse, and put up other homes. By mid-1795 a little hamlet of log or square-hewn timber houses was clustered in the middle of the town plot, around what was to be the main east-west, central artery of King Street, thanks largely to the work of Berczy, his axemen and carpenters.[7]

Meanwhile, Simcoe had often been absent on military concerns, or touring his forest domain and ordering strategic trunk roads to be cut by the Rangers. Most significantly for York, he planned a better version of the old Toronto Trail, Yonge Street, named after Britain's secretary of war, primarily as a military link with Lake Huron. It would run north to gain the Holland River and Lake Simcoe, but not by the former Humber path, being directed instead closer to the Don and the town of York within the guarded harbour. The Rangers began hewing a road line; Berczy and his Markham settlers were contracted to work on the route. By the spring of 1796, Yonge Street was roughly useable as an ox-cart track extending thirty-three miles to a landing on the Holland, where that stream became navigable to Lake Simcoe.[8] It was a mere track indeed, full of stumps, roots and streams to ford. Still, this was another vital beginning, opening lands above York to wider settlement, and in due course to the markets of the town.

Early in 1796, moreover, the governor ordered the Rangers to erect public buildings at York. Two one-story brick structures would house the provincial legislature, which thus far had met at

Smith house in York, built 1794. Government officials might first inhabit town homes like this one — but D. W. Smith, surveyor-general, soon remade his into the more imposing Maryville Lodge.

William Berczy, artist, settlement agent, contractor, architect and pioneer builder of the Town of York.

Niagara, and provide for law courts and religious services also. In short, Simcoe was about to move the capital. He instructed the Niagara officialdom to transfer to York, "the present seat of this Government."[9] Yet while the public officers had long known of the impending move, they still delayed in facing the discomforts of a tiny bush settlement, so that the transfer actually took some two years to complete. Simcoe returned to England on leave in the fall of 1796, and there was reappointed as general in command of forces in the West Indies. And despite some later talk of Kingston, the province's capital stayed where he had left it, at York, where parliament began meeting in 1797. Thus was illustrated a principle in urban growth, as well as physics: inertia. Once started, things tend to move on in the direction set — unless deflected by some strong external force, as John Graves Simcoe had been.

In the year following his departure, there were about forty houses at York, and more under way as the officials' families continued to arrive. Apart from them, there were a few small shopkeepers and millers, contractors like Berczy, some farmers, house-building artisans, labourers and servants. In all, 241 inhabitants were enumerated at the first town meeting, held in July 1797 to elect town officers, almost four years after Simcoe had landed at Toronto Bay.[10] In one sense, this was a pretty modest achievement. In another, it was a critical head start. Through Simcoe's impetus, York had received initial advantage, another key consideration in urban development. Made garrison centre, it gained a lead in road access to the interior just because it was the command base. Ordered into being, it had equally been made a place to which Upper Canada had to look because of its role in legislative decisions or in the administering of law and land grants, not to mention its influence as the focus of imperial connections. Little York might yet be only a half-built forest hamlet, its public pretensions sneered at in older Kingston or Niagara. But it existed, with inset advantage and authority, in time to demonstrate yet another significant principle in urban growth: "Them as has, gits."

In all then, the city of Toronto needs pay respect to Simcoe, without forgetting others who shared in its foundation, from Dorchester at the inception of the idea to Berczy who worked to materialize it in town construction. Yet Dorchester, once the idea moved to implementation, did little that was positive, while Berczy as a town builder lacked Simcoe's powers over crucial policy decisions. The last-named remains pre-eminent. Once overpraised for his far-sighted vision (often wrong), he has since tended to be underrated as a caste-bound military Tory — a very partial verdict. But whatever his views, Simcoe deserves due recognition in the city that grew from his imperial base on Toronto Bay.

SETTLEMENT GROWTH AND EMERGENCE OF AN URBAN ECONOMY

The Simcoe years had produced a political headquarters. It was really the following period, from the late 1790s to the War of 1812, that saw York become a distinctly urban community, that is, with economic activities and social concerns differentiated from the rural areas that now were growing up beyond it. The rise of this town community with its own life and interests was certainly associated with the whole upsurge of settled society around the Lower Lakes. But to begin with, it was more immediately affected by the influx of officials and their families into York. The salaried and fee-receiving bureaucrats required materials and workers to build their homes and develop their estates, and their demands for goods and services were on a scale well beyond those of frontier farmers. Consequently, York could better attract storekeepers and labourers, and in addition a significant proportion of skilled craftsmen and specialized retailers. By 1812 its urban offerings included those of watchmaker, chairmaker and apothecary, hatter, tailor, hairdresser, brewer and baker, besides the general stores, mills, taverns, and blacksmith shops found also in rural hamlets.[11] The official class, then, not only put a political stamp on York; they helped energize and specialize its economic growth as well.

Economic growth brought an increasing population at the government village, from 241 in 1797 to 703 by 1812.[12] That still was small within Upper Canada in general, whose total population advanced by almost wholly rural settlement from some 14,000 in 1791 to around 90,000 in 1812.[13] Nevertheless, this farming spread necessarily impinged on York's own rise, particularly as districts around it were increasingly cleared. Numbers of settlers came in via York as an already established place, and took up land in its vicinity because it could offer them a market for produce as well as providing store supplies and a range of services. In short, town and country were starting to function in the essentially complementary, or symbiotic, relationship of service centre with hinterland. For years yet, however, the relatively thin spread of pioneer rural

Council-Office, Dec. 29, 1798.

YONGE-STREET.

NOTICE is hereby given to all persons settled, or about to settle on *YONGE-STREET*, and whose *locations* have not yet been confirmed by order of the PRESIDENT in council, that before such locations can be confirmed it will be expected that the following CONDITIONS be complied with :

First. That within *twelve months* from the time they are permitted to occupy their respective lots, they do cause to be erected thereon a good and sufficient dwelling house, of at least 16 feet by 20 in the clear, and do occupy the same in *Person*, or by a substantial *Tenant*.

Second, THAT within the same period of time, they do clear and fence *five* acres, of their respective lots, in a substantial manner.

Third, THAT within the same period of time, they do open as much of the Yonge-Street road as lies between the front of their lots and the middle of said road, amounting to one acre or thereabouts.

JOHN SMALL, C. E. C.

Regulations for settling and developing Yonge Street, 1798, issued by the Clerk of the Executive Council of Upper Canada.

settlement and the primitive state of inland communications meant that any hinterland trade remained restricted. York still lived a good deal unto itself, and from its own internal activities. But developments strongly to affect it in the long run grew, as migrants flowed into Upper Canada from the United States on through the 1790s down to 1812.

These newcomers came in the wake of the original Loyalist movement. American land-seekers pushing westward with Great Lakes frontiers brought with them a rough-and-ready pioneer individualism with small esteem for rank, and an expanding Methodism in popular religion. Broadly speaking, they filled in settlement eastward from York along Lake Ontario to Loyalist farms around the Bay of Quinte: they took up lands around the head of the lake or moved westward into the Grand and Thames valleys. More directly important for York, these post-Loyalist Americans also settled in farming townships above the town up Yonge Street, where mill-seats and little neighbourhoods began to emerge.[14] By 1812, accordingly, when war with the United States brought an abrupt end to the inflow, Upper Canada had acquired an agrarian population that was in large majority American, while the Loyalist minority among it differed more in allegiance than lifestyle. The province as a whole seemed fast becoming just another segment of the advancing American–Great Lakes world. And that marked another kind of differentiation between the Upper Canadian countryside and the small York urban centre, which remained predominantly British in make-up and convictions.

Nonetheless, the town's own economic development began to reflect the rising frontier life beyond it. York harbour attracted a growing traffic in batteaux and schooners, in part to supply its own residents, but also because it was a useful transshipment point, as crude roads extended its communications inward. Yonge Street was intermittently "improved" over the period, though remained incredibly bad by later standards. West of the town, a track was opened to Dundas and Ancaster at the head of the lake, linking there with the shore path around to Niagara and with Simcoe's Dundas Street, the route he had cut westward to the Grand and Thames. In 1799 the provincial authorities also had a road made eastward from the capital to the Bay of Quinte settlements and Kingston, in use by 1801. All these through routes could be reached from York harbour, if by rough connecting trails. At that port, accordingly, as the new nineteenth century got under way, ship-masters, shipwrights and sailors gathered; a commercial wharf was built, and flour and potash started going out, though at first irregularly. In effect, a transport pattern was forming for the town, thanks to the location of York's harbour at the centre of outreaching land lines. An official port-of-entry since 1801, its significance indeed was marked by the stone lighthouse raised on Gibraltar Point in 1808 and still standing today.

Merchants, too, began to concentrate at Little York. Rousseau, the long-established fur trader, started running a little general store once settlement took root. He formed a partnership with Thomas Barry (named first town clerk in 1797), but shortly after left the store to Barry and moved to Ancaster, where he continued to prosper.[15] Other small general storekeepers also appeared, trading in goods purchased in Kingston or Montreal. Owing to the absence of banks, the shortage of ready cash so characteristic of frontier areas, and the diversity of several accepted "currencies of account" for business transactions, local trade was mainly carried on by means of barter and credit, which often tied farmers deep in store debts and overextended the storekeepers. Then three particularly enterprising merchants arrived around the turn of the century, to gain ground by capturing much of the trade of the town elite. They were William Allan and Alexander Wood, both Scots, and Laurent Quetton de St. George, one of a group of French royalist emigrés who unsuccessfully attempted a settlement up Yonge Street.

As larger merchants with bigger and more varied stocks to furnish, these three began buying directly from Britain or New York to save on middlemen's costs. Through them, York was thus striking out for a commercial position of its own, no longer to be just a sales outlet for Kingston or Montreal businesses. Allan and Wood dealt more with British suppliers, perhaps because of their own origins and past contacts, but consequently incurred the still slow and often damaging transport of cargoes sent in via the long, rapids-impeded St. Lawrence route. St. George instead ordered largely from New York. It was near enough for goods sought there to be inspected by visiting buyers, goods that could then be forwarded by a shorter route of river, road and lake transport to arrive in a better state at York.[16] Political or tariff problems could still disadvantage shipment from New York, and since many of the items bought there were originally of British manufacture, they were often more expensive than if purchased from Britain direct. In

York in 1803, a village spreading along the shorebank, fronted by square-built wooden Georgian homes. The Don end is at the right side of the picture.

either case, however, York's commerce was shaping long-distance relationships with two external, and alternative, metropolitan sources of supply.

The physical enlargement of the town also reflected its material progress. On Simcoe's departure in 1796, his receiver-general and right-hand man, Peter Russell, carried on as administrator of the province. Because Simcoe's original town plot was fast being taken up, Russell in 1797 extended the townsite north to Lot Street and west to Peter Street, while between this planned New Town and the Old he reserved space for a jail and a courthouse, a market, hospital, school and church.[17] Only a log jail was actually erected during his administration — the rest came later — and the whole new area was slow to develop, being somewhat too ambitious for the time. Still, Russell did proceed with military construction, putting up a blockhouse at Garrison Creek and one near the eastern outskirts of the Old Town to guard the Don. Moreover, troubles with disapproving senior military officials at last were ended when another full-fledged governor, General Peter Hunter, arrived in 1799. In his alternative role of commander-in-chief of the British forces in the Canadas, Hunter ruled that York definitely would stay a garrison centre. Though its defences remained far from formidable, the would-be imperial fortress had moved a step ahead.

Under Hunter in 1803, a public market was established at its planned central location near the waterside, to which cattle and produce were brought in growing quantities on weekly market days, although for years it operated amid makeshift shelters.[18] Inns and hotels were added as well in the decade before the War of 1812. Some were little more than barrooms or small bedding-places for migrants in transit. Others, like Jordan's and Frank's, offered well-utilized ballrooms or assembly chambers, where York's first-known public theatrical performances were presented in 1809 and 1810.[19] There were hotels frequented by labourers and Garrison soldiers, by legislators attending parliament, or, as in the case of the Red Lion built around 1810 on Yonge Street north of the town, by farmers coming in to market. In the growth of its hotel trade, York was further benefiting from both its political role and enlarging economic facilities.

By 1812 that centre had not only gained sizeably in range and number of offerings, but had also considerably improved its town landscape. Board and often picket fences were replacing rough split rails, enclosing lots with cultivated gardens and orchards instead of stumps and brush. Streets were losing their ramshackle look, though their mud remained notorious: frogs, it was said, constantly chorused "knee-deep, knee-deep."[20] The town's buildings assessed in 1809 numbered 107: comprising 14 still made of logs, 11 one-storeyed square-timber houses and 27 two-storeyed, and 55 of more up-to-date frame construction, generally with one and a half storeys.[21] A number of respectably imposing Georgian wooden mansions had gone up, including the large but plain residences of Secretary William Jarvis and Judge William Dummer Powell. More handsomely designed was Peter Russell's home, produced in the late 1790s by William Berczy. A broad frame bungalow with wings, "Russell Abbey" fronted on the lakeshore in neo-classical dignity. The first brick residence in York was built in 1809 for St. George, the merchant. And the first church (Anglican, and later denominated St. James) was opened on King Street in 1807. Originally designed in stone by Berczy, costs compelled that a plain wooden building had to do instead.

Viewed from the water, Little York had thus acquired quite an attractive appearance; it stretched, half-canopied in trees, along the harbour front from near the Don towards the Garrison, but straggled out well before the western limits of the New Town were reached. The finest houses looked almost pastoral in their gardened settings, and apart from a few ship-landings with nearby storage sheds, there was no evident clustering of workplaces, for shopkeepers and craftsmen mainly carried on business within their own homes. The white or light-hued wooden residences in the forefront largely screened the lesser cottages or still crude cabins from the lake prospect. And even humbler backstreet dwellings were far less gloomy or harsh in their environment than were isolated frontier bush shanties or crowded hovels of the poor in contemporary European cities. For all its mud and straggle, York appeared a prospering small place — as indeed it was by the time of war in 1812.[22]

SOCIETY AND CULTURE IN PREWAR YORK

The officials who settled down in York from the mid-1790s, not only carried on its main political function and fostered initial economic growth, but also directed the urban society and set its cultural tone. They established long-significant families — as did English-born Thomas Ridout and William Chewett in the

The first government buildings near the Don mouth held parliaments from 1797 till burned in the American raid of 1813. Rebuilt following the war, they were abandoned after burning again in 1824.

Russell Abbey was affectionately so nicknamed by relatives of top official Peter Russell. Built in the late 1790s at the corner of later Front and Princess streets, it later became town residence of the first Catholic bishop, Alexander Macdonell.

Initially a private home, this became the Court House after the destruction of York's government buildings in the War of 1812. It was later made the "House of Industry" — the local workhouse.

York's first church, 1807, was generally just "the English Church" until dedicated to St. James in 1828. Set at the planned core of the New Town, it began in this clearing north of King.

surveyor-general's office; William Jarvis, provincial secretary for a quarter century, a New England Loyalist who had served with the Queen's Rangers in the Revolution; and Christopher Robinson, a Virginia Loyalist whose son, John Beverley Robinson, became a leading figure in the official class of the next generation. There was John Small from England, clerk of the Executive Council for nearly forty years, and, too, the Scottish army surgeon Dr. James Macaulay, whose own park-lot estate ultimately gave rise to the town's first suburb, Macaulaytown. Above all, there was Peter Russell, the Anglo-Irish administrator who emerged as one of Upper Canada's largest landowners well before his death in 1808. By laying out the New Town, extending roads, amassing properties, and making the home he shared with his sister, Elizabeth, one of the top social gathering-points in the young community, he left a strong mark on prewar Little York.

Russell had been on staff in America during the Revolution, but like most of the chief British "founding" officials who had come into Upper Canada with Simcoe, he was not of Loyalist background. In its earliest days, the town of York did contain a number of American Loyalists, some of whom continued to be prominent there. Yet unlike Kingston, York was never really a Loyalist foundation. By the time the latter started to grow, the Loyalist movement was all but over. Less than a quarter of its inhabitants as first enumerated in 1797 could also be found on Loyalist lists, and this proportion declined further as population mounted.[23] Moreover, as for the Queen's Rangers at York, though originally a Loyalist unit during the revolutionary war, it had been freshly recruited in England to accompany Simcoe to Upper Canada. Still further, after the Rangers were disbanded in 1802 (many to settle in the province), soldiers from regular British regiments formed the garrison at York. All in all, Loyalism at York became more an acclaimed attitude or an esteemed public virtue than a historic link with old colonial America, for this was truly a new town, one closely tied in its society and outlook to Britain.

Generally speaking, there was no mass British migration overseas during this era, the time of the far-reaching French Revolution during the 1790s and of the Napoleonic Wars that only ended in 1815. The relative few who did reach Upper Canada from Britain in these years were considerably drawn from the upper or middle classes: persons who came to fill military or civil posts, find a professional position, seek preferment through connections, or

make their way in trade or a skilled craft. Yet their qualitative impact went well beyond their restricted numbers. Whatever their possible failings, they brought some measure of cultivation, business enterprise and specialized skills to a raw, agrarian frontier province, not to mention a general belief in a ranked, hierarchical society and conservative British institutions. And they ended up far less often on backwoods farms than in Upper Canada's incipient urban communities — particularly in its political power centre, York.

In the upper ranks of York society, well-connected or acceptably talented arrivals from the British Isles thus reinforced its dominant patterns. They often gained important places of their own, although members of the governing circles continued to come numerously from the town's already established official families. Moreover, at the apex of both the political and social elite in York stood the ruling representative of Britain's Crown — from Governors Simcoe and Hunter to Francis Gore, whose own term of office lasted right from 1806 to 1817. Amid vice-regal ceremony and Garrison parades, the social leaders of Little York, a village of clapboard houses, squared-log cabins and mud streets, firmly upheld its position as a British imperial buttress in the backwoods of America.

Among the influential British arrivals in the prewar town was the well-connected Anglo-Irishman Dr. William Warren Baldwin, who settled in York as a physician in 1802. He further became a lawyer, architect, judge and parliamentarian — as well as a wealthy landholder through managing Russell properties, which his wife inherited. The previously mentioned Scottish merchants, Allan and Wood, were made magistrates and held other posts, while the Boultons from England, lawyers, judges and politicians, grew as prominent at York as did the Baldwins. But in due course, strongminded, energetic Dr. John Strachan emerged as the most eminent of all these upper-level British immigrants. A Scottish university graduate, Strachan from 1799 taught school at Kingston and Cornwall, and also entered the Anglican ministry. In 1812 he was appointed rector at York, but when he moved there, he was already well known, since the sons of leading citizens had regularly been sent to study at his highly reputed Cornwall school.

What of the rest of society in this British-led, rank-oriented capital village? It contained an element of German origin, dating in part from William Berczy's settlers of 1797, but also drawn more widely from nearby Great Lake states. Also worthy of note were some non-Loyalist American landholders, hotel-keepers and craftsmen, such as the tanner Jesse Ketchum, later active in both politics and philanthropy. Furthermore, a few French Canadians were present, often as batteaux men, and a small number of blacks, chiefly servants, some of whom had first arrived as slaves. None of these groups, however, altered the British context of the community. Many of its early farm-settlers (like the Denisons from Yorkshire) were of British birth as well, as were varied tradesmen and labourers, including discharged soldiers. Indeed, the largest single element in early York seems to have been of English extraction, with far fewer Scots and still less Irishmen.[24] In the era before the War of 1812, the urban York community developed as manifestly distinct in its preponderantly British society and culture from the Loyalist or post-Loyalist rural areas outside it, or beyond them, from the republican American states.

The cultural context of the town was also demonstrated in religion. Anglicanism was strongly rooted there, not the Methodism or other evangelical forms of Protestantism more widely found in the countryside. No doubt the fact that the only church built in prewar York was Anglican owed much to the strength of the ruling order in the capital, which deemed the Church of England to be the official religious authority as in the English homeland; yet thus far other religious groups in York were not sufficiently numerous to set up churches on their own. Anglicanism had popular adherence as well as high-level influence in that community, expressing loyally British values in church no less than state. Moreover, when an act of 1807 established provincially supported grammar schools, Anglican clergy largely directed them, including that at York. Here the government grammar school, providing secondary education that stressed the classics, considerably improved on shaky little private ventures, especially from 1812 under the capable care of John Strachan, now schoolmaster as well as rector of York. Though this institution chiefly dealt with the children of the well-to-do, it marked a bare beginning of urban public schooling. And schooled or not, children were assuredly not left idle. In a small society with a limited labour supply, they worked (no less than their mothers) for the family unit, in homes, plots or workshops — as was often so even for the young of the estate-owning gentry.

Another important social and cultural institution appeared at York, the press. The *Upper Canada Gazette* was transferred there from Niagara in 1798, to follow the officials and the parliament. Largely a government organ, its local news, advertisements of new store stocks or reports of public meetings were nevertheless of eager interest to the capital community. A critical press with conflicting political opinions was still years away. Provincial politics in prewar York might see some passing stirs, but they scarcely shook the established regime. Accordingly, the *Gazette* sufficed until a later day of sharpening partisan discords and debate.

As for civic politics, there were none, in that the little capital had no municipal organization of its own at this stage. It is true that local institutions of a sort had come into being in 1797 when a town clerk, town wardens and other minor local officers were elected at York's first town meeting. But the powers of these officers were very restricted, as were those of town meetings themselves, which in the young province dealt largely with matters such as fence heights and straying animals. Real local power was vested in the magistrates provincially appointed for the districts, the administrative units into which Upper Canada was divided from its start; counties then were mainly just parliamentary constituencies. The district magistrates met regularly in courts of quarter session (in York's case, for the Home District) within a long-set English form of local government. The Home District magistrates levied small local taxes, looked after the jail at the district seat of York, or appointed a paid high constable and unpaid annual constables to maintain the public peace. They also supervised taverns, made fire regulations and required street upkeep by residents — along with taking a vague responsibility for the poverty-stricken or insane, directing York's public market, and doing even more. But while their broad and far-from-democratic sway extended well beyond the town, they were closely linked to it personally. The Home District magistrates named by the provincial officialdom included leading York inhabitants, in a kind of elite local directorate. Among those active in the quarter sessions of the prewar years were such York notables as William Allan (also collector of customs), Alexander Wood, William Jarvis, William Willcocks (Peter Russell's cousin) and Thomas Ridout.[25] On the whole, they gave conscientious, if conservative and constantly underfunded, administration to their town.

In a real way this paternalistic local rule by traditionally appointed authority fitted the world of prewar York. Though the system would subsequently undergo some refinements, and face strains on its capacities, it was to last without substantial questioning until the 1830s. Little York, in sum, was still a village community, and in spite of notions of grandeur it accepted habitual village controls. The role of families, close or extended, was paramount in its upper-class society, within which women from Mrs. Simcoe to Elizabeth Russell might wield conventional influence, while sons took places suitable to the family, as daughters married, with due filial obedience. In the absence of much record, it can still be presumed that those of the "generality" below endorsed similar modes of behaviour. At any rate, the populace at large was acquiescent under the customary rule of its betters, evidently satisfied to sustain them in provincial politics, to take the magistrates, the official gentry and the Anglican clergy in the places God had awarded them — and inherently suspicious of Yankee republicanism and loud noises of self-congratulating liberty from across the Lakes. York was, of course, no vibrant centre of urbane culture: an outpost on the shaggy edge of civilization still. Nonetheless, as such, it had no fixed or crowded mass of poverty and misery. Fish from the lake and game from the woods were near to hand; there was in general sufficient food, work and space for humble inhabitants.

As for the privileged group, their life was none too onerous: short work days for officials, ample time for tea or sherry with the ladies, rounds of social dinners and assemblies for both, along with rides out the breezy peninsula, or salmon-fishing and pigeon-shooting around the harbour reaches. They had "musical evenings" and a small subscription lending-library to keep in touch with fashionable works from England.[26] All the same, theirs was a narrow world of petty cliques, hemmed in by isolation and stiff social distinctions, rife with gossip as its one abiding entertainment. And so this controlling prewar York society did remain in a village state — self-centred, conformist, and by no means exciting in its ordered pace.

WARTIME SHOCKS AT YORK

By 1812 there was a good deal of unwanted excitement: the signs of approaching war with the United States. Accordingly, it might seem fortunate that the government of York had now come under the authority of General Isaac Brock, commander of British forces in Upper Canada, Governor Gore having departed for leave in

England. Brock believed, with Simcoe, in the strategic value of York. He began looking to its defences; it was agreed that the naval base should be moved there from exposed Kingston, and the building of a ten-gun schooner was started in York harbour. The plans, however, to move the naval dockyard to York and erect a strong new fort to replace its inadequate, poorly kept up blockhouses had not time to be effected. War began in June; Brock died in the battle of Queenston Heights in October; and the demands of the conflict on his military successors left little possibility of achieving the designs intended for the capital. Three small batteries, a powder magazine, the earthworks of an unfinished fort, and the embodied companies of York militia — 120 men under Major William Allan who were ordered to the Garrison at the outbreak of the war — these comprised about all that could be done to strengthen York's own defences.[27]

The town's inhabitants still felt few qualms during the opening stages of the struggle, confident of Britain's protecting imperial power, even though its small forces in Canada were stretched perilously thin, depending much on Indian aid. Moreover, the early British victories at Detroit and Queenston, in which York militia played an active part, only enhanced patriotic pride, aided by the ardent eloquence of Reverend Dr. John Strachan. But the next year the war came home to York directly. On 27 April 1813 a strong American force of fourteen ships and 1,700 troops raided the town, particularly to seize the large, thirty-gun warship, the *Sir Isaac Brock*, under construction there. Landing to the west outside the harbour, the Americans overwhelmed the advanced positions held by the defending forces — in all, some 300 British regulars, a similar body of militia, and a smaller group of Indians. The invaders swept onward to the uncompleted fort. There, as they poured in, the magazine was blown up, killing numbers in a devastating blast, including the American field commander, General Zebulon Pike. The British general, Sir Roger Sheafe, retired towards Kingston from a totally untenable position, burning the *Brock* and leaving York to make what terms it could with the incensed attackers. The next few days saw looting and destruction of public property, and the burning of the Parliament Buildings by unknown hands; but there were no organized American military reprisals. In fact, reasonable terms of capitulation were reached in negotiations led by an undaunted Dr. Strachan, who thus gained a reputation as the town's resolute spokesman.[28]

The raid on York, 27 April 1813. Owen Staples's reconstruction shows the American fleet engaging shore batteries around the harbour entry, while troops land in the woods outside. The Gibraltar Point lighthouse is at the right of the picture.

Early in May the raiders departed; still, the shock was lasting. York had found how exposed it was to American dangers. Most of its public buildings had been destroyed, the landing fight had been particularly bloody, and pillagers had widely robbed the town, of even its little library. On the one hand, there was anxious criticism of the British higher command. On the other, there was fear and suspicion of American sympathizers in Upper Canada. Undoubtedly considerable disaffection existed in the countryside, where the recent American settlers felt no strong grievances against British rule, but equally no great disposition to fight for it. In the capital also, where more Americans had been congregating by the time the war began, there were those who expected an inevitable takeover by the republic, and there had been the initial, alarming breakdown of public order after the fighting at York. Almost surely, this breakdown can be attributed far more to the opportunity for plunder by lawless elements than to the expression of pro-American sympathies. Still, if the loyal citizenry did not quite

picture traitors behind every bush, they could envisage them plotting or fostering sedition. York's mood had been hardened. Pro-British loyalty had been redefined more sharply and prejudicially in anti-American terms.[29]

The rest of the war intensified these feelings. The tide of battle turned at least against any likelihood that the Americans could take Upper Canada, what with their own military setbacks and the strengthening of British regular forces. Nevertheless, a still defenceless York was again briefly seized by U.S. troops in the summer of 1813, to heighten bitterness against suspected American collaborators. At last, by July 1814, a much more defensible fort had replaced the shattered remnants of the old Garrison, and that fall, the war moved to an end. Peace was signed in December, although this news was not known at the inland capital until February of 1815. There, the chief officials consolidated power as a firmly anti-Yankee oligarchy, which soon gained leaders tested in the war — notably, young John Beverley Robinson, who had fought under Brock, and John Strachan, York's champion in the raid of 1813.

The war brought more to York than military attack and political hardening. It also brought considerable economic growth. The supply purchases of the British commissariat led to high profits and much speculation among the town merchants. The greatest returns went to the more prominent men such as Allan, St. George and Wood, but others also gained in wealth, like Jesse Ketchum or the Yorkshireman, Joseph Cawthra, who had begun with a little apothecary shop.[30] War prices soared, partly because of costly transport problems. The New York route was cut off, and that of the St. Lawrence was dangerously open to assault, especially from American ships on Lake Ontario. The resulting uprush of inflation led the magistrates to fix provision prices. Town workers at least got higher wages and full employment in the wartime boom, but it suddenly collapsed when peace returned. Prices dived as military buying ceased and "army bills," a reliable kind of British-backed paper currency, were withdrawn. Nevertheless, the boom had created a more widely based middle class, and left a small but influential moneyed group at York with expanded financial connections and expertise. The town's inhabitants, however, still only numbered 720 in 1816, since population had been almost at a standstill in the war years, with immigration virtually halted.[31] Moreover, Indians, once frequent visitors to early York, now began to disappear beyond the town's horizons — displaced to reserves on frontier fringes as their military value faded at the peace.

POSTWAR ECONOMIC DEVELOPMENTS

After the war, immigrants began coming anew to Upper Canada, but now in a growing mass movement from across the Atlantic. Henceforth the lands of the province were increasingly to be occupied by settlers from Great Britain and Ireland. From the ending of the Napoleonic conflict in 1815, the oceans lay open once more to peacetime shipping, while the people of the United Kingdom, rural and urban, were facing the harsh dislocations that accompanied the ever-spreading Industrial Revolution. The resulting flow of transatlantic migrants began for Upper Canada with only a trickle in 1815–16, but despite some fluctuations, it took an ascending curve. With population pushing out settlement again, or filling in earlier-opened districts, Upper Canada's grain and timber yields expanded,

as did their exports to Britain; and in the process, the economies of little business centres like York enlarged as well.

The full tide of overseas immigration would not be reached till the late Twenties and early Thirties. Yet even in the more immediate postwar years, it rising effects were felt in the Upper Canadian capital. The British settlers came to the province by waterways, up the St. Lawrence or inward from New York. Often they then landed at York as a central transit point, before proceeding to farming areas beyond, thereby fostering the business of its stores and inns. Some of the newcomers, in fact, remained in the town, investing new capital and skills there, though others who stayed might have had little other than their physical labour to offer. Many of the latter came ill-adapted for a life of pioneer farming. Through unpreparedness, lack of funds or sheer misfortune, some of these British immigrants failed to make a way in the countryside or never got there, adding instead to the lower ranks of the town. Here they might raise problems of urban poverty scarcely evident before, but on balance York clearly gained from its gathering numbers — from the enlarging work force, internal markets and potential enterprise they represented.

All the same, the town's economic growth did not proceed smoothly but fluctuated as did the settlement stream itself. Phases of good years and bad, wherein trade and immigration largely rose or fell together, marked the increasing influence of world business cycles on outlying Upper Canada and its capital. The very fact that long-distance trade was expanding through the mounting production of wheat and timber staples tied colonial economic life more closely to outside market conditions. A world cycle of high wartime prices had ended with the close of the Napoleonic struggle, far wider in its impact than the minor War of 1812. Readjustments that followed, adding to the derangements of the Industrial Revolution, brought recurrent periods of distress to Britain, and thus to the imperial economy on which Upper Canada now increasingly depended. As part consequence, the years 1819 and 1822 were much depressed at York, and the better times that followed were checked again by the serious British commercial slump of 1825, which only lifted slowly. Moreover, the complex workings of Britain's Corn Law of 1815 at times could all but exclude colonial grain from the British markets, until from 1822 the granting of imperial preferential duties gave it surer access.[32] This certainly benefited merchants at York, among other Upper Canadian outlets. In fact, it

Postwar York, around 1820: the newer western frontage from Peter to John streets, featuring, left to right, Cruikshank and Beikie homes, military storehouse, and Half-Way Tavern, a resort of Garrison soldiers.

promoted increasingly substantial grain exports from York harbour, despite short-term ups and downs.

The main functions of York merchants, however, lay less in the export trade than in supplying the markets of the town and its vicinity. Here again they felt the force of external economic factors, as when depressed prices for consumer goods in Britain led to their being dumped cheaply at Montreal and other ports of entry. As a result, York traders largely ceased direct purchase from British suppliers of items which they could obtain at about the same price in Montreal.[33] This effectively placed their commerce back under Montreal dominance, for while there was the alternative supply source of New York, it generally remained more expensive, especially because of increased American tariffs. Still, the postwar generation of York merchants chiefly took up ordering through Montreal houses. And in some respects this was indeed a new generation, since the three chief commercial figures of earlier days — Quetton St. George, Wood and Allan — all wound up their businesses between 1815 and 1822. William Allan nevertheless continued to be active in key official and financial circles. He became president of York's first bank, chartered in 1821, plainly because of his position as the town's leading capitalist.

The creation of this Bank of Upper Canada was undoubtedly a major economic advance for postwar York, and essentially displayed the leverage it had through being seat of government. A business group in Kingston, still by far the biggest town and trade centre in the province, had already secured an act to incorporate a bank and issue notes there; but by the time that act finally received royal assent in 1819, its terms had expired. Another very different measure was pushed on the governor (now Sir Peregrine Maitland), backed by a body of York's elite under the driving force of John Strachan, who had become a powerful executive councillor. Through fast work and successful pressure, an officially connected bank issue was incorporated at the capital instead.[34]

Now there might have been good arguments for this more solidly backed York enterprise, which had one-quarter of its stock subscribed by the government and four government directors on its board of fifteen. But it was no less the achievement of the closely interlocked York political oligarchy — soon to be dubbed the "Family Compact" — and it gave the capital a provincial bank which held a virtual monopoly, backed by government sanction, during its early formative years. Led by William Allan as president till 1835,

with directors drawn from the town's official and merchant leaders, and with large amounts of shares held by members of the ruling Compact, the Bank of Upper Canada served as a powerful agent of York's interests, facilitating trade with its notes or credits, fending off banking interventions from Montreal or elsewhere, and gradually spreading its own branches out across the province. Once more through being the governing village, York had gained special vantage and wider economic prospects.[35]

Other wider prospects were indicated by the new steamboats that appeared in growing numbers in the harbour in these postwar years, initially products of Kingston and Niagara, but in 1826 the first one was built at York — all offering greater scope to port traffic and shipping investment. The harbourside itself was building up. Already in 1816 three additional wharves were under construction.[36] Ship carpenteries, lumberyards and more storehouses followed, to give the waterfront an increasingly commercial character, as functional patterns of land use took stronger hold. Nevertheless, some of the best homes in York continued to be found on Palace or Front streets, which looked out on the harbour. There was not much residential segregation still, and there seemed plenty of room for dockside sheds and storehouses along with mansions and their gardens. In 1818, however, the strip of open land along the harbour edge was vested in perpetuity in William Allan, John Beverley Robinson and several other leading citizens, in order to preserve a public promenade in front of the town — a sign of some awareness that growth was beginning to affect York's former semi-rural scatter.[37]

Within the town also, a significant amount of new construction went on. The burned legislative chambers were rebuilt in 1819, and the next year a brick General Hospital was erected; only to be needed for the legislature when the Parliament Buildings burned down again in 1824 (Map 3, page 38). A larger Government House, a Masonic Hall, and a new jail and courthouse went up, as did a steeple for the Anglican church. Seen from the lake, York still looked somewhat rustic and unfocused as it spread out along the shore, and there were empty gaps yet between Simcoe's original plot and the New Town. But from near the Don west past Yonge Street, and from Palace and Front back to the park lots, there was a reasonably built-up area, centring around the public market south of the intersection of King and New (now Jarvis) streets. King Street traversed this urban core, and linked with the Kingston

The town market, at King and New (Jarvis) streets, was built in wood in 1820 and replaced in brick in 1831. The first public pump (1823) is in the foreground.

The Bank of Upper Canada opened in temporary quarters in 1822, but in 1825 bought land at the corner of George and Duke to erect this fine stone structure — symbolizing the growing business power of York.

John Strachan in 1818 built this leading town house, popularly called the Palace, on property originally reaching from Front to Wellington, and York to Simcoe. The photograph dates from days past its grandeur, not long before demolition in the 1890s.

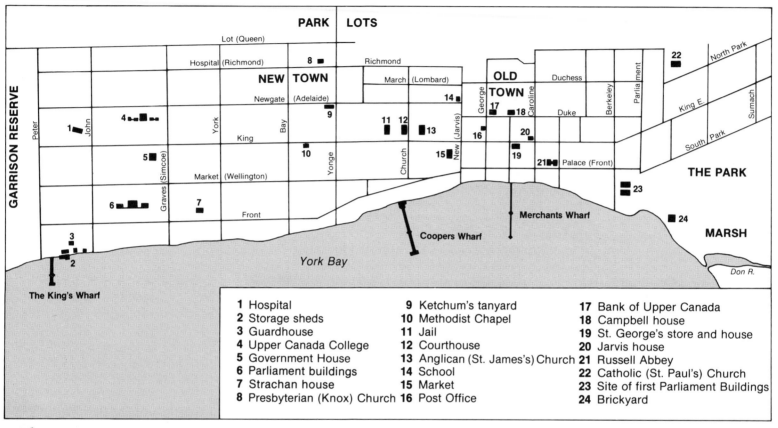

PARK | LOTS

Lot (Queen)

Hospital (Richmond)

NEW TOWN

Newgate (Adelaide)

Richmond

March (Lombard)

OLD TOWN

Duchess

GARRISON RESERVE

Peter

John

4

1

York

Bay

King

5

Graves (Simcoe)

Market (Wellington)

6

7

Front

Yonge

10

9

8

11 12

13

Church

15

16

New (Jarvis)

George

17

18

Caroline

14

Duke

Berkeley

20

19

21 Palace (Front)

Parliament

22

King E.

South Park

North Park

Sumach

THE PARK

23

24

MARSH

Merchants Wharf

Coopers Wharf

York Bay

The King's Wharf

3

2

Don R.

1 Hospital	**9** Ketchum's tanyard	**17** Bank of Upper Canada
2 Storage sheds	**10** Methodist Chapel	**18** Campbell house
3 Guardhouse	**11** Jail	**19** St. George's store and house
4 Upper Canada College	**12** Courthouse	**20** Jarvis house
5 Government House	**13** Anglican (St. James's) Church	**21** Russell Abbey
6 Parliament buildings	**14** School	**22** Catholic (St. Paul's) Church
7 Strachan house	**15** Market	**23** Site of first Parliament Buildings
8 Presbyterian (Knox) Church	**16** Post Office	**24** Brickyard

3 The Town to 1830

Road, over which in 1817 a stage coach first began winter service to Kingston on sleigh runners.[38] When bridges over the Don and Humber were reconstructed after the war on the Kingston and Dundas routes, they served as well to feed more business into the stores collecting along King.

Private building also proceeded; brick had become the fashion for finer residences. John Strachan put up a grand home on Front in 1818, while about 1820 Judge D'Arcy Boulton completed an elegant red-brick mansion in his park lot northward: The Grange, still standing in its classical symmetry. On his own estate further northwest, on the rise above the Shore Plain, Dr. William Baldwin

built "a very commodious house in the Country — I have called the place Spadina, the Indian word for Hill."[39] And Chief Justice Sir William Campbell in 1822 erected a graceful example of a late Georgian town house, which also survives, though moved from its original Duke Street site. Despite their formal poise, however, these gentry homes first rose in park-lot pastures or on unpaved town streets near rough sheds and simple cottages. Here there was no manicured English countryside or the terraced urban order of Jane Austen's Bath. These were urbane transfers to very different frontier surroundings. Yet they put some distinction into the York landscape, and in themselves expressed the urbanizing process under way: from village existence into full town life. By 1825 the little community had 287 private buildings to assess (compared with 139 in 1816), 132 of them one-storey houses, 107 two-storey, and 48 shops.[40] It was passing over the threshold of its rustic state — as social developments made plain as well.

IMMIGRATION AND A CHANGING URBAN SOCIETY

The postwar expansion of York's housing stock obviously reflected its rise in population, which reached more than 1,600 in 1825, by which time the provincial total stood at some 157,000.[41] The town's numbers thus were still a small fraction of the Upper Canadian whole; but they had more than doubled since 1816, while the province's population had grown only by about half.[42] Despite a shortage of statistics, one can interpret this differential growth. In prewar times, the American wave of pioneer farmers had gone overwhelmingly to open backwoods districts. But after the war, the British influx brought a significantly larger element of townsfolk, while urban attractive capacities were steadily enlarging. Hence a higher proportion of the incoming British could effectively end up in centres like York. Though natural increase played some part, the greater growth rate in that town's postwar population was essentially linked with its mounting intake of immigrants.

The lack of adequate records prevents precise statements as to how many newcomers actually settled in York, moved on or later returned; and transiency, difficult to measure, is a perennial feature in urban demography. Migrants to a new land, moreover, were often highly transient, shifting their locations as need or opportunity dictated. Nevertheless, it is beyond doubt that the British settlers, the bulk of whom landed at St. Lawrence ports of entry, came on in sizeable numbers to Upper Canada, and to York specifically,[43] so that their annual landing figures at Montreal or Quebec (mainly the latter) provide a kind of demographic barometer of the pressure moving inland, and an index also to the accretion of British migrants in Upper Canada's capital.

York's rise in population became most marked, to repeat, after 1825, for within eight years following, its numbers nearly quadrupled. Yet the impact of the annual overseas intake was already plain in the postwar town — for instance, in the problem of relief raised by the least fortunate among the arrivals. As early as 1817, the Society for the Relief of Strangers was formed at York to deal with distressed immigrants, the sick and helpless, perhaps left abandoned through the illness or death of their breadwinners.[44] For years this organization remained the main charitable agency in the community, suggesting that in this village-shaped society resident families were expected to cope with their own needs and that a growing group of migrants, not fitting into that pattern, required different treatment.

More notably, however, British newcomers to York helped expand an already emerging middle class, between the urban labouring strata and the ruling order. Within this leading segment, the associates of officialdom shared the interests of the estate-owning Family Compact, at times building up their own large, speculative landholdings. But many of the postwar middle-class arrivals from Britain looked to other means of advancement than government ties or patronage, striking out on their own in commercial or professional ventures, and often displaying an increasingly critical view of the entrenched colonial regime. Some had already derived a new and different outlook from the Reform movement now swelling in Britain. Others developed it at York, feeling the narrow confines of its existing political and social structure.

Religious connections were also influential here. Non-Anglican British immigrants to the town might well dislike the transfer of Church of England official privileges to a new country, regarding them as outmoded pretensions. And there was besides a significant leaven of Americans with Methodist or other evangelical backgrounds among the gathering middle class, for enterprising Yankees still found business opportunities in growing Canadian centres. In general, however, the rising York middle class kept its British make-up, with a large component that also held to conservative and/or Anglican persuasions. Nevertheless, it constituted a changing, dynamic factor in society. It also brought English Non-Conformists, Scots Presbyterians, Protestant Irish Methodists and Irish Catholics into increasing evidence in town — inevitably to question, though not yet to endanger, the older established order.

Some among this incoming element were to figure strongly in the York community. One such was Francis Collins, a Catholic Irish journalist who arrived in 1818, and in 1825 launched his Reform-spirited *Canadian Freeman*. There was William Draper from England, who became a leading lawyer; the Scots stationer James Lesslie, who took to reforming politics and later to radical journal-

Bridges over the Don and Humber were vital to York's east-west land links. Flimsily begun, they were not too impressive after postwar rebuilding. The Humber bridge seen here connected with Lot (Queen) Street, the Don with King.

ism; and, above all, another keenly critical Scot, William Lyon Mackenzie. Arriving at York in 1820, Mackenzie entered storekeeping, then moved onward and started a newspaper in Queenston. In 1824 he returned to York, bringing his *Colonial Advocate* with him to make it the most vehement public voice for change in Upper Canada. Urban British immigrants like these would do much to shape a less inbred and parochial York society.

Church growth also showed the more varied community that was emerging. The American-linked Methodist Episcopals, the principal Methodist body in Upper Canada, in 1818 erected a small chapel on the western outskirts of York, while the Roman Catholics began building St. Paul's Church in 1822 at the eastern edge of town.[45] A minor Presbyterian sect proceeded in 1820 to raise a little church on lands at Lot (Queen) and Yonge donated by the prosperous American tanner, Jesse Ketchum, who had his reeking tanyard in this low-price area.[46] Scots Presbyterians who held to the Church of Scotland, the state-established denomination in their homeland, continued, however, to worship at the officially recognized Anglican church for some years more. At official behest, the government-aided elementary school set up at York in 1818 was also assigned to Anglican control. As a result, this Central School became a fresh source of friction in an increasingly sectarian environment.

Furthermore, a growing concentration of Protestant Ulster Irish at York was manifested in the emergence of the Orange Order, transplanted there from Northern Ireland roots. In 1822, on July 12, the Orange festal day, John Strachan delivered a sermon to about one hundred parading Orangemen from the town and vicinity.[47] And the defence of British ties and Protestant religion fervently proclaimed by the Order attracted some non-Ulster adherents as well at York, including established middle-class citizens. But Orangeism remained more widely based in lower-class urban ranks, where its conservative loyalties offered a popular offset to any too insistent reforming forces — a fact that would give it increasingly political significance in the town.

Politically speaking, York still remained under the local rule of the Home District magistrates, who were given increased policing powers in 1817. In 1820 its growth at least gained it a seat of its own in the provincial parliament. At the election of that year, the seat was won by acclamation by John Beverley Robinson, now Upper Canada's attorney-general and the ablest member of the Tory-minded governing oligarchy. In adjoining York County, however, another prominent townsman there elected, Dr. Baldwin, began showing a remarkable readiness to talk of reform. Moreover, at the next election held in 1824, while Robinson again won the town seat, he had to face a real contest with a York storekeeper, George Duggan, an Ulster Irishman who stood against some government policies and was actively supported by Orangemen.[48] Politics were showing signs of social change; the long Orange Walk through Toronto history was already under way.

In the main, this was yet the ordered world of Little York, still dominated by the social attitudes, political and religious precepts of its ruling Compact officialdom. But the very enlarging of the newer groups in the community challenged the old stability in state, society and church. The different incoming ethnic and religious elements brought their own beliefs and biases, and there were other stirs in opinion deriving from American democratic doctrines as well as British Reform.

Consequently, times were decisively changing at York by 1825, what with Collins's *Freeman* and Mackenzie's *Advocate* launching vigorous censures of the status quo, and social and political feelings growing warmly partisan. The complacent little town was becoming a far more vibrant, interesting place. In short, Simcoe's imperial military base, Russell's clannish official village, and the postwar Compact capital now stood on the verge of a whole new stage of troubled but lively expansion.

York from the peninsula, 1828. While rather romanticized, this painting does denote the rising port town. St. James, with steeple, centres an urban shoreline, and an up-to-date steamer traverses the harbour. The advent of steam navigation enhanced the port's activities: by 1834 the new Cobourg *of 418 tons (owned in Toronto and with twin engines built there) was making 15 m.p.h. on its three-hour crossing to Niagara.*

Chapter Two
The Commercial Port-Town, 1825–47

The new stage did not start suddenly for York. Following depression in 1825–26, British immigration — the impetus to Upper Canadian growth in general — only began a rising sweep in 1827, when arrivals at St. Lawrence ports, which had averaged about 9,000 yearly from 1822 to 1826, increased to 16,000.[1] In 1829 almost that many landed at Quebec alone, the prime gateway, as 28,000 did in 1830.[2] Their number swelled to nearly 52,000 in 1832, continued high to 1837, then rose anew in the Forties.[3] As a result, settlement across the period greatly enlarged the Upper Canadian farm frontier, from the Ottawa Valley in the east to the Huron Tract and Lake Erie districts in the west. Agrarian expansion in turn promoted urban development; service-and-supply hamlets multiplied in the interior, providing general stores, mills and taverns. And along the older settled fronts, previously established places developed on a larger scale to furnish goods, credit and market services for the proliferating little inland centres behind them. This typified a basic feature in North American urbanization: the growth of prosperous commercial towns with the spread of hinterland settlement. In Canada it appeared in the Maritimes as well as in the St. Lawrence and Great Lakes regions, and later across the farming West. But no place gained more than York in its own day, as it rose as a trading focus for a thriving, fast-populating farm hinterland. Already an established port, the advance of rural settlement beyond it in the late 1820s and early 1830s brought on its rapid growth as a commercial town.

URBAN ECONOMY: A COMMERCIAL CENTRE TAKES OFF

The new phase for York was witnessed by an upsurge in its population. Starting in 1826 with 1,719 inhabitants, it had 2,335 by 1828, and 5,505 in 1832, by which time it had outpaced Kingston to become the largest urban community in the province.[4] Though a late starter compared with earlier centres like Niagara and Kingston, York had definitely surpassed them by the mid-1830s, essentially because it found a wider countryside to deal with as a growing commercial town. Its two older rivals were by no means as well placed to exploit new tributary areas. Niagara did have the richly fertile Niagara Peninsula around it, but this was a set-off pocket of the province. Districts beyond could be better dealt with from other locations, so that Niagara was soon outdone. As for the erstwhile commercial leader, Kingston, while it remained a significant trading entrepôt at the entry to the St. Lawrence route, the outlier of Montreal in that commerce, its own surrounding countryside was fairly early occupied and contained a good deal of rocky terrain. And Kingston, too, could not effectually expand its reach, lying as it did well to the east in Upper Canada away from the fastest-growing, fertile central and western areas. The port-town of York, instead, not only had its more central situation, but could also extend its own farm hinterland over the very road system that its role as capital had given it.

Among the roads to the hinterland, Yonge Street served York best. While the town's trade did stretch out eastward beyond the nearby Scarborough and Pickering settlements, or westward towards the head of Lake Ontario, the land routes here paralleled the lakeshores and could be tapped by competing little ports along the way. But York itself commanded Yonge Street, the highway northward. Local traffic grew particularly in this direction as the townships on either side of Yonge filled in, villages sprang up along the route to Holland Landing, and bush farms reached Lake Simcoe shores. Note that this assuredly was local traffic: Governor Simcoe's vision of re-establishing the old Toronto Passage, of reopening its access to the great northwest, was one of his many hopes that had not materialized. About the only long-range transport that moved by way of Yonge Street had come during the War of

A citified King Street, 1835. The second court house and jail (1826 and 1827) adjoin a new brick-and-stone St. James, opened in 1832. There is artistic liberty, however: the planned church tower had not yet been added in 1835.

A main corduroy road, making plain that winter sleighing would be far preferable on highways out of town. But stage coaches did negotiate these routes.

Sleigh-coach of the noted William Weller stage line. Weller ran stages to Hamilton and Montreal, and Charles Thompson those north to Holland Landing.

1812 when the North West Company made some use of this route to its western fur empire, since the way along the Lower Lakes was open to attack. In any event, the amalgamation of the North West Company with the older Hudson's Bay Company in 1821 switched the main fur transport route to Hudson Bay, closing off Canadian links with far-spread territories above the Lakes. The Toronto gateway to a huge northern and western hinterland again became a dream — though not to be forgotten. Meanwhile, at least there was Yonge Street.

Like most of the land routes of early Upper Canada, when capital and labour both were scarce, this allegedly improved road still posed fearsome challenges. "Corduroy" stretches of logs laid across swampy areas readily shifted or rotted, leaving gaps that could topple carts or break bones. Spring thaws and fall rains could make poorly drained, rutted surfaces impassable, although the winter freeze-up brought sleighing and was the best time for moving farm crops to town. Nonetheless, while mired and pot-holed, Yonge Street carried a rising traffic: by foot, on horseback, in freight wagons, and even by clumsy, lurching stage coach — which ran regularly between York and Holland Landing from 1828, and soon provided daily service.[5] Moreover, the rise in the hinterland population and the increasing demands of its little trading centres gave York merchants good reason to expand their business dealings up Yonge.

Bigger merchants with large stocks at York had regularly both retailed goods to the town market in their own shops and sold supplies wholesale to small country stores in the near vicinity. But now that the country market was growing so rapidly, wholesaling became increasingly important in its own right. New stores under new men sprang up in York from 1828, some dealing only wholesale, the chief area of expanding wealth.[6] The new men generally had good connections with Montreal or British houses, and could buy on large credits. Many themselves were recent British immigrants, like the young Scot, Isaac Buchanan, who came out in 1830. He built a major York wholesale business, which largely ordered through a partner-firm in Glasgow, and by 1836 had branches at Niagara and the rising head-of-the-lake town, Hamilton.[7] There were also Joseph and George Percival Ridout, English relatives of Surveyor General Thomas Ridout, who in 1832 began a long-lasting wholesale (and retail) hardware firm at York; and Francis Hincks from Ireland, who set up a wholesale warehouse in 1832,

though he shortly turned to banking, then to Reform journalism and an ascending political career. The bigger wholesalers handled dry goods, groceries, liquor and hardware in bulk; but smaller stores also began to specialize out of general trading: as book and stationery dealers, china merchants, druggists, drapers and iron-mongers.[8] York's commercial operations were multiplying apace.

Accordingly, the York *Courier of Upper Canada* could proclaim in 1832 that "we fairly now look on our town as a second Montreal in point of commercial and mercantile importance. Country merchants need now no longer look to Montreal for their supplies, as these can be obtained in quantity, quality and price, at York, at least equal to the Montreal markets!"[9] In actuality, some of the chief new firms were branches of big Montreal houses. Yet that helped to demonstrate that the lake port had become a sufficiently significant commercial centre to attract capital and enterprise from outside. Moreover, constant efforts were being made to bring country dealers to order their goods through York, not Montreal, which reasserted a pattern among York merchants of importing direct from Britain — and to much less extent, New York — in order to keep down costs and improve service. The imports themselves, of course, still mostly came via the St. Lawrence, and so paid trans-shipment and forwarding charges at Montreal. Nevertheless, the further mark-up of Montreal wholesalers was thus avoided, while York trade became less subject to the control and credit of its bigger rival.[10] No doubt the presence of the Bank of Upper Canada also helped York finance its own commercial enterprises. In any case, as they advanced, the Montreal branch stores either withdrew or became York-based themselves. And even the powerful Bank of Montreal withdrew after a brief attempt in 1829 to establish a branch at York. In short, York was winning a greater business sphere — and basically because of its expanding hinterland trade.

Commercial expansion was still far more evident than industrial activity in the port-town, during an era when the demands of a young farm economy for manufactures were simple and when York itself was mostly importing such factory products as were required from the potent coal-and-iron technology of Britain. Still, apart from essential saw and grist mills, the town by the early 1830s had cabinet and carriage makers, leather works, iron foundries, and plough and axe manufactories. There was a paper mill (up the Don); Knott's and Freeland's competing soap factories, begun in 1830 and 1832; and two plants that made steam engines —

The Fish Market below Front, where hotels and office blocks were appearing. Lake fishing was an important local activity, largely conducted from the peninsula. William Weller's stage service centred in the "Coffin Block" (so called from its shape), which appears to the right of the picture, at Front and Market (Wellington).

one, printing presses as well.[11] Most of these establishments were small-scale, deriving from artisans' shops, and consequently employing only a limited labour force. Yet some new ventures did point to larger investments and developments: notably the wind-driven flour mill set up in 1831–32 by two English immigrants, James Worts and his brother-in-law, William Gooderham. Their milling business led to profitable distilling and then to a variety of manufacturing, mercantile and financial operations undertaken by successor Gooderhams and Wortses. Their tall windmill near the Don, for years a commanding landmark, was actually soon replaced by steam power, as noted by the *Colonial Advocate* in 1833, which added that steam saw mills were also now "the rage" in a booming York, where water power from slow rivers had become inadequate for its needs.[12]

What capital there was available in the town, however, was invested mainly in commercial growth and related developments in transport. Improving the main land routes was difficult, given the heavy expenses involved and the dependence on the reluctant labours of adjoining property-holders as prescribed by law. Then in 1833 a group of prominent York citizens became trustees of a scheme to surface the trunk roads leading out of the town, provincially empowered to raise funds and erect toll gates, through which the outlays were ultimately to be returned. By 1835 Yonge Street, as a result, had been macadamized (surfaced with crushed, packed stone) up to the third concession line, and work was probing onward.[13] This was obviously slow and costly, and both use of the highway and complaints about it continued to increase. More noteworthy were improvements in water transit, which, after all, concerned a far wider area of traffic, opening the port of York to the world outside until each winter froze it in.

Through most of the year, larger, faster steamers brought comfortable and regular passage around Lake Ontario, so that travellers and immigrants still moved by water when they could. Bulk goods now largely went by sailing schooners, which steadily displaced the row-and-sail batteaux or Durham boats of earlier days, and dealt with Kingston, Cobourg and Port Hope, head-of-the-lake and Niagara River ports, as well as Rochester and Oswego. To handle the enlarging water traffic, more wharves and warehouses were erected along York harbour. There, dockhands and carters congregated in a rowdy work force, while steamer captains, ship-owners and port officers became important adjuncts of York com-

merce. One in particular was steamboat owner Hugh Richardson, who put lights and buoys at the port at his own expense, and in 1833 was made a harbour commissioner with a small public grant to effect other improvements.[14]

Exports from the harbour still mainly consisted of wheat, flour and potash, with some lumber and lesser farm products for more local trade. But such exports went out from many another port along the lake. York's more significant role was as an importing and distributing centre, having the advantages of its expanding hinterland and radiating roads, its already well-provided business facilities, and its aggressive, diversifying mercantile community.[15] The lead it thus was winning as a commercial town would only hold and lengthen. It would also gain from the canal-building now under way.

In 1825 the Erie Canal had been opened from New York to Buffalo on Lake Erie, with a side-cut to Oswego on Lake Ontario completed in 1828. The Erie, affording through-water access from the Great Lakes to the Atlantic, did not immediately affect York's trading pattern; but in the long run it offered far easier contact with the markets and supplies of New York.[16] Moreover, by 1833 Upper Canada's Welland Canal across the Niagara Peninsula provided a ship route to Lake Erie and beyond, or to the Erie Canal entry at Buffalo. Meanwhile, the Lachine Canal had been built above Montreal, although the full canalization of the upper St. Lawrence route would take till 1848. All these projects promised York far better links with distant markets and supplies, and lower, competing transport rates. If the consequences for this aspiring commercial town were not immediately felt, their gradual effects and even expectations of them surely marked its growth. In hopes of improving main-line bulk transport, York's men of property invested in various canal schemes, not always well chosen in the boom-time optimism, while its Family Compact officials steered loans through the legislature for the Welland Canal especially, and ended up deeply involved as stockholders and directors in that enterprise.

The boom years, which continued till the onset of another world depression in 1837, also brought significant financial developments. In 1834 the British American Fire and Life Assurance Company was incorporated in York as a competitor of British and American firms, offering both more efficient local coverage and lower rates. Under directors who included major business figures

Jesse Ketchum's tannery at Yonge and Newgate (Adelaide). Ketchum arrived from New York State in 1799 and moved back (to Buffalo) in 1845. A Reform member of parliament from 1828 to 1834, he was also prominent in the Mechanics Institute, the Temperance Society and the Common School board.

Another early town "industry" was Peter Freeland's soap and candle works at Yonge and Front. Freeland, a Glasgow Scot, moved to York from Montreal, relocating his factory as well. In York he was active in founding the Congregational Church.

like William Allan, Isaac Buchanan, George Ridout and William Draper (already a prominent town lawyer), the company soon flourished — and survives today within a later combine.[17] Because, however, it was very much dominated by allies of the government, opponents of the Compact were led to found the rival Home District Mutual Fire Insurance Company in 1837, with directors drawn from such recognized Reformers as Dr. Baldwin (president), Francis Hincks (secretary-treasurer) and James Lesslie.[18] This enterprise also survived for years as part of the town's increasing financial services.

At the same time, both political rivalries and larger business possibilities inspired fresh banking ventures. The Bank of Upper Canada, whose branch offices now extended from Niagara to Brockville, faced constant Reform hostility as the overfed creature of a ruling Tory Compact.[19] Consequently, the Farmers Bank came into being in 1835 under a largely moderate Reform directorate, with Hincks as managing cashier. A few months later, a still more partisan-pure Reform institution, the Bank of the People, appeared as well, to which Hincks transferred his services as manager. Still further, the Commercial Bank of Kingston, which had finally been chartered in 1832, opened a York branch in 1833, as did the wealthy British-based Bank of British North America three years later. These last two banks were clearly drawn by the business concentrating at the thriving commercial town. In any event, thanks to its range of banking and insurance services, the one-time village of York had by 1837 become the largest financial centre in Upper Canada.[20]

A different development that bore on economic growth was the advance of York's press, inherently related to the town's role as provincial capital. Since political action centred there, an increasingly partisan Upper Canadian society hung on the words and doings of the key men at York, all closely reported in its newspapers, which thus acquired a widening popular hold. William Lyon Mackenzie's case revealed as much. In 1826 the office of his *Colonial Advocate* was ravaged by a mob of "well-bred" young York gentlemen connected with the leading families, in retaliation for its anti-government diatribes. The result, however, was to make Mackenzie a martyr of Reform, and enhance his paper's standing with dissatisfied elements in the countryside. Entering parliament for York County in 1828, he strengthened his popular following

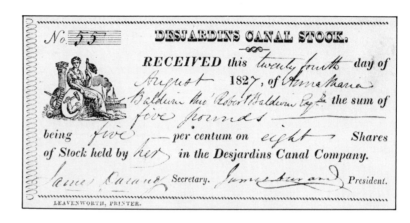

Financial aspects: the Desjardins canal project near Hamilton failed, and the Baldwins' stock (top) proved a bad investment; but the notes of the Bank of Upper Canada (bottom) stayed sound.

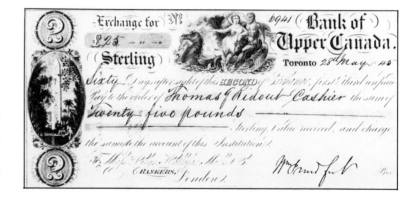

both as a Reform politician and leading capital journalist, each role interacting.

By 1834 there were seven newspapers at York: Mackenzie's *Advocate* and the official *Gazette*; the pro-government *Patriot* and *Courier*, published respectively by the Englishmen Thomas Dalton and George Gurnett; Francis Collins's *Canadian Freeman*, not as adamantly radical as the *Advocate* but still potently reformist; the *Christian Guardian*, begun in 1829 under the able editorship of a young Methodist minister of Loyalist descent, Egerton Ryerson, as the York organ for Upper Canada's main Methodist element; and the *Canadian Correspondent*, started in 1832 by William O'Grady, an Irish Catholic priest who turned political radical. The *Guardian* plainly looked to a province-wide audience, one not solely religious in interests, since the paper also voiced considerable political criticism — as the *Canadian Correspondent* decidedly did also. The fact that four of these seven newspapers were variously oriented to Reform in a town still dominated by the Tory-minded outlook of its ruling order, further demonstrated that they were appealing well beyond York — that it had indeed become a central political headquarters for the press. Yet more than this, the same journals as readily purveyed the notices and advertisements of York business to the countryside, extending its commercial communications as well as its political and social influence. In every way the town was enlarging its economic grasp, increasing its regional stature — and not the least through the dissemination of information and opinion.

THE SHAPING OF A MUNICIPAL STRUCTURE

York's vigorous growth through the earlier 1830s no less strained its established framework and raised new public needs. Furthermore, the tide of immigration did not just bring it purchasers, workers and investors, but disease and distress as well. In the summers of 1832 and 1834, cholera came with the immigrants to York, a deadly scourge ascribed to foul air or "miasmas" — not to microbes (then unknown) spread by contaminated drinking water. During the epidemic of 1832, 273 deaths were recorded; that of 1834 killed over 500, among them Francis Collins, the journalist.[21] Urgent but piecemeal efforts were made to deal with the contagion by cleaning up filth and waste, held to generate miasmas. In 1832 York for the first time got daily garbage and sewage collection, ordered by the Home District magistrates, who also had small drains built in the dirtiest, poorest parts of town.[22] They appointed a temporary Board of Health, composed of physicians and leading citizens under Dr. W. W. Baldwin; but it lacked compelling force and funds, while the General Hospital that had finally opened in 1829 was a veritable plague pit, which sufferers dreaded to enter.[23] Hence, the epidemic of 1832 virtually ran unchecked until the colder days of autumn arrived. It harshly underlined the inadequacy of existing local government for a town which, thanks to its very expansion, faced serious shortcomings in financial and administrative powers as well as in public services.

Municipal change was in the offing. Politics had much to do with it, besides. York Reformers attacked the civic rule of the appointed district magistrates as much as the provincial rule of the Family Compact, seeking to bring both regimes under popular, representative control. Yet the established structures of authority also won support. Many anxiously loyal townsmen rallied against the appeals to American democratic models made by more radically minded advocates of Reform like William Lyon Mackenzie, preferring accepted British ways to headlong, republican-sounding proposals. In point of fact, the moderate bulk of Upper Canadian Reformers in both town and country desired less-sweeping changes still within a British colonial framework. Nevertheless, radical rhetoric roused anti-American apprehensions in York, still sensitive to its border position and memories of the War of 1812, and its attitude was shown in the provincial elections of the time.

In 1828, John Beverley Robinson again took the town seat, beating Dr. T. D. Morrison, a Radical associate of Mackenzie's. In a by-election of 1830 — after Robinson had been named chief justice — Robert Baldwin, son of Dr. Baldwin, did defeat a Compact Tory stalwart, Sheriff W. B. Jarvis. But Robert, like his father, was a firmly pro-British moderate Reformer, and his ruling-class background scarcely opened him to charges of Yankee democratic leanings. In any case, in general elections later that year, Jarvis won York, only to lose it in 1834 to James Small, another leading family offshoot become a moderate Reformer. The upshot was that York went Tory-Conservative, or at most middle-road Reform, even when Mackenzie and his left-wing allies were winning in the countryside. Of course, one might expect that the capital's gentry-officials and government retainers would take the establishment

William Lyon Mackenzie in later years: first city mayor, urban journalist and fiery hero of agrarian radicalism.

John Strachan, also in later life: warrior churchman, Compact champion, and promoter of education and economic power in young Toronto.

John Beverley Robinson: attorney-general, chief justice, and patrician Tory.

Robert Baldwin: leading Torontonian, Reform party chief and premier.

side. So would most of its commercial elite, who backed orderly rule and government aid to business, not the populist, pro-farmer militancy of Radical Reformers. Yet on evidence, too, a strong segment of the town's lesser shopkeepers and skilled artisans (those with the franchise) sustained the government cause, as largely did "loyal" immigrants, and there was no sizeable urban proletariat, whether or not it would have gone to the Radicals if it could have voted.[24]

In sum, a broad cross-section of York's political society endorsed the powers-that-be or wanted only to modify them. This may well have reflected British background traditions besides anti-American sentiments, and also a practical disbelief in vociferous Radicals who, when seated in a provincial assembly with much restricted powers, could do little more there than denounce and obstruct. At any rate, it seems clear that the town stayed pretty conservatively inclined. The presence of a faithful Reform contingent in the capital, and of such provincially significant left-wing figures there as Mackenzie, Jesse Ketchum, Dr. Morrison and the capable but devious Dr. John Rolph, could seldom alter the dominant complexion of York itself.

All the same, when it came to civic government, Tories and Conservatives as well as moderate Reformers and Radicals could be led to conclude that changes were required in the local regime at York. The elements on the right began to see the existing rule by appointed magistrates as too limited in powers and finance to supply effective services; while those to the left regarded it as corrupt and wrong in principle. The former mainly wanted a well-funded, efficient authority, but one naturally still based on reliable propertied interests. The latter sought a progressive new era of popular urban government, but naturally without increasing taxes. Despite these differences, however, both sides grew ready for a crucial step: the incorporation of York as a municipality with power over its own local concerns.

By the 1830s, in fact, the difficulties of a swelling urban centre being run by part-time magistrates, authorized merely to tax a penny on a pound of assessed property, were all too glaringly apparent. In 1827 the magistrates had had to borrow funds to pay for a new courthouse and a still inadequate new jail. By 1830 better market buildings were desperately needed, but could only be undertaken by raising another large loan.[25] The administration was continually on the edge of bankruptcy because of public needs. It had also had to establish a full-time police clerk, organize a volunteer fire company and lay some primitive sewers, all in the later Twenties, but had no funds left for major improvements, such as draining the main streets effectively. Accordingly, Henry John Boulton, Tory attorney-general, in 1830 proposed an incorporated, elected, municipal government for York with greater taxing power. Partisan debate stalled his scheme in parliament, until in 1833 a committee of Robert Baldwin, Dr. Rolph, James Small and George Ridout produced an amended draft bill that finally passed. Taking effect on 6 March 1834, it incorporated the first city in Upper Canada.[26]

Under this chartering act, the new city was to consist of five wards, bounded by Parliament Street on the east, Bathurst on the west, and extending from the lake to a line 400 yards north of Lot (Queen) Street. (See Map 7, page 126.) Beyond lay the city "liberties," in which new wards could be erected, reaching east to the Don, west to the present Dufferin Street, and north to Bloor, largely covering the Shore Plain area. Each of the five wards was annually to elect two aldermen and two common councilmen, with sizeable real-property qualifications. All adult male resident house or lot holders, being British subjects, received the civic vote. A mayor, salaried and chosen yearly by the aldermen out of their own number, would preside over and vote in the City Council, composed of both aldermen and common councilmen. That body would now take over duties formerly held by the magistrates, from dealing with public works, police, and fire prevention to controlling the market, taverns, public nuisances and the harbour, not to mention Sabbath observance and the licensing of theatrical performances. And the council could now levy taxes up to fourpence on the pound in the city, twopence in the liberties, while the municipal corporation was given increased borrowing powers. Finally — and quite significantly — the city's name was changed to Toronto, the older, more distinctive name that avoided the connotations of "Little" York.[27]

The charter of this new City of Toronto unquestionably had its failings. If a camel is a horse designed by a committee, so it had camel-like awkwardness, the results of trade-offs by contending factions. It provided elective control, but well qualified by property ownership; a mayor safeguarded from popular democracy by in-group selection, but with little real authority of his own. It left both Radicals like Mackenzie and Tories like Sheriff Jarvis considerably unhappy, and even moderates who stayed with it tended to see it as

the best of a dubious job. Above all, owing to legislative restrictions, the charter still provided insufficient sources of revenue for the enlarged municipal services that were hopefully expected from the new regime. Financial problems, quarrelling mayors and councils, public reluctance to meet the real costs of running a fast-growing city, were the vexed consequences of the incorporation act of 1834. And yet, like a camel, this municipal creation showed remarkable endurance, plodding on across the years, full of noisy grumbles but performing its tasks. A pragmatic recognition of civic responsibility, a political compromise largely between moderate Reform and Toronto Conservatism, the municipal system thus established still gave the city its own directing organization for an increasingly complex urban life.

LANDSCAPE, SOCIETY AND CULTURE IN A FRONTIER BOOM TOWN

Toronto in 1834 was beginning to look like a city. That June, its population was recorded at 9,252, though this near doubling since 1832 was partly due to the extension of its boundaries.[28] King Street, the main commercial thoroughfare, was now quite solidly built up from Caroline (Sherbourne) west to York Street, beyond Yonge. It displayed a mixture of structures that still included small wooden shops and frame houses, but consisted more and more of closed ranks of brick stores with dwelling quarters above, for both retail business and land values were steadily climbing on King. The large and handsome Chewett's Buildings were under construction at King and York, their architect a talented recent arrival from England, John Howard, who was to leave his mark on Toronto's built environment.[29] In the central King Street area, new brick market buildings had been completed in 1833, containing a public auditorium and now housing the City Hall as well. (See Map 3, page 38.) Rows of three-storey residences and stores were being promoted or erected elsewhere in this central neighbourhood, to give it an increasingly "downtown" character. On King Street at Church a new stone and brick Anglican St. James had been opened in 1832. Across Church Street from St. James was the courthouse, and north of this the second most socially significant Toronto church, St. Andrew's Presbyterian, begun by Church of Scotland adherents in 1830. A large new Methodist chapel stood a street away. And in this central section there were also major hotels like the

Bishop's Buildings at Newgate (Adelaide) and Simcoe: sizeable homes for the well-to-do. Built by 1833 (though seen here in a later photograph), these attached houses were not only indicative of the Thirties' building boom, but of a new urban pattern in residential living. The youngster at right evidently could not hold his pose.

four-storey North American, together with manufactories both large and small, since any sorting out of land uses had still not proceeded much beyond the rough distinction of a core segment from adjacent, supporting sections.

On the east of the central area of mercantile, civic and religious leadership, the original Old Town now merged into it. The Bank of Upper Canada lay here, and some imposing private mansions like that of Joseph Cawthra, a wealthy merchant. But poorer elements also tended to congregate in this section, many of them immigrants or transients, filling older, run-down little cottages on back lanes, often living in near-slum conditions. On the other side of the central area, the Macaulaytown fringe of humble homes spread into the park lots west of Yonge and above Lot. Yonge Street nearer the harbour was a rising focus of cartage, storage and workplaces. As the link between the port and the trunk route northward, it drew such concerns to its vicinity; and habitations as well were scattering up its course towards the tollgate at Bloor Street, the limit of the city liberties. North of this limit, Joseph Bloor, a prosperous local brewer, and Sheriff Jarvis (whose country seat, Rosedale, lay nearby) were planning out the future village of Yorkville.

The main thrust of development, however, was westward towards the Garrison. In the western area, fine residences fronted on the water, as they still did along the eastern shoreline. But to the west, the houses and properties tended to be larger; besides, the provincial government establishment was now centred in this section of the New Town, a prestige-factor influencing land use. Here on Front Street, three red-brick, plain but ample late-Georgian edifices had been constructed between 1829 and 1832 to house the provincial legislature and offices. Their grounds backed on those of Government House, since 1815 set in this location. East of the political complex stood John Strachan's resplendent mansion; and nearby, Henry John Boulton's stuccoed Holland House, erected in 1831 as a first attempt in Gothic Revival style at Toronto, with pointed arches and mediaeval ornamentation.[30] On Lot Street above lay Osgoode Hall, a stout brick block built by 1832 for the benchers and students of the Law Society of Upper Canada on a portion of John Beverley Robinson's estate. Beside Osgoode, broad College (later University) Avenue ran northward to the lands of the projected provincial university, for which Strachan had obtained a royal charter in 1827. Though planted and landscaped,

this road led nowhere, since chartered King's College would not be constructed at its head for another decade. West of College Avenue, however, lowlier, wooden dwellings spread unevenly along Lot Street towards another impressively wide roadway, Spadina Avenue, laid out by Dr. Baldwin below his hillcrest home. And while scarcely yet developed, both grand avenues pointed plainly to future extensions of Toronto's growth.

In many ways the new city was a frontier boom town, pushing, clamorous and cluttered, full of energy and land speculation, considerably different from the placid Little York of early years. Its older gentry families might still look to keep the lid on, but they were no less busily engaged themselves in developing and speculating, reaching after wealth and progress. And the increasingly strong and assertive business classes, the annual inundations of immigrants, the growing needs of municipal services and budgets, all testified that the stable state of official and gentry leadership was passing beyond recall. The very existence of the new, elected civic regime was further evidence. Toronto indeed had become a commercially oriented community, growing with the Upper Canada frontier, and thanks to the boom of the Thirties, no longer so greatly dependent on its old official ranks.

New cultural developments marked this larger society, improving its bare frontier plainness. In education, the failure of the provincial university to materialize was partly offset by the opening, with eighty-nine boy pupils, of publicly endowed Upper Canada College (UCC) across from Government House in 1830.[31] Governor Sir John Colborne, who had replaced Maitland, considered that a university would be premature until a fully qualified secondary school could prepare students for it, and used his still compelling authority to get his way. Directed mainly by Anglican clerics, graduates of British universities, the new institution aimed at cultivating future leaders for society. Its stress on classical studies, however, and the non-Anglican predilections of some of the city's growing middle class, fostered the appearance of private, more practically oriented academies for the sons of commerce, though age-old patterns of apprenticeship continued for professions and crafts. The old York grammar school also resumed, while primary education largely stayed with the government-supported Central School well into the 1840s. It was still generally deemed unnecessary to educate girls much beyond the primary level, though there were some private girls' schools, as well as other small

The new Parliament Buildings by J. G. Chewett, erected 1829-32, lay in a square at Front and Simcoe overlooking the water. Artistic licence again: the central portico was never added.

Upper Canada College, opened in 1830 north of the Parliament Buildings and Government House. A main school building was flanked by houses for masters and boarders.

and dubious private elementary ventures that charged little and provided less for either male or female children. The lower orders often had only church Sunday schools, which did impart some reading and writing as means to scriptural study. Toronto's educational facilities were not impressive. Yet the staffing of UCC to train a provincial elite at least planted a modest kernel of intelligentsia that would grow in years ahead.

The formation of the Literary and Philosophical Society in 1831 evinced fresh cultural stirrings, as did the Society of Artists and Amateurs, which in 1834 held an exhibition of 196 paintings at the legislature, promoted by John Howard, the architect, who was also drawing-master at UCC.[32] The tastes of the upper class still ran more to subscription balls and card parties; those of the lower to taverns for social recreation and release; while the righteous middle class largely frowned on dancing, cards and drink, and looked to church gatherings or elevating lectures as suitable social amusements. Nevertheless, the theatre also became a more regular means of public entertainment, if not of high cultural edification. Companies of American actors, travelling up the Erie canal route to Great Lakes centres, included Toronto increasingly in their tours. Moreover, instead of playing in hotel assembly rooms, they now could perform in the Theatre Royal, which acquired its own frame building at King and York in 1836. Despite its name, this was a makeshift structure that drew an unruly audience, and was continually decried by Toronto's Calvinists and Methodists, who saw theatre as mid-way between the temptations of taverns and the sins of bawdy-houses (the latter then centred on Lombard Street). All the same, the Theatre Royal provided a resident base for plays from excerpted Shakespeare to popular farces.

But for the middle class in particular, there was the Mechanics Institute. It was founded in 1830 to emulate English examples by such earnest moral uplifters as James Lesslie, and was intended primarily as a means of self-help for aspiring workers, to enable individuals to better their position through instruction in practical arts and sciences. But it soon became a middle-class institution that presented public talks in the Masonic Hall on broader philosophical and scientific topics, that ran classes on drawing or the musical arts, and that began collecting a library more suited to entertain well-to-do subscribers than meet the technical needs of artisans. Hopeful shop clerks and apprentices did attend its evening classes, yet generally most workingmen showed small interest. Nonetheless,

after a shaky start, the institute was flourishing by 1837, to be patronized by Toronto's respectability for its lecture series and social gatherings, and in time its library, which became the nucleus of the city's future Public Library.[33]

The local mechanics themselves tended to show livelier interest in collective action than individual self-help, that is, in forming trade unions of their own. Because there were no large industrial work units in this mercantile city, however, such efforts were limited to a few more-skilled, craft-conscious trades. In 1832 a printers' union had been formed; in 1833, benevolent societies among groups of building tradesmen.[34] The printers went on to set union wage levels, and in October 1836 all of them in Toronto struck when their increased rates were not accepted. William Lyon Mackenzie, one of the press owners thus affected, sounded a lot less like a friend of the people than an embattled employer defending the sanctity of the free labour market when he denounced "such an ungrateful and censurable proceeding."[35] But the strike was over in a few days, with only a general amnesty to end it. Another by journeymen tailors in November also quickly closed in failure. Evidently both the numbers and organization of labouring elements in the city were yet too weak to have much impact.

CIVIC POLITICS AND REBELLION DANGERS

Growth, thanks to the boom years, was really the basic problem that confronted the city administration inaugurated in 1834, pressing the need for better public service. Instead of decisively responding, the first municipal government became embroiled in clashes stemming from the sharp political divisions of the day. The initial civic elections of late March 1834 had produced a City Council split between twelve decided Reformers, including Mackenzie, Lesslie, Dr. Morrison and brewer John Doel, and eight staunch Tory-Conservatives, such as George Gurnett, editor of the *Courier*, George Monro, a leading wholesaler, and Colonel George T. Denison, an eminent militia officer. The fact that Reformers nevertheless won the first civic contest in this more usually Conservative community requires some explanation. At that point in 1834, local feeling against the old rule of district magistrates was more likely to hit Tory candidates at the municipal polls; Reformers, indeed, might have seemed to deserve the chance to launch a new era of civic progress. Besides, the fact that Mackenzie had recently been repeatedly and vindictively expelled from the Tory-dominated provincial assembly of the day brought him and his associates a surge of popular sympathy. At any rate, the balance did shift to Reform for Toronto's new civic regime of 1834, though only briefly as it transpired. And Mackenzie was chosen as first mayor by the council's Reform majority.[36]

From the start this regime ran into quarrels over disputed elections, during which an irate Mackenzie had Alderman George Monro forcibly ejected from the council chamber — shades of his own expulsions. Something was accomplished in establishing standing committees of council for finance, fire and water, roads, markets, police and prisons, the harbour and more; and a number of basic by-laws were passed dealing with fire or market regulations, garbage collection, Sunday observance, and so on. But few other advances were made, except in providing plank sidewalks on main streets, for besides the handicap of party strife, civic financial powers still proved inadequate to meet major needs.

The dread return of cholera in August of 1834 raised a more urgent problem. The Board of Health set up by the city corporation had scarcely more success in coping with it than had that named by the district magistrates two years before; yet it undoubtedly was hampered by its own deep factional divisions, which led to the board's recasting as a wholly Reform group. And after the disease subsided in the fall, the city government returned to heated wrangling, to wind up the year frustrated and considerably in debt. The initial Reform dominance had not had high success. Moreover, as a seasoned battler, Mackenzie did not adapt easily to presiding office, and his impetuous temperament hardly fostered concord.[37] In any event, Tories swept the civic elections of January 1835. Robert Baldwin Sullivan became mayor (a brother-in-law of Robert Baldwin, though a moderate Tory himself), while Mackenzie instead turned back to provincial politics and the fiery probing of popular grievances.

Under a solid council majority, new headway was made by the civic corporation, notably in building trunk sewers of brick under the chief streets.[38] But its deficit was thus enlarged, and attempts by this Tory council to have the city's tax base in its charter widened were held up in a provincial assembly now dominated by Mackenzie's friends. Accordingly, faced with debts from improvements while lacking an improved assessment law, a disgruntled citizenry swung back to the Reformers. They were returned

twelve to eight again on the council for 1836, which chose Dr. Morrison as mayor.[39] Whether or not Mackenzie's absence helped or the rival factions were now more chastened, this regime also made material progress, particularly in macadamizing main arteries like central King and Yonge streets. Moreover, the need to deal with growing numbers of helpless urban poor led to a civic grant for a House of Industry, which was opened the next year (under a volunteer citizens' group) to provide permanent, institutionalized poor relief on the English workhouse model.[40] Yet the hard question of municipal debt and reassessment remained unanswered. Despite its useful service, the Reform administration in turn was replaced by an all-Tory council in 1837 under George Gurnett as mayor, now one of an emergent breed of "regular" municipal politicans.

This Tory civic victory in Toronto also reflected a provincial shift; for in the election of 1836, Tories had again won control of parliament, swept on by extravagant appeals to British loyalty made by an intemperate new governor, Sir Francis Bond Head, who proved as inflammatory as Mackenzie. Still, the city did benefit from the Tory legislature. William Draper, the skilful Conservative lawyer who now sat for Toronto in the assembly, steered a measure through it by March 1837 that set up a wider system of assessment for the city, raised the maximum tax rate in its wards to one shilling sixpence on the pound, and increased its borrowing authority.[41] Hence, that spring prospects might have looked bright for Mayor Gurnett and the municipal corporation, except that, by then, a spreading world depression was making inroads at Toronto.

In consequence, the city's revenues were increasingly hit: building, street and sewer projects were cut back, and the municipal regime sank into the doldrums for months to come. All this, however, was soon overshadowed by far graver financial and political developments. Deepening depression in trade, shortages of cash and credit, led to business failures and heavy drains on the city's banks, which shook confidence in them by the summer of 1837.[42] The Reform banks were hard put to survive, though the far stronger government Bank of Upper Canada continued to meet its obligations. And many farmers who could not extend their notes in this financial turmoil were left distressed and debt-ridden, a steaming hotbed for the appeal to force which an exasperated Mackenzie and Radical comrades now worked to promote.[43] Rebellion was in view.

As the bad times worsened across the autumn, unrest deepened in the countryside. Then in November the outbreak of revolt in still more troubled Lower Canada brought Upper Canadian Radicals the signal for action. Following secret leadership meetings in Toronto, they called for armed insurgents to assemble on the capital. Governor Head had done his bubble-headed best to encourage violence by sending the troops of the Garrison off to help in Lower Canada. Hence, by early December Toronto lay open to attack — just as in 1813 — as several hundred prospective rebels collected outside the city at Montgomery's Tavern, some miles north up Yonge Street above present-day Eglinton Avenue. On the night of December 4, alarm bells rang out in Toronto when word of the massing at Montgomery's came in. Alderman John Powell, who had been scouting up Yonge Street and there been seized by a rebel party, had shot his guard with a hidden pistol, then ridden hotly for town with the news. Actually, Colonel James FitzGibbon, the veteran officer of the War of 1812 commanding Toronto's citizen militia, had already learned of the rebel gathering from other sources, and a superbly overconfident Head finally took the danger seriously. As for John Powell, he became a city hero, and a future mayor.[44]

The next day the rebel forces marched on Toronto, led by Mackenzie and Samuel Lount, a substantial North York blacksmith. They showed no clear direction, stopping to parley ineffectually with emissaries sent by Head. By nightfall their vanguard had plodded down Yonge into the city liberties to be ambushed by a picket under Sheriff Jarvis. After an excited exchange of shots, both sides fled back the way they had come. But this clash in a bush field became a turning point. The following day, December 6, the attackers did little but capture the mail coach out on Dundas Street; and many of them were already deserting in discouragement. Finally, on December 7, loyal militia who had been collecting in Toronto took the offensive. Some 900 men, with banners, two bands and, more important, several small cannon, advanced up Yonge towards Montgomery's on a crisp, sunny winter afternoon.[45] There they quickly scattered the ill-armed rebel remnants, and put cannon shots through the tavern, whereupon their enemies ran off wildly. The Yonge Street rising was over, Toronto saved from fire and sword — although, except for the few casualties in the skirmishing, it was more a comedy of errors than an epic

drama. Still, the rebellion period itself was not over, and its results would be telling.

Within the city, fears and enmities led to charges against leading Reformers like Dr. Morrison, who was deeply implicated, but escaped, and James Lesslie, who was not, but still was jailed for thirteen days without warrant. Dr. John Rolph, the secret co-designer of revolt with Mackenzie,[46] successfully took off for the border before being found out; Mackenzie, too, reached the United States after a flight to the Niagara River. Now American sympathizers backed his call to free (or conquer) Canada, and their border raids which went on through 1838 cost far more in casualties and damage that the abortive original rising had done. Consequently, warlike tensions and an inevitable Tory reaction gripped the province as rebels and raiders were hunted down, suspicions ran riot, and Lount and a Yonge Street rebel comrade, Peter Matthews, were hanged at the jail in the capital in April 1838.

Nowhere was the Tory reaction more evident than in Toronto, bastion of the Family Compact and British loyalism, which now felt the alarms of 1813 sharply revived. Clearly too, the rebel movement had found few followers in the city, although some there quite likely had had no chance to join it. On balance, however, it seems evident that the possessing classes and their "respectable" supporters upheld a loyal consensus in the capital, and that the strength of any rebel sympathy lay in the hinterland. In any event, one consequence of Radical revolt was a drastic setback to the whole Reform cause in Toronto.[47] Reform papers there went out of print, while moderate party leaders like Dr. Baldwin and Robert Baldwin had publicly to disavow any links with the rebel faction. And for years to come, while Toronto necessarily served as provincial headquarters for a reviving Reform party, the city itself returned a succession of Tory or Conservative members to parliament, with only a few moderate business Liberals as exceptions to the rule.

If anything, therefore, Toronto moved decisively further right after the Rebellion of 1837. The shift showed most plainly in civic politics. Far from having any left-wing city administrations, however transitory, there would not even be a moderate Reform mayor until the 1850s. Meanwhile a string of Tory-controlled municipal governments ran Toronto, beginning with John Powell, the war hero, who proved an unimpressive mayor in 1838–40. These civic

Reaction to rebellion as envisioned by C. W. Jefferys: loyal volunteers muster at Toronto's Parliament Buildings, December 1837.

regimes often had their own contending in-group cliques, but then they did not have to fear Reform party opposition. In fact, while parties in municipal affairs might still have provided more healthy alternations, party politics as such became considered factious and unnecessary in the civic sphere. But who needed party labels when only one set of partisans ruled thereafter? Tory Toronto and Conservative civic mastery owed much to the events of 1837.[48]

THE CONSOLIDATING COMMERCIAL CITY OF THE FORTIES

Unyielding depression and border troubles that possibly threatened a new American war imposed a gloomy interlude on Upper Canada's capital, one lasting into 1840. That demographic barometer, immigrant arrivals at the port of Quebec, fell to 3,200 in 1838, rose only to 7,400 in 1839, and did not recover, to 22,000, until the year after.[49] And in the waning Thirties Toronto's civic administration stayed hard-pressed for funds, as the city's poor strained all-too-limited means of relief, and its businesses remained severely short of credit, a lack which drove more under. Ambitious projects put forward in the good times had to be adandoned, from lighting the city with gas to planning a railway north to Georgian Bay. Nevertheless, the basic commercial or municipal achievements of the preceding boom persisted, while gradually border violence was checked, tense relations with the United States were eased, and political passions lost some of their vehement heat.

A new political era, in fact, was opening. Lord Durham came out in 1838 to investigate Canadian ills. At Toronto in July he interviewed Robert Baldwin, among others, who pressed his own cherished remedy, responsible self-government on British lines. Earlier in July, Francis Hincks, by now Baldwin's close associate, had launched a newly constructive liberal paper, the Toronto *Examiner*, also dedicated to responsible rule. Under this renewed Toronto leadership, a Reform resurgence began spreading in the province, heightened by Durham's weighty Report of 1839, which endorsed responsible government, urged other reforms and condemned the old Compact's grasp on power. In the autumn of 1839, Governor-General Poulett Thomson, later Lord Sydenham, arrived to effect some of the proposals, particularly a union of the two Canadas, which could effectively develop their joint St. Lawrence waterway

and commercial system. In 1840 an imperial Act of Union followed, to take effect early in 1841.

Assuredly, a different period was under way. Within the new United Province of Canada, an alliance of French and English Reformers was to obtain responsible rule before the decade closed. But whatever else transpired, not only did the former province of Upper Canada now cease to exist but Toronto also ceased to be a capital. Governor Sydenham considered that the city lay too far west in the extended Province of Canada to be its ruling seat, and chose Kingston instead. When his decision was made public, just before the United Province was proclaimed in February 1841, Kingston was gleeful at the downfall of its old rival, while Toronto was full of protests and dismay. Its press predicted ruinous declines in property values as provincial bureaucrats began to pack up for the move.[50]

And yet the change proved to have remarkably small effect. For one thing, the law courts, land agencies and some other government offices were not moved; Toronto still remained a provincial administrative centre. For another, Upper Canada did not wholly disappear, but stayed a distinctive section of the new Union — one very different from the Lower Canadian, largely French half — and although it now might be known on maps as "Canada West," the term "Upper Canada" continued in popular as well as some official use. Equally, Toronto continued to be an established focus within this section: a centre of Upper Canadian private and public elites, where the main churches, social organizations, chief newspapers and even party headquarters were still located for the western sectional community. But most important of all, Toronto by now had gained such a lead as a western urban centre, in population growth and commercial development, that the loss of its status as a capital made little serious difference to its fortunes.[51]

It also helped considerably that by the time of the move, world depression had lifted at last. With reviving export markets, imports for Toronto's hinterland correspondingly went up, and credit began to flow readily once more. By 1841, in fact, the city's commerce was on another ascending curve, to run to 1847. Enlarged wholesale, banking and insurance operations, increased harbour facilities and improved roads (especially the new plank roads), all strengthened Toronto's hold on a freshly prospering countryside. The results were displayed in more urban affluence, amenities and

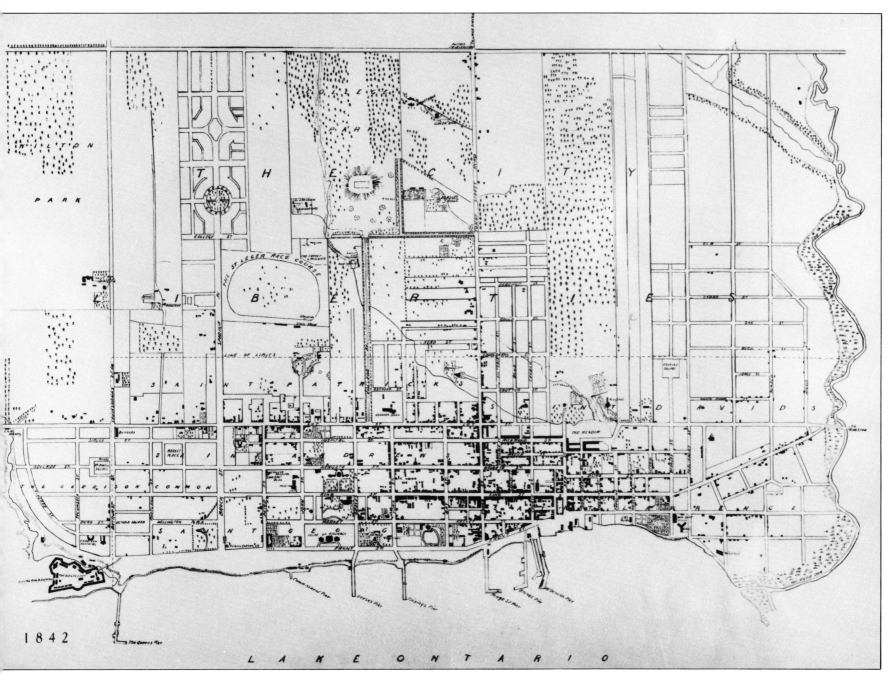

1842

Toronto by 1842. The built-up city had already reached above Queen, especially up Yonge in the Macaulaytown area, but much vacant land remained in the "liberties" to east and west, and particularly north to the Bloor Street limit.

construction — and perhaps in the incorporation of the Board of Trade in 1845 as the city merchants' own power and pressure group.

A better-off civic government looked to developing gas and water services, pushed on by Alderman George Gurnett as a leading advocate. In 1841 it franchised Albert Furniss of the Montreal Gas Light Company to supply the city.[52] The main streets were gas lit by the next year, and the waterworks were completed the year after, although there were constant complaints about inadequate water pressure for fire-fighting.[53] The city also built its own City Hall below the central market in 1844 — more elaborately styled, with its domed cupola and "Italianate" arcaded wings, than most Toronto public structures up to that time.[54] John Howard's massive new stone city jail and his handsome classical Bank of British North America were further additions. So were the attractive Gothic Revival Anglican churches, Little Trinity and Holy Trinity, by Henry Lane, the City Hall's architect: the first out eastern King Street, the second west off Yonge above Queen (as Lot Street became in 1843). A good deal larger, however, was the impressively Gothic Roman Catholic cathedral, St. Michael's, built by William Thomas in 1845 above Queen near Church.

A pillared Methodist church on Richmond west of Yonge (1844); the stately, domed Provincial Asylum by Howard well west out Queen, begun in 1846 but not finished until 1850; more downtown rows of houses and shops; and new mansions on emerging streets to northward: these, too, were products of the flourishing Forties. Still further, the university, King's College, opened in 1843, was temporarily housed in the former Parliament Buildings until new quarters were completed on its College Avenue grounds. Generally speaking, the whole ambience of Toronto altered over these years. A shambling boom town was already becoming a respectably integrated "city in earnest" — one linked by the electric telegraph to New York and Montreal in 1847.[55] Its affluence showed in the busy docks and customs house at the port, where Toronto shipowners now controlled a substantial fleet, notably of modern steamboats. Hugh Richardson's line boasted the new *Chief Justice Robinson*, while Donald Bethune's eight vessels made him by 1845 "the largest steam boat proprietor in Canada West."[56]

Throughout the period, the city government remained firmly in Tory hands: Mayor Powell being followed by George Monro in 1841, succeeded by Henry Sherwood, then William Henry Boulton,

and back to veteran George Gurnett as mayor from 1848 to 1850. Sherwood and Boulton, besides, were not just civic politicians, but also represented Toronto in the provincial legislature. The city had been given two parliamentary seats in the new United Province; these two staunch Tories held both of them for most of the decade. They won them, for example, in 1847 despite a Baldwin Reform sweep elsewhere, which led to fully operative responsible government in the province by 1848. The Tory pair even won Toronto again in 1851.

This prevailing political response (which Charles Dickens on a visit of the early Forties termed "the wild and rabid Toryism of Toronto")[57] was not wholly the consequence of British traditionalism, anti-American attitudes and acute memories of armed raids and revolt. It stemmed also from Toronto's very demography. In the continuing British immigration, the city had still collected a high proportion of Protestant Irish and Anglican English, both elements largely inclined to Tory-Conservatism. The weight of English massed, conceivably, because many of them were already urbanized, more adapted to city needs than were rural Scottish crofters or Catholic Southern Irish cottagers, and most of them could find congenial settings in the established patterns of Toronto. The sizeable Northern Irish contingent also included numbers of town-dwellers with urban-oriented skills; but whether these and more rural Ulstermen were drawn to the city by its British-Protestant affinities may scarcely be estimated. What can be noted is that the Ulster Orange Order continued to spread in Toronto as a benevolent association and tribal shelter for incoming Northern Irish. And the vehement pro-British loyalties and biases of the Order provided a powerful underpinning for Toronto Toryism, supplying rambunctious shock troops for election campaigns, besides political links reaching well into the lower classes.

Orangemen had played a stormy part in the provincial elections of 1836, although there was not much to choose then between their cudgels and those of Radical farmers. Orangemen were central in election rioting of 1841 in Toronto, which left one man dead, and in many other public disorders for years to come.[58] In any event, the Orange Order became a prominent feature in civic life from the Thirties onward, buttressing Conservative predominance and repeatedly influencing politics. But the point to note is that this was indeed a popular, mass force that inevitably widened the base of Toronto Toryism beyond a deferential support of established

City Hall of 1844, by H. B. Lane, facing north on Front, west of Jarvis. The centre block still exists, with its Council Chamber now a city art gallery.

Lane's Holy Trinity, erected in 1847, gave Macaulaytown its own Anglican church. In 1845 a Mrs. Lambert Swale of Yorkshire, England, gave the funds for this edifice, to have its seats free "forever" for the poor. A counterpart for the Anglican poor of the eastern end of town was Little Trinity.

John Howard's monumental Provincial Asylum (1846–50), out Queen West north of the Garrison. The tall dome actually concealed a water tank for this most "modern" structure.

The dignified Bank of British North America, raised in 1845 at the corner of Yonge and Wellington, was another of the many buildings in the young city designed by Howard.

Howard, seen in old age, also made many sketches and paintings of Toronto, collected art, and built a picturesque home, Colborne Lodge, on his High Park estate west of the city. His subsequent gift of magnificent High Park to Toronto in 1873 was a present beyond price.

old-family leadership. Family Compact patrician Toryism and Orange plebian Conservatism were not the same; and truth to tell, the former was fast running out, even before the revolt of 1837.

Compact officialdom, in fact, was not just a casualty of Durham's Report and the movement to responsible government, but also succumbed to a rising business and professional class leadership with popular mass backing. Toronto politics demonstrated as much in the 1840s. Tories might rule the city, but while they yet included gentry names, they reflected changing political and social patterns that affected town and country alike. Chief Justice Robinson might yet inveigh eloquently but fruitlessly against the Canadian Union that had ended his old provincial bailiwick; John Strachan, a bishop since 1839, was still an undaunted champion of Anglican vested interests. But neither sat in governing councils any more. In the city, Mayor W. H. Boulton, MPP, was still lord of The Grange with its carriage society and fine dinners, but he had to deal with shop-owners, building contractors and Orange chieftains to function in office — in politics that were often less than gentlemanly.

In sum, while the old-family presence still persisted, particularly in social repute, both politics and society in Toronto were increasingly finding new directors. In provincial circles, William Draper (who now became a Conservative party leader) exemplified the change: acceptably a Toronto gentleman and successful lawyer, he was a postwar English immigrant, not a descendant of old official-dom. In the city community, also, there were rising figures like the Ulster Irish wholesaler, William McMaster, the biggest Toronto capitalist of the coming era, and the Scottish Liberal journalist, George Brown, whose *Globe*, founded in 1844, was to be the most influential newspaper in English-speaking Canada for some forty years ahead. Not just the capital had departed Toronto, but the former government village society; and the consolidating commercial city was shaping a bourgeois leadership drawn mainly from the British immigrant influx that had swelled its numbers so significantly.[59]

The immigrant tide ran on quite steadily and with no great problems down to 1847: Quebec landings reached 44,000 in 1842 and 32,000 in 1846, by which time Toronto's own population, around 11,000 in 1837, was passing the 20,000 mark.[60] The year 1847, however, brought both renewed world depression and the startling arrival of nearly 90,000 migrants at Quebec.[61] The over-

The south side of King Street looking east towards St. James, 1847. A comparison with the picture of King in the 1830s, on page 44, conveys how the city's central core had grown and consolidated since then.

whelming majority of them were impoverished, disease-stricken refugees from an Ireland devastated since 1845 by famine. Faced again with bad times and an unprecedented flood of human misery, Toronto saw its integrating span of the 1840s come swiftly to an end. Nevertheless, some other, more long-range developments promised better things instead.

In 1846 Britain had adopted free trade, removing its tariff controls over colonial commerce. The consequent ending of imperial preferential duties was a hard blow to Montreal and Kingston merchants, along with those in other centres who had been mainly engaged in sending staple Canadian exports via the St. Lawrence route to protected British markets. But Toronto had its Hudson–New York links as well, and after the initial impact of depression, stood to benefit increasingly from the newly opened state of trade. Besides, the American Drawback Acts of 1845–46 had remitted tariff charges on goods in transit between U.S. Atlantic ports and Canada, so that Toronto business could now freely use American routes to send products outward, or as freely use them to bring imports direct from Britain. Cross-lake traffic would hence develop in new volume with American towns like Buffalo and Oswego, which gave access to the New York entrepôt via the direct, efficient Erie Canal. Thanks to the lifting of trade controls, Toronto might utilize either the St. Lawrence or Erie routes with almost equal facility, could even play one off against the other, and so enhance its own trading position at a breakpoint between the rival Montreal and New York systems.[62]

In fact, the coming of imperial free trade and the new ease in trans-border commerce virtually made good Toronto's potential advantages of site as a major focus of traffic on the Lower Lakes. In the economic growth that resulted, it was to fill out its commercial metropolitan role, add railway transport, and become the business nexus of most of Upper Canada. Accordingly, the city was on the verge of another era of rapid development by the late Forties, however grey and foreboding conditions might have looked just before the approaching dawn. The commercial town that took off was now heading towards much wider control of the Ontario lakelands. A consolidated, bourgeois Toronto was soon to be caught up in eagerly welcomed change.

Even amid signs of looming trouble in 1847, there was optimism.

That May a rising young city lawyer, trained in Draper's firm, Larratt Smith, wrote cheerfully to a relative in England:

> Canada is not such a wilderness as some imagine, and when you tread the gas lit streets of Toronto, and look into as many handsome shops with full length plate glass windows as there are in Bristol or London you will not look upon us as many of your countrymen do; when you see steamers entering our noble bay as comfortable as magnificent in their internal arrangements, the bay wharves, the thousands and thousands of passengers arriving hourly from the United States and all ports, the electric Telegraph almost from one end of the Province to another every moment conveying intelligence with the rapidity of thought, you will have every reason to be proud of your country and her glorious dependencies, if you never were before, and to thank God that you were born an Englishman.[63]

What more need anyone say?

The city in 1854. Growing fast in the new era of railway building, but not yet marked by tracks along the harbour, which would line the open stretch below Front Street, to be the Esplanade. The first train from Toronto had actually run in 1853, northward about twenty miles to Aurora. The early depot and track of this Northern line lay towards the left (west) end of this scene, but are not visible here.

Chapter Three
The Railway and Regional Hub, 1847–71

Mid-Victorian Toronto saw the advent of the railway, one of the nineteenth century's greatest instruments of change, which conquered continental land space and tied together existing populated areas. From the 1850s in Canada, extending rail lines fed and supplemented waterways, enabling far greater traffic flows and fostering much bigger urban centres at focal points on transport routes. For inland regions, moreover, this new technology overcame the annual winter closing, when shipping by lake and river ceased. And rough, inadequate roads, all but unusable during spring thaws and autumn freezes, no longer dictated the timing, reach and carrying capacity of traffic by land, since now both goods and passengers could move year-round by rail, on regular journeys across wide distances. The consequences for an advancing urban place such as Toronto were powerful and pervasive. Like other leading Canadian towns, it rose as a railway city during the mid-century era, pulsing with fresh activity and building. And it did particularly well as a rail transport hub by gaining much-improved lines outward, expanding hinterland links inward, and through its own vigorous enterprise. The years down to the 1870s thus saw striking growth in Toronto as this emerging transport metropolis became a commanding centre of regional life in general. But first the city faced grave social strains at the end of the Forties: strains that would by no means vanish, even with the climbing sweep of rail prosperity.

POPULATION CHANGES AND ETHNIC STRAINS IN SOCIETY

In June of 1847 young Larratt Smith had sent a less cheery letter overseas to England, this time describing the impoverished Irish famine immigrants who then were daily flooding into Toronto on their way westward from Quebec and Montreal:

They arrive here to the extent of about 300 to 600 by any steamer. The sick are immediately sent to the hospital which has been given up to them entirely and the healthy are fed and allowed to occupy the Immigrant Sheds for 24 *hours*; at the expiration of this time, they are obliged to keep moving, their rations are stopped and if they are found begging are imprisoned at once. Means of conveyance are provided by the Corporation to take them off at once to the country, and they are accordingly carried off "willy nilly" some 16 or 20 miles, North, South, East & West and quickly put down, leaving *the country* to support them by giving them employment.... John Gamble advertised for 50 for the Vaughan plank road, and hardly were the placards out, than the Corporation bundled 500 out and set them down.... It is a great pity we have not some railroads going on, if only to give employment to these thousands of destitute Irish swarming among us. The hospitals contain over 600 and besides the sick and convalescent, we have hundreds of widows and orphans to provide for.[1]

Smith's account was more matter-of-fact than sensitive — the response of the city corporation, more concerned with controlling the problem, and passing on as much of it as possible, than with relieving the misery of the sufferers. Nevertheless, these attitudes were widespread in the Toronto of the time, confronting social needs on a scale it had never before experienced, sharing assumptions that work and settlement in the rising countryside was the ever-present remedy for want in a new land, and possessing few means of public welfare, or even private assistance, within the inundated host community itself.

The rapid spread of typhus brought with immigrants who had often sailed in "floating pesthouses" made Toronto's difficulties far more acute.[2] As in the cholera epidemics of the Thirties, a temporary Board of Health had to cope with the emerging crisis. Annually

Appeal to the Citizens of Toronto, on behalf of the Widows and Orphans of Destitute Immigrants Dying here.

The Managing Committee of the Society for the relief of Widows and Orphans of destitute Immigrants, who have died in Toronto, feel persuaded that they have but to state to the citizens of Toronto the objects which they contemplate, and the means which they propose adopting to carry out those objects, to insure the warm co-operation of every benevolent individual in the community.

The number of orphans, as nearly as it can be ascertained, left at this moment in total destitution by the deaths of their natural protectors in this city, does not fall short of 140, and the helpless widows amount to at least 30. It is to provide temporary shelter and food for these unfortunates, until they can be distributed among those who are willing to receive them; providing for them in the mean time, as far as possible, such occupation as will tend to make them useful members of the community, that this society has been formed.— The committee intend devoting their best energies to procuring the permanent settlement of these helpless objects throughout the city and surrounding country, and are sanguine that in this their efforts will prove successful.

The committee have the gratification to state, that the gratuitous use of the barracks at the corner of Bathurst and Queen streets, has been granted to them, and the building is now being fitted up as a house of refuge. By this arrangement, the only item of expenditure, beyond mere necessaries of life for the inmates, will be the salary of the Superintendent. To this office an individual and his wife have been appointed, who, besides possessing valuable experience, acquired as overseer and matron of a Poor Law Union Work House in the old country, presented the most satisfactory testimonials as to character and conduct. The house will be under their management—open to the inspection of the public every day, and regularly visited by the committee. It is also hoped that many benevolent ladies will kindly take a part in the superintendence. But although the expenditure of the institution be narrowed to providing mere necessaries of life for its inmates, yet the great number to be supported will entail a very large expense, to meet which the committee make this appeal to the benevolence of their fellow citizens. —Subscriptions in money to an amount exceeding £300, have already been received, a quantity of clothing and flour are also at the disposal of the Committee, and every facility will be afforded to the humane to contribute to this work of charity. Articles of clothing and bedding, remnants of woollen and cotton materials, and food of all descriptions, will be gratefully accepted at the house, or sent for, upon due notification to the Superintendent. Mr. C. Foster has been appointed Collector, with instructions immediately to enter upon his duties,—in the discharge of which the Committee feel well assured he will be cordially and liberally met.

The poor were always with them. At right, Toronto's British Colonist *of 20 August 1847 calls for aid for Irish famine immigrants in that typhus-laden year. Top, the big charitable Roman Catholic House of Providence of the 1850s reflects enlarged Catholic numbers in the city. Above, the separate charities of the Protestant majority are evinced in this 1870 ball for the Orphans' Home.*

appointed by the council, its role had been only nominal since the last epidemic in 1834, but as reorganized under Alderman George Gurnett, the board of 1847 strove its best in the face of an economy-minded civic government and a citizenry fearful of contact with infected immigrants. The General Hospital was soon overflowing with sick and dying, and the board had to seek more funds for additional quarters.[3] By September close on 30,000 immigrants had reached Toronto, more than double the previous year's arrivals for the same period.[4] By mid-October there had been 3,300 admissions to the hospital and 757 deaths there.[5] The hospital's final mortality rate was about 29 per cent — a good deal lower, at least, than the 47 per cent at Kingston.[6] Meanwhile, Torontonians who sought to care for the stricken newcomers succumbed themselves, including Dr. George Grasett, the hospital superintendent, and the Catholic bishop, Dr. Michael Power. Aside from the devastation wrought by typhus, there was also the question of its helpless leavings: whole families, wrote Sheriff W. B. Jarvis to Mayor Boulton, "lying under the shelter of fences and trees, not only on the outskirts, but within the very heart of town — human beings begging for food, having disease and famine depicted in their countenances and without a shelter to cover them."[7]

Private charity did what it could; public meetings raised money to supply relief and work to survivors. The Toronto Destitute Widow and Orphan's Society provided aid through its subscriptions, larger sums coming from such as Bishop Strachan, Chief Justice Beverley Robinson and Robert Baldwin.[8] But only the winter 1847–48 ended the typhus epidemic and the worst suffering, as the immigrant season closed down. By that time 38,560 migrants had passed through Toronto, and 1,124 persons had died there, when the city then had but some 21,000 residents.[9]

There was not to be so bitter a plague experience as this in following years. In the 1848 season, the entrants at the port of Quebec comprised less than a third of the famine wave, and no great outbreak of disease accompanied them inward. The next year, however, the older enemy, cholera, invaded again, and in Toronto killed 424.[10] In 1854 it returned anew, to carry off close to 500.[11] But it did not threaten once more till 1866, and then turned out to be a scare, not a scourge. Thereafter, advances in medicine and sanitation largely brought an end to such drastic epidemics in the city. By then, moreover, the influx of transatlantic immigrants, so often associated with the fearsome spread of contagion, had long since ceased to be an annual flood.

In sum, the mass exodus to Canada from the British Isles that rose in 1820s had sharply dwindled by the 1860s as the supply of fertile colonial wild lands ran out, and as urbanized Britain now increasingly adjusted to its industrial existence. Through the late Forties and early Fifties, however, a still deeply blighted Ireland continued to send by far the biggest numbers across to Quebec yearly: altogether some 126,000 between 1848 and a final crest in 1854.[12] And during this last sweep of the great transatlantic movement, the heavy outflow from the desolated Irish countryside, mainly from the Catholic South, added to the famine survivors of 1847 to reinforce the Irish presence in Canada. Specifically in Toronto, the Catholic Irish ingredient in the community expanded sizeably, certainly contributing to the city's growth, and to its social and ethnic tensions as well.

The provincial census of 1851–52 recorded the Irish-born as already the largest single ethnic element in Toronto. Altogether they now constituted about 11,300 in a total city population of some 30,000, over a third. The English-born residents numbered 4,958, the Scots 2,169, and there were nearly 10,000 Canadian-born of "non-French" origin, 467 of French descent, 1,405 American-born, and a scattering of "other origins," including about 50 Jews.[13] In point of fact, the Anglo-Protestant ascendancy remained firm in the city, since the great majority still were English-speaking Protestants and the Irish-born themselves included many staunchly Orange Ulstermen. But the religious census for 1851 helped to reveal more. Although Anglicanism continued to be the largest denomination in Toronto (then having 11,577 adherents, to 4,123 for Methodism and 4,544 for Presbyterianism), the Roman Catholic church stood second, with 7,940 followers, mainly comprised of Irish Catholics.[14] By 1861, in a city that had now enlarged to over 44,000, the Roman Catholic element had climbed to 12,135 and the Anglicans held a much smaller lead at 14,125, though Methodism and Presbyterianism had also increased their proportions.[15]

These mounting Catholic Irish numbers made mid-century Toronto more than a little uncomfortable. They represented a challenge to its ruling Protestant patterns and presumptions. The newcomers required, and soon obtained, more Catholic churches and clergy; and the latter pressed demands for publicly organized, state-supported Catholic separate schools. The Orange Order grew freshly vigilant against papist threats, and the ancient homeland feud of Orange and Green took on new heat, recurrently erupting in mob violence. Moreover, wider anti-Catholic sentiments in the established community reflected current Protestant reactions in Britain and America against the anti-liberal papacy of the day, while "voluntaryism" — the view that churches should be voluntary associations of faith not backed or aided by the state — was also strong among the more evangelical Protestants in the city.[16]

In consequence, Protestant and Catholic spokesmen in Toronto were drawn into sweeping doctrinal disputes. A sectarian war of newspapers broke out, to be waged recurrently through the 1850s and beyond, waged especially by a powerful Liberal *Globe* (under the resolutely voluntaryist Presbyterian, George Brown) against an ardent Irish Catholic *Mirror* and its religious allies. The dominant majority came broadly to regard the Catholic Irish as an obstreperous, discordant block, and anxious eyes were drawn to the "Catholic vote," locally or provincially. But beyond these religious and political troubles, the fact that the Irish influx largely went to swell the unpropertied element in Toronto further sharpened urban social tensions.

That the arriving Irish massed generally and for years ahead in the lower ranks of civic society was none too surprising. Those who had fled famine in 1847, and survived typhus to be dumped destitute in or out of town, were unlikely candidates for starting farms or launching city enterprises — or finding much more than day-labour for men, household or laundry work for women. From about 1850 a newly rising boom did open many pick-and-shovel jobs in urban construction, or soon in railway building. Yet even after the worst hardships had passed for the Irish arrivals of 1847, their countrymen who followed them were not much better equipped to advance economically and socially. They came mostly from a deprived, parochial rural tenantry, ill-conditioned for a starkly strange new world. The strength of their family, locality and religious ties, still helped them to cohere, to look after their own, and in time to adjust to their new environment. In all this, in fact, the experiences of the Catholic Irish were not too different from those of later disadvantaged ethnic elements who settled in

Toronto. At least they had English (though not all did) and were already British subjects — however much some of them might harbour dark memories of that fact.[17]

At any rate, the reactions of established Toronto society to the displaced Catholic Irish collecting in its midst were a good deal like those the host community would show to subsequent ethnic groups who also entered at near-bottom levels. These newcomers seemed entirely too cohesive and distinctive as they crowded into mean shanty dwellings. At one extreme, indeed, the Irish might be sentimentalized as naturally humorous and good-hearted; but at the other, the possessing order in Toronto quite readily regarded them as ignorant, feckless and a threat to lawful peace. In fact, such prejudiced opinions had some basis, given the harsh background of these immigrants and their difficult, often demoralizing, conditions of life in the urban setting. Irish names loomed on police records or among jail inmates (and certainly were so noted), especially in cases of disorderly conduct or personal assaults. Irish drunkenness in squalid little tippling shops, Irish vagrancy and illiteracy, drew the attention of the temperance advocates, moral reformers and apostles of mass public schooling who rose vigorously in the city from around the mid-century onward. At root these problems were the general troubles of a massing urban society. Yet a bottom class provided underdogs to whom social faults were regularly attributed; and in the 1850s the Catholic Irish were conspicuously represented in it in Toronto.[18]

During the same period, there was also a much smaller black migration into the city. While never numerous, blacks had been present there from the founding days of York; but in the early Fifties the drastic Fugitive Slave Law in the United States brought hundreds of refugee slaves to seek haven in Upper Canada, the final terminus of the celebrated "Underground Railroad." Many of them came on to Toronto, about as destitute as the famine Irish has been; yet the strength of local abolitionist sympathies brought them aid, particularly from the earnest Toronto Anti-Slavery Society.[19] Charity, however, cooled in time, especially after the Civil War of 1861–65 did away with slavery in the United States. Still not that numerous, some blacks moved off to farm-settlement projects; some returned to the republic after the Civil War; and others stayed on in Toronto, where colour prejudice surely helped to hold them largely at low levels. The "respectable Negro" might

Queen's Birthday celebration at Government House, 1854. Whatever the ethnic strains in mid-Victorian Toronto, its British loyalism remained fully apparent, as suggested by this early work of the Toronto painter Lucius O'Brien, then twenty-two.

aspire within much restricted limits; by contrast, the Irish immigrant experience was an open-ended exercise in upward social mobility.

As for the bigger Irish influx, it not only anticipated the heavy immigrant intakes and resulting social reactions known to the twentieth-century metropolis, but through its powerful impact on the Victorian city was also highly consequential in its own right. In Victorian Toronto, the Irish were long to form a major part of the urban masses. Working-class movements, civic politics, public education, would all be deeply affected by Catholic-Protestant divisions. So to some extent would residential location, as markedly Catholic Irish neighbourhoods emerged at the eastern and western ends of town.[20] So would public order — during Orange-Green antagonisms expressed in election clashes, at celebrations of Catholic festivals, or at Orange parades on the "Glorious Twelfth" of July. And so would the treatment of civic welfare needs, largely handled through dual Catholic and Protestant-majority services.[21] The altered population pattern of the mid-century, the Celtic-Catholic qualification on an Anglo-Protestant city, left a strong mark on its social responses also.

Nevertheless, owing to the drop in transatlantic migration over the later Fifties and much of the Sixties, mid-Victorian Toronto had some interval in which recent comers and older residents could gradually adjust to each other. At the same time, its non-immigrant, native-born element steadily expanded in proportion, almost tripling between 1851 and 1871, and constituting over half the population by the latter date.[22] Of course, many of these native-born in 1871 represented the children of earlier British immigrants. Still, while Toronto consequently retained its basic British ethnicity, it was steadily being Canadianized as well. In the later Sixties, it is true, the intake of immigrants began another rise, largely because of job opportunities in a city then entering another boom phase; but it scarcely attained its earlier levels. Notably, too, of those British who did come after 1866, the English again became the largest group. In 1869, for instance, out of some 20,000 departures from the British Isles for Canada, over 7,200 English picked Toronto for their destination compared with about 1,550 Scots and only 811 Irish.[23] Once more we cannot be sure how many of these departing actually arrived and stayed. Yet their relative ratios are significant, and they represent a continuing trend rather than special examples.

The census of 1871 showed Toronto with a total population of over 56,000: among them, in rounded numbers, 11,000 English-born, 10,300 Irish-born Catholics and Protestants, 3,200 Scots, nearly 2,000 Americans and about 29,500 Canadian-born; the remainder being mere handfuls, mainly of northern Europeans.[24] In religious affiliation, there now were about 20,600 Anglicans, 11,800 Roman Catholics, 9,600 Methodists, 8,900 Presbyterians and 1,900 Baptists, plus other small Protestant groups.[25] Plainly, this Anglo-Celtic city had remained overwhelmingly Protestant, but with a strong Catholic contingent and a continuing Anglican lead. Thus had demographic and ethnic change worked out over the whole mid-Victorian period: to strain and yet confirm the dominant patterns of the Toronto community.

URBAN ECONOMY: THE COMING OF THE RAILWAY

Population strains might have proved still sharper, had not Toronto's economy also grown so extensively over the period. Following the late-Forties' depression, prosperity returned to world commerce around 1850, backed by California gold discoveries, industrial expansion in western Europe and the eastern United States, and by generally strong demands for staple goods. In Canada a mounting inflow of British capital soon fed railway building, while in Upper Canada a veritable wheat boom arose in its more recently settled, fertile western peninsula. Still further, the Reciprocity Treaty of 1854 brought free trade with the United States for basic products like grain and lumber. Business and prices climbed swiftly, and in an increasingly inflationary but keenly optimistic era, Toronto's own economic life surged forward. One indicator, city assessments, shot from £132,359 to £186,983 just from 1850 to 1851.[26]

Aided by the American bonding system completed in 1852, the city took full advantage of its trans-lake and Erie Canal trade links. Import trade, its leading commerce, rose fivefold in value between 1849 and 1856, from some $1,200,000 to over $6,600,000 — a figure not to be surpassed till 1867.[27] Its export trade, while of lesser weight, also made it a major port in shipping grain and wood. "It seems like magic!" declared the *Globe*. "We question whether there is a town in the world which has advanced more rapidly than Toronto."[28] For the well-to-do, the good times meant opportunities for investment and development, for entrepreneurship and speculation. For poorer citizens, however, they also spelled inflating costs of living and housing, even though jobs grew more plentiful and money wages rose.

Skilled workers in particular felt prices pressing on their established craft status, and made fresh attempts at trade unionism to protect their positions, raise pay or shorten hours.[29] A series of sporadic strikes ensued, most notably by printers at the *Globe* in 1854.[30] That journal, now the strongest voice of Liberalism in the city, was no less directed by a thorough economic liberal, George Brown, who vigorously fought these assaults on the masters' freedom of contract. By and large the unionizing efforts faded out, though wage levels did go up markedly over 1853.[31] The city's industrial work force was still too limited and dispersed for unions to take firm hold. Nevertheless, some wider trades organization did subsequently appear when a branch of the British Amalgamated Society of Engineers was set up by machinists in Toronto in 1858; while in 1860 the American-based Iron Moulders laid foundations for future "international" unionism in the town.[32] And in any event, if not yet unionized or industrialized, Toronto's whole economic life was being sweepingly altered during the Fifties.

The lands beyond it were fast filling in. Frontier farm extension had met the rugged barriers of the Precambrian Shield, and intensive rural growth took over more and more. The consequences appeared in well-tilled acres that replaced stump fields, in brick and frame farmhouses instead of squared-log cabins, and in thriving villages that had been bush hamlets, now linked by improved roads, mail services and spreading newspapers to local commercial towns. As a major centre, Toronto profited increasingly from this hinterland progress, drawing on the gains of the farmsteads and lesser country places. Its own core area of trade by the early Fifties covered an Upper Canadian central zone roughly extending east to Durham County, north to around Barrie on Lake Simcoe, and west into the grainfields of Peel.[33] Further westward, the enterprising head-of-the-lake town, Hamilton, offered strenuous competition; further eastward there was Kingston still, while on the north, much of Simcoe County up to Georgian Bay was as yet little developed. Toronto's economic hinterland was hence still very much smaller than the whole Upper Canadian region. But this hinterland assuredly was flourishing, was generally well tied to its commanding city — and the advancing means of land transport, the railway, could powerfully enlarge it. And so Toronto in its fresh phase of growth turned heartily to railways.

In 1853 a line opened from Montreal to Portland, Maine, gave St. Lawrence transport an ice-free Atlantic outlet. By 1855 the Great Western (GWR) had built from the Niagara River via Hamilton to the Detroit River, connecting the American rails to New York at the one end with track westward across Michigan at the other (Map 4). But much the largest line was the Grand Trunk, chartered in 1852–53. When complete in 1860, this railway, capitalized in London but centred on Montreal, spanned United Canada, from Quebec to Montreal and Toronto, then on via Guelph to Sarnia at the foot of Lake Huron. Though enmeshed in politics and loaded with debt, the great transprovincial rail route provided all-year land transit between the Canadian interior and the St. Lawrence ports, effectively opening the "spring trade" of Toronto merchants two months earlier.[34] The city would gain abundantly from its new Grand Trunk access far to east and west. Yet other lines also came to serve it well, especially the Northern Railway, a Toronto-based venture backed by civic loans, which built to Georgian Bay on Lake Huron, thereby renewing the old Toronto Passage.

The Northern, initially named the Ontario, Simcoe and Huron, began construction in October 1851 at a gala ground-breaking ceremony on Front Street. Its track reached Barrie in 1853 and Collingwood, the newly laid-out terminal port on Georgian Bay, in 1855. The route soon began to flourish as the lands of Simcoe County were thereby opened up, and not only farm produce but lumber from huge Georgian Bay forests came down to Toronto by rail. In truth, this expanded hinterland freight traffic proved far more substantial to the city than the envisioned wealth to be won from a re-established passage to the great North West.[35] Nonetheless, Toronto business leaders looked to develop shipping services on the Upper Lakes out of Collingwood, to link one day with the western plains still ruled by the Hudson's Bay Company, and so win a vast new commercial empire for their city.[36] Meanwhile, a wide area northward had been tapped by rail into Toronto, making it a much bigger port for lumber shipments to the United States, and, by the Sixties, attracting a wheat flow down the Northern from American ports around the Upper Lakes that brought grain elevators to rise beside Toronto Bay.[37]

The same year that the Northern was completed, 1855, the Great Western Railway was extended into Toronto from Hamilton. This Toronto "branch" was largely viewed by the Hamilton-based GWR as an outthrust to tie the Toronto market into its rail

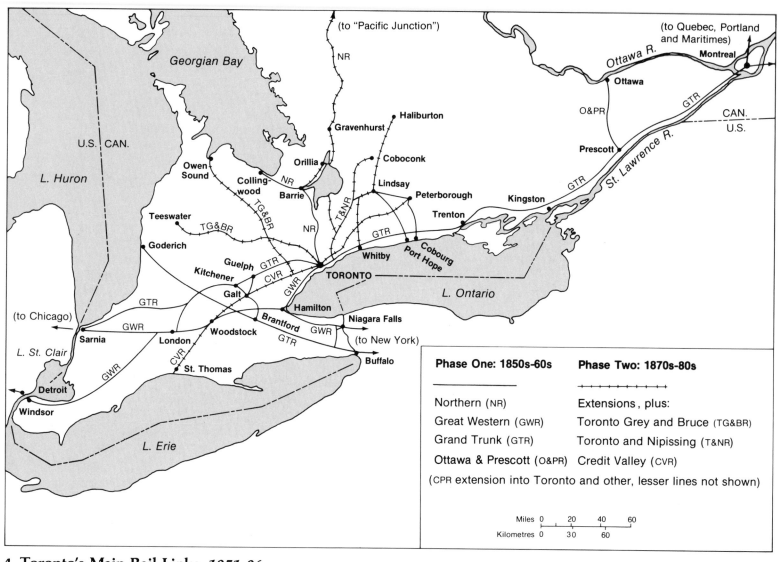

(to "Pacific Junction")

NR

Georgian Bay

(to Quebec, Portland and Maritimes)

Ottawa R.

Montreal

Ottawa

O&PR

GTR

CAN.

U.S.

Prescott

St. Lawrence R.

Haliburton

Gravenhurst

GTR

Coboconk

U.S. CAN.

L. Huron

Owen
Sound

Colling-
wood

Orillia

NR

Lindsay

Barrie

Peterborough

T&NR

Kingston

Teeswater

TG&BR

TG&BR

NR

Trenton

Goderich

GTR

Whitby

Cobourg
Port Hope

Guelph

GTR

CVR

GWR

TORONTO

Kitchener

L. Ontario

Galt

GTR

Hamilton

(to Chicago)

GWR

Brantford

Niagara Falls

GWR

Woodstock

Sarnia

London

GTR

(to New York)

L. St. Clair

CVR

St. Thomas

Buffalo

Detroit

Windsor

L. Erie

Phase One: 1850s-60s	Phase Two: 1870s-80s
Northern (NR)	Extensions, plus:
Great Western (GWR)	Toronto Grey and Bruce (TG&BR)
Grand Trunk (GTR)	Toronto and Nipissing (T&NR)
Ottawa & Prescott (O&PR)	Credit Valley (CVR)
(CPR extension into Toronto and other, lesser lines not shown)	

Miles 0   20   40   60

Kilometres 0   30   60

4 Toronto's Main Rail Links, 1851-86

*The first locomotive on the first railroad out of Toronto, the wood-burning **Lady Elgin** was named for the wife of the then governor-general. She lifted the first sod for the Ontario Simcoe and Huron (from 1858 the Northern) on Front Street in October 1851. This engine (costing $9,000), however, proved too light for all but construction work, and was soon superseded by those from James Good's foundry on Queen Street.*

Davenport Station on the Northern, a rural location now deep within Toronto. The station building was a model in its day.

system across southwestern Upper Canada. Instead, Hamilton and the whole Southwest found themselves increasingly tied into Toronto. The much larger centre, with its greater trading facilities, business resources and market demands, exercised the stronger focusing power. In effect, the fast-rising western peninsula beyond Hamilton was opened to Toronto as never before, through Woodstock and London by rail to Windsor, where train ferries crossed to Detroit and American tracks to Chicago. Furthermore, since the Great Western also joined with lines to New York, Toronto equally gained direct rail access to the giant American supply and market centre, a major supplement to the Erie Canal route.[38] No wonder the jubilant city celebrated a "Great Railway Festival" when the link to Hamilton was opened in December 1855 with a banquet and ball for 5,000 guests, held in the big new Northern Railway workshops, lavishly decorated for the occasion.[39]

The next year the Grand Trunk reached the city from Montreal, then built on westward towards Sarnia. The long Sarnia section of the line extended Toronto's traffic hinterland along a more northerly route across the broad western peninsula, on a direct course running from Toronto harbour. The track to Sarnia was not completed until 1859, by which time Canada's first railway boom had collapsed, following financial crashes in London and New York in 1857. But though depressed times lasted on into the Sixties (until the American Civil War revived market demands), the exuberant rail-building years left far more behind them than heavy loads of public debt, bankrupt schemes and strained finances — all of which certainly affected Toronto, along with other centres hit still harder.

To begin with, the city's commercial and financial growth had been strongly stimulated. Its trading activities essentially had mounted as its transport hinterland spread out by rail. Nor was this only through the wider reach of its wholesale imports. Toronto also increasingly took command of the western Upper Canada grain export trade, wresting much of it from Hamilton, for which town the building of the Grand Trunk behind it — from Toronto right to Sarnia — completed its downfall as a serious commercial rival in the 1860s.[40] Hence, still-larger Toronto mercantile houses developed in keeping with the greater scope of business. Prominent among them was that of John Macdonald, a Scot who rose with the dry-goods enterprise he began in 1849 to become a "merchant prince," whose firm occupied a city block by 1865, a capitalist-politician and ultimately a senator.[41] The Toronto Stock Exchange began in 1852, ministering to the city's grain dealers and wholesalers, and further promoting its role as a commercial metropolis. And during the Fifties the Toronto Board of Trade became a powerful rostrum for the urban mercantile elite.[42] At the same time, the capital and expertise required in large-scale trade, or in the corporate dealings of railway companies, fostered new joint-stock financial and investment enterprises. The Bank of Toronto was founded in 1856, also serving grain and wholesale interests, with J. G. Chewett as first president, J. G. Worts as a major shareholder, and from 1862, William Gooderham as one of three successive presidents drawn from his family.[43] Insurance companies, building and loan firms multiplied as well, the most significant among the latter, the Canada Permanent Building and Savings Society, incorporated in 1855 under directors such as Chewett and Worts again.

This wave of entrepreneurship produced new prominent figures of the railway age. There was Frederick Capreol, the initial driving force behind the Northern Railway — who indeed sought to finance it by a public lottery, an idea sharply rejected by righteous mid-Victorian Toronto.[44] He subsequently lost control of the project, but it was effected under Frederic W. Cumberland, another Englishman, long influential in his adopted city as an engineer, architect and director-manager. And the Scot, Sandford Fleming, who became the Northern's chief engineer in 1857, went on thereafter to construct other lines, to survey the Canadian Pacific Railway (CPR) across the West, and pioneer the idea of Standard Time that would end the chaos of "local-time" railway schedules. Then also there was Casimir Gzowski, originally an exile from the abortive revolution of 1830 in Poland. He organized his own heavy construction company in 1853, which largely built the Toronto-Sarnia line of the Grand Trunk. In his engineering career, Gzowski later erected a massive new international bridge at Niagara, and wealthy, subsequently knighted, he long remained a leading figure in Toronto's inner circles.

Railways also laid foundations for new industrial growth. They tended to foster concentrations of industry, since the vastly improved land transport they provided invited economies of scale, whereby more could be done efficiently and cheaply by larger producing units in major places than by a host of little mills or workshops strung out across the country. This concentrating nevertheless took time. It only saw its beginnings in Toronto of the

Casimir Gzowski, with his family in the 1850s. Builder of the St. Lawrence and Atlantic, the Grand Trunk west from Toronto, and the Esplanade that brought tracks to the harbour, he also developed the heavy Toronto Rolling Mills to produce iron rails. His elegant Italianate residence stood on Bathurst.

Frederic Cumberland, Toronto entrepreneur of the railway era, managing director of the Northern, major city architect, and later member of parliament for Algoma — an early linking of Toronto interests with the Ontario north.

1860s, though ardent boosters then sought a cotton mill, a sugar refinery and a large new brewery, unsuccessfully. The change from localized patterns of merely minor manufacturing would not occur overnight; and it was risky to undertake big industrial enterprises, especially after the severe crash of 1857 cut down credit and investment funds for some years. Still, the change went forward. It was evidenced, for instance, in the fine five-floor, stone Gooderham distillery of 1859, and especially in the Toronto Rolling Mills set up by Gzowski and his partner, D. L. Macpherson, in 1857 to supply rails for their Grand Trunk contract. By the mid-Sixties the Toronto Mills near the Don's mouth turned out tons of manufactured nails as well as railway iron.[45] This was a pioneering plant of large-scale metal industry — and a clear product of the railway.

The railway, after all, was the first direct major impingement of the Industrial Revolution on Toronto. In comparison, the earlier wooden steamboats of the waterways had had far less effect, requiring merely a limited amount of machine and metal technology. Not so the locomotives, cars and iron road on land. They demanded far more from the metal trades, and so laid a broader basis for mechanized industry. On the Northern, for example, while its first small locomotive had been brought complete from Portland, the second was produced by James Good's foundry in Toronto.[46] Other engineering enterprises followed as railway work enlarged technical capacity, pointing onward to much fuller later industrialization.

But for the Toronto of the Fifties and Sixties, the most sweeping effect of railways was undoubtedly the remaking of its whole land transport system. To the north, this system had reached the rim of the Upper Great Lakes basin. To the west, its traffic now extended to the bounds of farming Upper Canada; western towns like Hamilton, Brantford or London might still control a good deal of local activity, but could not contend against the overall transport mastery of Toronto. Eastward, its one-time rival, Kingston, had declined still further. The Grand Trunk's line lay inland behind that town, but in any case, the "focusing" tendency of rail transport, to feed to and from main centres, effectively diminished Kingston's own realm. Instead, Toronto's distributing trade spread on eastward into the upper St. Lawrence area. Here, however, and in the Ottawa Valley, the commercial grasp of Montreal remained powerfully felt. But for the bulk of the region, the strategic web of tracks that now radiated southwest, west, north and east from that city's harbour made Toronto the railway hub of Upper Canada, and greatly thanks to this, the main regional business hub as well.

Toronto still had to contend with Montreal on varied fronts, while equally dealing with it as a major outlet and source of supply. The older, much bigger urban centre, with 90,000 inhabitants in 1861 to Toronto's 44,000, was at least as well served by rail and water transport, had far greater wholesaling, banking and processing facilities, and still exercised wide influence across the whole Upper Canadian business realm.[47] In the depression of the late Fifties and early Sixties, Toronto's import trade even lost some ground to Montreal's, but by the end of the decade it had regained the loss, particularly in higher-value goods.[48] Above all, Toronto consistently made use of its alternative links to New York for market and supply. It continued to play off the Erie "ditch" (down which travelled most of Upper Canada's grain crop in these years) against the St. Lawrence route, and now it had its own rail connections southward as well. Consequently, the city's businessmen and politicians fought attempts favouring Montreal interests to set preferential provincial duties on transport by way of the St. Lawrence.[49] Its Board of Trade and press generally voiced righteous free-trade principles. They opposed the placing of any barriers to the ready flow of goods to and from the United States, which might — worst of all — invite an end to the Reciprocity Treaty and the return of high American tariff rates. For reciprocity and railways had facilitated the burgeoning Lake Ontario city's access to the American seaboard, giving it a still stronger offset to either rail or water dominance from Montreal.

Toronto also had to fight the power of Montreal finance. During the stringent early Sixties, its own key Bank of Upper Canada became seriously embarrassed, in part the result of poor management and overinvestment in unrealizable land and railway assets.[50] Further damage was done when provincial government accounts were withdrawn for safety from the troubled bank in 1863. And under a sharply restrictive credit policy now really directed by the biggest Canadian bank, the Bank of Montreal, as government agent, the Bank of Upper Canada floundered more and more. In 1866 it had to close its doors. Toronto businessmen widely saw the failure as deliberately engineered. But out of it came a more aggressive enterprise founded in the city in 1867, the Canadian Bank of

Toronto Rolling Mills, 1864. The importing of steel rails by the 1870s removed the need to re-roll iron ones grown brittle in use, and so ended this early example of industrialism, luridly painted here by William Armstrong.

The Exchange Building, erected in 1855 on Wellington east of Yonge, testified to the growth of milling, transport and banking interests in the railway city. This is a notably early photograph, of 1856, by the "photographists" Armstrong, Beere and Hime.

Commerce, pushed on by the powerful wholesaler William McMaster. With McMaster as first president and John Macdonald and H. S. Howland (a leading wholesale hardware merchant) among its directors, the well-funded Commerce was soon to become Toronto's prime banking house and spread its branches widely. Moreover, between 1869 and 1871 the city's financial interests mounted a strong campaign to secure new legislation that would save note-issuing chartered banks from the sway of one paramount, government-favoured bank of issue — namely, the Bank of Montreal. They succeeded through measures now put forward by Sir Francis Hincks as minister of finance. In banking as well, then, Toronto business defended and advanced its own domain.[51]

Port activities, however, advanced far less in the urban economy. Over the period, Toronto's harbour traffic certainly enlarged to serve the expanding community, drawing ships from Kingston and Oswego, Cleveland and Chicago. Yet rail competition and the depression of the late Fifties took a heavy toll on the city's own shipping. Toronto-owned steamboats nearly disappeared; by the early Sixties steam service was virtually left to Kingston, Montreal or American-registered boats, while resident shipmasters retreated to sailing craft.[52] To an extent, this was a practical conservatism: sailing vessels still handled a major share of bulk water-carriage, and they were much less costly — and explosive — than steamers. Nevertheless, it also indicated that Toronto investments in transport had now turned chiefly to land lines inward, leaving its outward water traffic far more to other centres. This same attitude was reflected in a relative failure to improve port facilities. In 1850 the province had set up a Toronto Harbour Trust with members from the City Council and Board of Trade. Its funds were small; the needs were large.[53] Spurred by Hugh Richardson as first harbourmaster, the trust did make some progress down to 1862, rebuilding the important but decrepit Queen's Wharf and dredging the main channel entry. But by then finances were still slighter, as was public interest. Any waterfront developments thereafter rested mainly in private hands, including railways like the Northern and Grand Trunk, which built their own dock facilities. Here, too, railways had their way at the port — another sign of the triumph of rail over older transport modes.

URBAN LANDSCAPE: BUILDING THE RAILWAY CITY

The buoyant growth of the rail-construction era also promoted a major phase of urban building in Toronto, much of which survives today to mark one of its best architectural periods, thoroughly derivative in styles, but happily adapted by a set of remarkably versatile architects. Almost at the outset, in 1851, William Thomas's St. Lawrence Hall was completed to provide a first-class public auditorium. Facing north on King Street, with a new market wing behind it, the grandly classic edifice further helped to focus communal activity around the area of central King. International artists played here: the "Swedish Nightingale," Jenny Lind, in 1851, Ole Bull in 1853 and 1857, Adelina Patti in 1853 and 1860. Leading politicians drew crowds to its main chamber; and balls, lectures, performances of the current hit, *Uncle Tom's Cabin*, or gatherings of the Anti-Slavery Society kept the hall in constant use.[54] It became the civic forum of the bustling mid-Victorian community.

The erection of St. Lawrence Hall was part of considerable new construction around central King Street, largely due to the Great Fire of 7 April 1849. The fire began in a stable, then swept over ten downtown acres, from Church Street on the west to George on the east, and from King northward to Adelaide. Winds, inadequate fire equipment and faulty water supply were chiefly responsible for the blaze's spread. At length, the open ground of St. James's churchyard, a brief shower, and the arrival of troops from the Garrison to help the exhausted volunteer fire companies, enabled the conflagration to be checked. Only one life was lost, and most of the structures destroyed were of a fairly nondescript commercial and storage character.[55] Nevertheless, the north range of the market had been burned out, as had St. James's itself and the offices of the Reform *Mirror* and Conservative *Patriot*. Accordingly, St. Lawrence Hall and Market arose instead, together with large white-brick blocks of stores and a lofty new St. James Cathedral of yellow brick, built in Early English Gothic by F. W. Cumberland and his partner, Thomas Ridout, and finally opened in 1853.

Major construction proceeded elsewhere, too. The handsomely classic Normal School (by Cumberland and Ridout) was built off Yonge at Gould in 1851, a teacher-training centre for the provincial school system being zealously developed from the mid-Forties under Chief Superintendent Egerton Ryerson. A large Mechanics Institute building (by Cumberland and W. G. Storm) went up at

King Street East, south side, winter of 1856. Another early streetscape by Armstrong, Beere and Hime, it shows not only prominent stores like the Golden Lion, at left, but also a plank sidewalk and a still-unpaved, muddy thoroughfare.

St. Lawrence Hall, by William Thomas, opened on the south side of King at Jarvis, 1851. Its tall classical cupola, columns and carved stonework expressed Toronto's rising prosperity and aspirations.

St, James' Cathedral, north side of King at Church: the large new Gothic structure by Cumberland and Ridout finished in 1853. Its present spire was not added till the 1870s.

Adelaide and Church in 1854, containing a library and music hall as well as meeting rooms. In 1855 a new General Hospital was erected east off Gerrard, in "modified Old English" by William Hay (Map 5). In 1856 William Kauffman's big Rossin House replaced the Chewett Block at King and York; it was a worthily metropolitan hotel in five storeys of freestone and white brick, boasting fifteen ground-floor shops with plate-glass windows and over 180 well-appointed bedrooms, plus reception hall, ladies' parlour and gentlemen's baths.[56] The same year a long-lived major rival appeared on Front — best known as the Queen's Hotel, it would last until the Royal York was built upon its site in the 1920s.

And since Toronto again became a political capital in this era, the seat of government (periodically) of the United Province of Canada, the former Upper Canada Parliament Buildings on Front were extensively refurbished, as was the adjacent Government House. Being renewed as capital affected the now high-riding commercial and railway city only temporarily, but it does need explaining. Small-sized Kingston had proved inadequate to house the provincial political establishment, and in 1844 Montreal had taken over as government centre — until a mob burned down its Parliament Building in April 1849. Afterwards, the capital of a sectionally divided province was shifted between Toronto and Quebec, the old governing seats of Upper and Lower Canada, mainly because neither section of the Union would willingly accept a permanent capital in the other. The prickly seat-of-government problem was finally resolved by the mid-way choice of Ottawa, but the government buildings erected there were only occupied late in 1865. Thus, Toronto served as Union capital in 1849–51 and 1855–59, after which Quebec did duty until Ottawa was ready.

In any case, Toronto remained the central judicial seat for Upper Canada, and Osgoode Hall, home of the Law Society, was much rebuilt to house the leading jurists in proper style. In 1857 Cumberland and Storm provided a lordly classical portico that unified the structure, and a magnificent, vaulted library within — thus to achieve one of the finest edifices in Toronto in that day or this. And the resourceful Cumberland also designed no less a distinguished home for the provincial university in a very different mode: University College, chiefly Norman mediaeval in form and massively reared in stone by 1859, in the university's estate that headed College Avenue.

That institution had known a trying career before its splendid new building put it squarely in the landscape. In 1849 the Baldwin Reform government of the day had transformed Anglican-dominated King's College into a secular University of Toronto, leaving Bishop Strachan denouncing the new "godless university." Indeed, the indefatigable bishop secured a royal charter for a new Anglican Trinity College, whose own sizeable building, in Tudor Gothic by Kivas Tully, was erected on Queen Street in 1851. Furthermore, other denominations' colleges in Upper Canada, especially the Methodists' Victoria College at Cobourg (backed by the influential Egerton Ryerson), continued to demand shares in the provincial university endowment. Only the construction of University College, as the teaching establishment of the degree-granting University of Toronto, literally placed the non-denominational state institution on firm ground, significantly confirming public university training in Toronto. Significant, too, as marking a development that in time would see other higher educational institutions gathering about this academic focus, Roman Catholic St. Michael's College settled itself to the east of the University grounds in 1856–57.

A big Masonic Hall by Kauffman, new churches, and much residential building further marked the railway city's growth. Homes for the rich tended to be Gothic-Romantic, with pinnacles, battlements and turrets, such as William McMaster's 1860 mansion on newly stylish northern Jarvis Street or John Macdonald's "Oaklands," set in a broad estate up Avenue Road on the rise beyond Bloor. Some larger homes adopted the increasingly fashionable Italianate style, like Casimir Gzowski's out west on Bathurst, featuring round-arched windows and overhanging cornices below low-pitched roofs, though others still were more classically derived. Many smaller houses also went up for the well-to-do middle class, particularly in dignified terraces along streets adjacent to the downtown core. Admirably proportioned, if plainly built in brick, with large shuttered windows and high ceilings, these row-houses offered ample room for the families of professional men, lesser merchants and officials.

As for the lower classes, they had mainly to be content with little clapboarded or rough-cast cottages still scattered throughout the city, but more especially located towards its edges. There, at least, they had gardens and some space around them, while yet being

An 1856 view of Trinity College by Kivas Tully, opened in 1852 on Queen West beyond Garrison Creek. This was the centre of Anglican university training well into the twentieth century.

University College: original architectural drawing before construction was begun in 1857, depicting what the architect Cumberland wanted and largely achieved, and also the ungroomed "campus" then.

Osgoode Hall on Queen: a west wing and centre block had been built in the 1840s, but Cumberland and Storm remodelled the whole, 1857-60, adorning it and creating its present fine facade.

The Rossin House, by William Kauffman — Toronto's first grand-scale hotel, 1856, not yet in business, at King and York. The downtown construction boom is suggested by the excavation in the foreground.

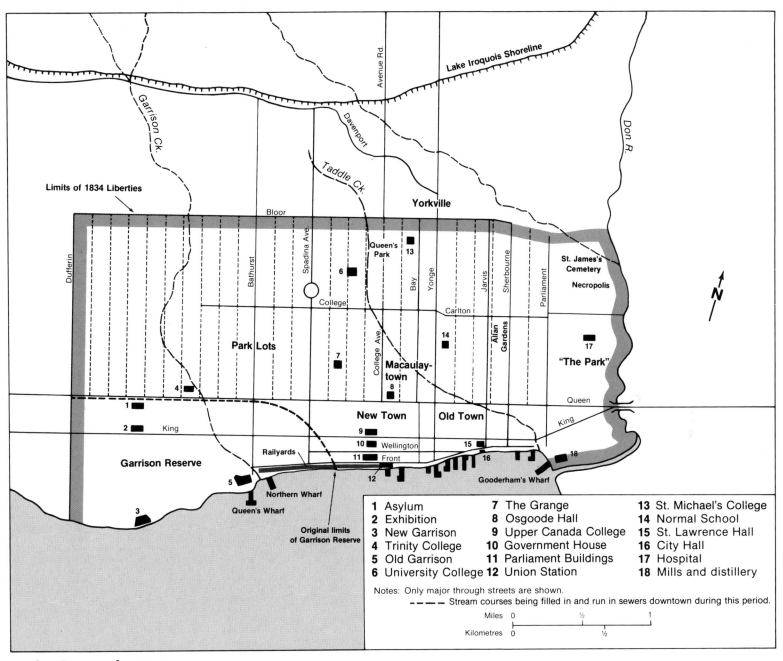

Limits of 1834 Liberties

Garrison Ck.

Lake Iroquois Shoreline

Avenue Rd.

Davenport

Taddle Ck.

Don R.

Yorkville

Bloor

Dufferin

Bathurst

Spadina Ave.

Queen's Park

13

6

College

Bay

Yonge

Jarvis

Sherbourne

Parliament

St. James's Cemetery

Necropolis

Park Lots

Carlton

College Ave.

14

Allan Gardens

7

Macaulay-town

17

"The Park"

8

4

Queen

1

New Town

Old Town

King

2   King

9

King

Garrison Reserve

10   Wellington

15

16

18

Railyards

11   Front

5   Northern Wharf

12

Gooderham's Wharf

Queen's Wharf

3

Original limits of Garrison Reserve

1 Asylum	7 The Grange	13 St. Michael's College
2 Exhibition	8 Osgoode Hall	14 Normal School
3 New Garrison	9 Upper Canada College	15 St. Lawrence Hall
4 Trinity College	10 Government House	16 City Hall
5 Old Garrison	11 Parliament Buildings	17 Hospital
6 University College	12 Union Station	18 Mills and distillery

Notes: Only major through streets are shown.
– – – – Stream courses being filled in and run in sewers downtown during this period.

Miles   0   ½   1
Kilometres   0   ½

5 The City to the 1860s

The Grange, one of the city's best elite homes since the days of the Family Compact, is seen in mid-Victorian years, when ex-mayor W. H. Boulton still occupied it. In the early twentieth century it became the initial core of the present Art Gallery of Ontario, and now is admirably restored.

Mid-Victorian in-town residences for the middle class: Sherbourne Row. A similar row-house on Bond Street, last home of William Lyon Mackenzie, has been restored through the Toronto Historical Board.

A cottage in lower-class Macaulaytown. Dating from earlier days, these simple, if often well-detailed, little homes long sheltered the poor, but continually deteriorated.

within walking range of work. For Toronto still was small enough and had sufficient room available to avoid, on the whole, the close-packed, noisome tenements that disfigured urban Britain, that rose in big American centres on the seaboard, and in due course developed in Montreal. The city's poor and needy, however, were generally left to shelter where they could, in dilapidated one-storey shacks that remained from an earlier day, more frequently found still in Macaulaytown or on back streets of the Old Town area. It can only be said that the poor were not so concentrated in mid-Victorian Toronto as to make their poverty blatantly apparent in what was yet a fairly unsorted, patchwork urban territory, apart from its few considerably Catholic neighbourhoods or the Macaulaytown tract, within St. John's Ward since 1853.

That city was nevertheless expanding beyond easy walking range, especially north along the main Yonge Street artery. Here above Bloor, Yorkville was now a prosperous village of storekeepers, artisans and suburban dwellers. Horse-drawn omnibuses ran from St. Lawrence Market up Yonge to the Red Lion Hotel in Yorkville from 1849, but in 1861 the horse-powered street railway made its first appearance in Toronto on the same route, to foster more growth in the northerly direction.[57] This improved facility for internal urban transport would, in fact, promote both the wider spread of the community and the sorting-out of business and residential districts within it, aided when additional lines were soon opened on King and Queen. The consequences took time to be felt, however. Of more immediate consequence to Toronto was the effect on its built environment of the street railway's big brother, the long-distance steam railway, whose tracks now penetrated to the very heart of the city, influencing land use along their converging paths.

Obviously the railway's influence was most strongly evident where the tracks came together at the harbour front. Land was in demand along the portside, where the Northern, Great Western and Grand Trunk located station buildings, sidings and transshipment facilities, and where more warehouses, cartage firms, lumberyards (and soon industries) came to cluster around the transport lines. On the other hand, living conditions obviously depreciated around this noisy, increasingly dingy area. Those who could, left its neighbourhood, though some were slow to abandon traditional, shore-view homes. Those who stayed close to the weedy desolation of the tracks and the drab walls of storage sheds more largely did so because they could not afford to do otherwise. Railways, then, forwarded a bleak kind of sorting-out around Toronto's once sparkling harbour. It was unplanned, in a happy-go-lucky day of faith in planless, wealth-producing "progress." But it ended in all but closing off the central lake frontage from the main mass of the town's inhabitants.

Paradoxically, one rare element of planning assisted this railway takeover along the shore. The undeveloped public promenade beside the water's edge, the open strip deeded in 1818 in trust to a leading group of York's early citizens, was in the prosperous early Fifties embodied in a grand new civic plan for an Esplanade: a landscaped walk and carriage drive to stretch along the harbour margin below Front Street on partially filled lands. In 1854 Gzowski and Company obtained a city contract for the work, but it soon transpired that this firm, which was also to build for the Grand Trunk, would obstruct water access by running that railway into Toronto right down the Esplanade. Public outcries arose, and in 1855 the City Council voted to cancel the contract, while the Grand Trunk threatened legislative sanction to build along Queen Street instead. More ferment followed, yet rail-boosting sentiment won out.[58] A provincial act of 1857 transferred the strip to the municipality, which granted the Grand Trunk right of way; and the Esplanade went ahead, with the other railroads also strung upon it.

By the Sixties the busily building city had reached the boundaries set out in its charter of 1834. Either its original wards — St. Lawrence's, St. George's, St. Andrew's, St. Patrick's and St. David's — had been extended into the city liberties, or new wards had been added — St. John's, St. James's and St. Thomas's — so that when the liberties were abolished completely by statute in 1859, there was little left of them to be taken in except for a margin on the east along the wet flats of the Don. Assuredly, most outer stretches of this civic territory still were sparsely occupied. But essentially it was already an urban domain, widely mapped out for streets and building lots, even where gardened estates, cottagers' cabbage fields or racetracks and amusement grounds as yet bordered on the built-up areas. And the city was steadily filling in westward, as well as northward towards the rise above its Shore Plain, where some of the rich found suburban refuge.[59]

To the west along the lakefront, the original Garrison Reserve

Above, towards the edge of the built-up town: Yonge Street looking north around Gerrard in the 1860s. The street rails were used by a horse-powered street railway that began service in 1861, replacing horse-drawn omnibuses like the one at left. The vehicle shown is one of four six-seaters brought into service in 1849 — Toronto's first "mass transit." To meet demand, four ten-seat omnibuses were added to the fleet the following year.

had long been dwindling, as from the mid-Thirties provincial authorities released tracts for development. Trinity College was situated on Queen just west of Garrison Creek; further west still stood the Provincial Asylum, open since 1850, itself on former Reserve land. South of the asylum gardens below Queen, the government in 1856 had turned over more Reserve land to the city for a park and exhibition ground. Here in 1858 Sandford Fleming co-designed the Crystal Palace for the annual provincial fair of "agriculture and the arts." It was virtually a commodious greenhouse, but did make Toronto a more effective exhibit centre. On the residual Garrison Reserve, a "New Fort" had been erected in 1841, west of the crumbling relic from the War of 1812. Yet enclosing fortifications for the new Garrison were never built. It remained a set of substantial but starkly plain, stone living-quarters for the military, to be later known as Stanley Barracks — a far cry from Simcoe's concept of Fortress Upper Canada.

On the west above Queen, city houses were spreading around Spadina Avenue in this era, on streets up towards Bloor initially planned by the Baldwins. But after Robert Baldwin died, his hillcrest property was sold in 1866 to James Austin, a wealthy wholesale grocer and financier of Ulster birth, who built a larger, still surviving Spadina House. Much more generally, original "park lot" gentry estates, stretching from Queen to Bloor, were increasingly being subdivided by their owners and would-be developers, Jarvises, Robinsons, Denisons, Boultons and others. Some of the park lots continued to hold large family homes with grounds. But to a great extent they were now laid out with transverse streets and ranges of building lots, just as their speculating proprietors thought best. The result was that east-west roads across a former park lot seldom met directly with those of its neighbours on either side, which still today cause main cross-town arteries through this area to take various bends, while north-south streets that once edged the estates basically run straight. Nevertheless, these almost ad-lib subdivisions often offered many small lots for lower-income homes, as was already the case in older Macaulaytown, near Yonge.[60]

East of Yonge above Queen, the same kind of subdividing and house-building went on in the park lots of this segment, eastward at least as far as Sherbourne Street. There, however, Moss Park intervened, previously the estate of banker William Allan (who had died in 1853), and now held by his son, the lawyer-politician George William Allan. Past Moss Park were mostly small fringe-cottage areas. The city's growth in this direction towards the Don continued to be slower, except for the General Hospital erected near the approaches to the river in 1855, and William Thomas's new Don Jail beyond, finally in operation in 1865. Further northward on the Don slopes were the Necropolis and St. James's new cemeteries, while beyond Bloor, Rosedale, an old Jarvis estate, was being plotted out as a high-class suburb. Otherwise there were no major changes in this eastern section down to the 1870s. Some of it had once been part of another government reserve, containing the first provincial legislative site at the foot of Parliament Street; and this district, often termed "the Park," largely a poorly drained backwater, did not readily attract boom-time speculators. Still, small cottages were spreading north of Queen from the poorer eastern reaches of the Old Town into the area later called Cabbagetown.[61]

It is all too clear that this sweep of mid-Victorian land development across Toronto took place as private enterprise, without significant public ordering or municipal design. A brief initial era of urban planning indeed had largely passed with early York: with Gother Mann's unrealized town scheme of 1788, Simcoe's Old Town plot, government reserves and park lots, and with Russell's layout for the New Town. Succeeding colonial masters had entertained more designs for land use, but public planning had essentially fallen victim to self-government and to the prevailing laissez-faire attitudes of the nineteenth century. It was scarcely to reappear in Toronto until the next century was under way. While there were a few limited attempts to plan by civic authorities, such as for the ill-fated Esplanade, and while private developers at times did plot out boulevards or crescents, physical urban growth, overall, went on uncoordinated and indiscriminantly. The cost was witnessed in confused street linkages or unrelieved, humdrum grids, made more apparent by the few exceptions like generous Spadina or landscaped College Avenue. It was seen besides in the spreading transport wilderness of the harbour front, in impressive central-district edifices mixed in with shoddy structures, and in the beginnings of upper-class, city-fleeing suburbanization.[62] These, too, were part of the landscape produced by an entrepreneurial railway city.

QUALITY OF LIFE AND SERVICES IN
THE MID-VICTORIAN CITY

And yet, amid the anarchy of get-rich individualism, surviving frontierism and incipient railway industrialism, the quality of life in this Toronto still won largely favourable opinions. William Russell, a leading correspondent of the London *Times*, visited it in the early Sixties. He observed:

> The city is so very surprising in the extent and excellence of its public edifices that I was fain to write to an American friend in New York to come up and admire what has been done in architecture under a monarchy.... Churches, cathedrals, markets, post office, colleges, schools, mechanics institute rise in imperial dignity in the city. The shops are large and well furnished with goods.... The people in the streets are well dressed, comfortable looking, well-to-do; not so tall as the people in New York, but stouter and more sturdy....[63]

Toronto, in fact, could make a good impression, at any rate along its main thoroughfare, King, lined with fashionable stores, on much of Queen, in the prosperous wholesale belt on lower Yonge, and in the emerging financial district around Wellington and Yonge, where most of the chief banking houses were congregating by the 1860s.[64] Formal streets of row-houses adjoining the central core, affluent mansions up Jarvis, Church and Bay, and well-kept smaller dwellings on many a leafy, quiet back road, all gave a substantial, ordered look to the community at large, overlying its frequent rough spots. Apparently the still conservatively cast city could avoid becoming hopelessly dishevelled by undirected development. By urban standards of the day, it was reasonably tidy and clean, and earnestly decent: a colonial town still, but by no means secluded, with real adornment, considerable wealth, and a generally thriving, solid citizenry. Nor had mass industrialism yet imposed its pace or problems on the city's life. There was time, and room, for cricket, boating and horse-racing in summer; curling, skating and sleighing in winter, often on frozen Toronto Bay.

But one particular amenity for urban living had not been produced by indiscriminate development — public parks, breathing spaces within the town for its inhabitants, above all for the less advantaged among them. In an earlier era, parks had hardly mattered, when the harbourside was easily at hand for any casual stroller, fisherman or boater, the wooded, sandy peninsula beyond gave still more rambling room, and the open countryside above the city was just a walk away. Now, however, the real countryside was more remote, while the lake frontage was being steadily taken up by rails and commerce. And the peninsula itself had decisively become an island when a great storm of 1858 cut a clear gap across its narrow eastern neck, through which ships could sail in nine feet of water. This was good for shipping access, but not for poorer citizens. They could pay to cross by ferry to the sandy strip, where hotels and amusement grounds had appeared, but the Island henceforth became increasingly a resort for those with some degree of means, where yachting and boat clubs developed, as did city-licensed private leasing.[65] Toronto began to look around for open public space within the town itself, to find that there was practically none.

Apart from the Exhibition parkland to the west — well out of the city then — there were only the limited grounds of the Parliament Buildings on Front Street, those of nearby Government House and Upper Canada College, and little else. However, in 1857, G. W. Allan had donated five acres north of his Moss Park property for the Horticultural Society of Toronto to develop gardens, and in 1862 he offered five additional acres to the city for use as the society approved. So emerged Toronto's first real in-town civic park, Allan Gardens, bordering Sherbourne and Carlton, but more through chance than any municipal initiative.[66] Queen's Park arose in a similar way. The provincial government appropriated for public purposes a sizeable eastern portion of the University's land tract, which stretched to Bloor from the head of College Avenue, and in 1859 this was passed to the city to tend.[67] In 1860 the property became Queen's Park, soon to be edged by well-to-do residences overlooking its trees and lawns, except on the western side, where the University's own buildings and grounds extended.

Along with these modest efforts to introduce public space, the city government did attempt some building regulation in the interests of fire control and safety within its ever-filling domain. It had prescribed, for instance, following the Fire of 1849, that only solid, first-class buildings could be erected in the downtown sector, a rule that led to the progressive disappearance of flimsy wooden stuctures there.[68] Lesser fires had a similar, if more random, clearing effect elsewhere. The city also retired its remaining old hand-

Winter recreation on Toronto harbour, 1853, towards the western end of town. In particular, sleigh-racing on the ice was popular among officers and the elite into the mid-century, but thereafter ice-boating increasingly replaced it.

Garden party at Sheriff W.B. Jarvis's residence, Rosedale, 1861. This Jarvis home gave its name to the fashionable new suburb of the next generation, one of the first laid out in a complex of curving streets. The guests at the party show many military uniforms, since the occasion was a prize-giving for the Fifth Militia District Rifle Association.

pumpers in 1861 in favour of steam fire-engines, already introduced, but went on largely relying on volunteer companies till 1874, and on all too undependable water mains for its fire-fighting service. In consequence, ravaging blazes continued, although fortunately did not reach the scale of 1849. It was rather in the related service to life, limb and property, police protection, that a community strong for law and order saw more significant developments.

Almost at the city's inception, full-time, paid police constables had been introduced, five being named under a high bailiff in 1835, thus making Toronto one of the first urban centres in America to found a regular police force. New York did not do so till 1844, but while it began with 400 members, Toronto by then had only 8![69] This little unit, gradually increasing and backed by part-time men for emergencies, continued under fairly casual supervision by successive high bailiffs into the 1850s. Then, however, the relative impotence of the police in riots — when troops from the Garrison had frequently to be called in — and the increase in crime in a much expanded city roused growing public disquiet. Some 5,000 persons came up on charges in 1857, for instance, over half the total charges involving drunken disorders.[70] At the same time, the ratio of policemen to citizens, 1 in 850 at the city's start, had sunk to 1 in 1,600.[71] Municipal concern and the anxiety of the respectable and propertied hence led to provincial enactments of 1858–59 that set up the Board of Police Commissioners for Toronto, consisting of the mayor, the police magistrate and a judge, with power to appoint a chief constable and recruit a larger force (paid by the City Council) as they determined.

The board went to work to build a new, trained body of over sixty men, and in this endeavour was influenced by two oddly diverse examples, the Boston police force and the Royal Irish Constabulary of Northern Ireland. From Boston they took the regular pattern of duty hours and patrol assignments. The Ulster Irish influence came largely through the newly appointed chief constable, Captain William Prince, a veteran of Britain's Crimean War of the 1850s. Prince wanted a well-drilled, semi-military formation, and chose a considerable number of men with army background, including ex-members of the Irish Constabulary. In any case, given the strong Northern Irish presence in Toronto and the influence of the Orange Order in civic affairs, it was not wholly astonishing that the Toronto force recruited a high proportion of Ulstermen. And despite a lack of due Catholic representation in this body, its stress on disciplined efficiency did make it a much improved instrument of order for the majority of the city's residents. It still had to face the City Council, which controlled its payroll, and Prince waged constant battle with civic politicians who sought to pare down his ranks. But long before he retired in the mid-1870s, he had shaped an adequate, essentially professional force to serve Toronto's policing needs.[72]

A considerable degree of ordered security (tempered by Orange-Green clashes) was thus sustained in mid-Victorian city life. But services for its poor were far less ordered. The House of Industry, a privately run institution with some municipal and provincial funding, had been operating since 1837, and in 1848 acquired a substantial new building designed by John Howard. It dealt, however, both with "deserving" and "undeserving" poor — a favourite Victorian distinction — and so mixed attributes of a refuge for the helpless with those of a place of correction for the idle. It came to administer both inmate and outdoor relief, not to mention serving as a way station for homeless transients; yet in the main it was a poorhouse with no instructive industrial activity much beyond housework.[73] In short, it was a catch-all, as was the similar Roman Catholic House of Providence. Nevertheless, from the 1850s, more-specialized developments tended to offer at least some charitable improvements for the life of the city's poorest inhabitants. The Orphans' Home and Female Aid Society was established in 1851, largely backed by women members of Toronto's old elite families. It pointed to a new awareness of the need for child care, which brought the Boys' Home of 1861 and the Girls' Home of 1863, to provide for vagrant or abandoned children and direct them to "honest industry."[74] All these were but small institutional beginnings, but they were accompanied by increasing public support, both municipal and provincial, which by the early Seventies produced a more structured welfare system under provincial regulation.

Charitable provisions such as these were no less influenced by the rising concern among the possessing classes over the dangerous potential for lawlessness that lay in the neglected and untaught. The filling city was generating a rowdy street youth from family breakdowns among its hard-pressed poorest elements, or from their need for every bit of income, which set poor children to work not just in homes or craft shops, but as newsboys, trifle-pedlars and the like. Some indeed were homeless cast-offs, managing to keep alive by ingenuity, thievery or prostitution. All could be seen as present or future threats to moral, safe society. In response, a rising faith was placed in general public education, not only as a wholesale means of betterment but also as a community bulwark against poverty and crime.

Literacy for the masses was the great answer, to be realized through public instruction. Accordingly, the city-wide elected Public School Board, set up in 1850 with a call on civic revenues, waged a successful campaign for free schooling over the next two years, while the *Globe* proclaimed, "Educate the people and your gaols [sic — that is, jails] may be abandoned.... if we make our people intelligent they cannot fail to be prosperous; intelligence makes morality, morality industry, industry prosperity as certainly as the sun shines."[75] Under that creed, eloquently upheld by key educators like Ryerson, new "common" or public elementary schools were spread throughout Toronto's wards. The old grammar school became the first public high school (admitting girls also from 1865); and state-aided Catholic separate schools multiplied as well.[76] In 1871 compulsory schooling began, setting the course from education as an individual need to education as a social dictate — and ending the open frontier realm of childhood, or so it was intended.

At any rate, educational services had decisively advanced in the city. Not so those of health and sanitation. Civic health activities remained negligible, ruled by indifference and tight budgets.[77] A minor committee of the City Council maintained a makeshift supervision over slaughterhouses, cattle sheds, and pigs running loose, but made little headway in dealing with unsanitary dwellings, flooding cesspools and private refuse dumps. Real improvements in Toronto's public health endeavours would not come till the following era. Under the circumstances, it is almost surprising that the mid-Victorian city, aside from its earlier Fifties' epidemics, had as reasonably good a mortality and morbidity record as it did have — but again its relatively small size helped.

Moreover, there was a further problem that affected sanitary conditions, the shortcomings of the city's existing water system.[78] By the 1860s Toronto Bay was polluted well out from the shore by sewage and uncontrolled waste-dumping, even though it was the source of the pumped water supply. The bulk of the citizenry nevertheless did not have piped water, mainly because of its charges and uncertainties, and instead used water carters or private wells, even when the wells were frequently contaminated by

nearby backyard privies. The "public" water supply chiefly fed fire mains and manufactories; its inadequate volume for fire fighting indeed roused more concern than its dubious quality. As a result, civic politicians waged a running battle with the municipally franchised gas and water company. In 1848, in fact, the Consumers' Gas Company was formed, headed by prominent citizens, which bought out the first gas works and in 1855 erected its own large coal-fired plant towards the eastern end of the harbour near the bottom of Parliament Street. Yet while this new private utility functioned effectively (and domestic gaslighting spread), water services remained at issue. In spite of newspaper campaigns, City Council oratory and engineering studies for larger facilities, the costs of major improvement or a municipal takeover still seemed insuperable to civic leaders and voters on through the 1860s.[79] The water company went its stumbling way, enlarging its steam-pumping equipment at the foot of Peter Street or pushing the intake pipe still further out into the bay when shortages or bad water quality became too flagrant to ignore.

More was achieved in civic draining and macadamizing streets, in paving crossings, extending plank sidewalks and putting flagstone ones in central sections.[80] The street railway helped somewhat after 1861, since by its charter it was responsible for placing pavements along its rails, for which, late in the Sixties, it took to laying cedar blocks. Yet its track also bisected streets where it ran into two muddy laneways, churned constantly by jolting wagons or spattering carriages, and pungent with manure. Such thoroughfares would not impress a later generation with the high quality of Toronto's urban existence. Still, it was acquiring a new tempo, for better or worse thrusting on to much more complex growth in city life and services.

POLITICS, CULTURE — AND REGIONAL COMMAND

The city's government over the period remained largely the preserve of a mostly Conservative coterie of lesser merchants and manufacturers, contractors and professional men. The first-rank figures in commerce and finance were seldom among them, though some prominent offspring of an older elite still appeared from time to time, such as G. W. Allan as mayor in 1855, John Beverley Robinson, Jr., in 1856, and the perennial William Henry Boulton two years later. In 1859 stirrings of municipal reform produced a mayoralty directly elected by the ratepayers, which brought to office the Reformer Adam Wilson, Baldwin's former law partner, who had led in the civic battle with the Grand Trunk over the Esplanade.[81] But though Wilson won another term in 1860, he still faced a well-established council old guard; and in 1866 the election of the mayor was once again made indirect, within the council itself. More conspicuous among Toronto's mayors of this mid-Victorian period was John George Bowes, first in office from 1851 through 1853, as a shrewd exponent of city-boosting "politics of enterprise."[82] An Irish Methodist wholesale dealer who had bought out Isaac Buchanan's Toronto business in the Forties, Bowes was active in railway promotion by the early Fifties, which helped to draw him into a notorious scandal, "The Ten Thousand Pounds Job." It was revealed in 1853 that he and Francis Hincks, then the provincial premier, had used inside knowledge to acquire and sell at a neat joint profit £10,000 of city debentures issued for the Northern Railway.[83] Yet Bowes soon regained popular acceptance in a day of flexible railway morality, and so returned to public life. Mayor anew in 1861, he was finally beaten in 1864 (largely for being insufficiently pro-Orange) by the provincial grand master of the Order, Francis Medcalf, who then held the mayoralty through 1866, and returned again in the next decade.

In spite of Bowes's passing notoriety, it would seem valid to assert that the municipal regime of this period was not blatantly involved in corruption, nor seldom even in extravagance. Rather, it was cozy, cautious and uninspired, not dynamically engaged — railways and private development drew the high-fliers. Quite evidently, however, the Loyal Orange Order operated close to the civic seats of power, and exercised its influence not only on the course of city elections but on municipal employment and contracts also. In "making it" in mid-Victorian official Toronto, one could scarcely forget that this still was a conservatively British and powerfully Protestant town.[84]

Toronto's part in the sectional politics of the Canadian Union reflected much the same pattern of Conservative predominance, from 1854 supported by a major city journal, the *Leader*. In the five Union elections after 1848, the city's two seats were won by a total of seven Conservatives to three Liberals. John G. Bowes was one such Conservative victor in 1854; John Beverley Robinson, Jr., another, both in 1857 and 1861. Yet in the election of 1857, the *Globe*'s George Brown, by then chief captain of the Upper Canada

Liberals or Reformers, gained a Toronto seat during a section-wide sweep by his newly reorganized "Clear Grit" Liberal party. In 1863 a similar Reform election sweep took both Toronto constituencies, putting into parliament wealthy John Macdonald and another city business Liberal, A. M. Smith. Still, these were the Liberal exceptions that proved the Conservative rule, and all three were anything but radical in viewpoint.

George Brown, in fact, had made his city the headquarters of an aggressive Clear Grit array dedicated to the "rights of Upper Canada": seeking representation by population in the Canadian Union, to realize the western section's greater weight of numbers, and the acquisition of the vast North West beyond the Lakes, both to serve land-hungry Upper Canadian farmers and to add a great new realm to Toronto's commercial dominance.[85] His *Globe* newspaper had now become big business, a daily by 1853, with steam-driven rotary presses, a large work force, and the widest circulation in British North America, especially throughout western Upper Canada.[86] Based on the *Globe*'s sway and his own parliamentary prowess, Brown built a party force that finally brought to terms the existing political masters of the Union, the Conservatives led by John A. Macdonald and George Étienne Cartier. Furthermore, the powerful Grit Liberal party he centred on Toronto made that city a stronger regional political focus than it had ever been before, certainly far more so than in the days of Mackenzie Reform. Undoubtedly Toronto's new railway network also helped in this regard — for example, in bringing train loads of rural Grits into town for mass Reform conventions in 1857, 1859 and 1867, each deftly managed by Brown and his urban headquarter associates.[87] By rail, press, and the bonds of party, a wide political hinterland was linked into the dominance of the Lake Ontario metropolis. And while Toronto's own preponderant local Conservatism was seldom shaken, it nonetheless became as well the centre of a Grit party empire. Thanks notably to Brown, the city thus developed its regional hold still further.

The Liberal champion and his journal in any case had a great deal in common with their own home city. Their pro-British, Protestant, anti-republican sentiments echoed strong chords in the community.[88] The *Globe*'s views on free trade, railway development and commercial policy were much as those then espoused by the influential Board of Trade, and the latter took up the former's North West campaign in 1857, calling for the annexation of the

The Globe.

By the mid-Victorian era, George Brown's widely read *Globe* made him a wealthy Toronto figure and powerful political force: leader of the Clear Grit Liberal party and a moulder of Confederation. The *Globe's* front page is shown in the year he first entered parliament, and the year before it became a daily (on large steam-driven presses). Characteristically then, the news and editorials lay within. The left side of the page is given over to ads; the right to a record of legislative debate on railroads involving Brown himself.

western territory to Canada. George Brown himself pressed for Toronto steamboats on the Upper Lakes, and for opening communications with the Red River settlement beyond, explicitly to enlarge the city's trading empire. In this he almost was a latter-day Simcoe, leading in recalling visions of the Toronto Passage northwestward to imperial greatness. His paper followed him: "There is no question that the merchants and other residents of Toronto are deeply interested in everything that will develop the resources of the North West route."[89]

At length, when by 1864 an all-but-equal balance of sectional forces in the provincial parliament had reduced the existing Canadian Union to deadlock, Brown also took the prime lead in bringing about a crucial coalition of parties: one that would work to recast the union in a federal form, assure the rights of Upper Canada, and incorporate the North West within a broad confederation of provinces. His approach in 1864 succeeded, the same year that the *Globe* opened imposing new premises on King Street.[90] By 1867 Confederation was achieved; and under it, the Province of Ontario came into being as old Upper Canada's successor, even as George Brown himself retired from active politics. One might reasonably suggest that his initiative not only led to the opening of the West to Canada and Toronto, but also to a fresh realization of his city's role as a political regional metropolis — for it now became the provincial capital of Ontario.

And so the first Ontario legislature met in Toronto's erstwhile Parliament Buildings in the closing days of 1867. The local citizenry (ungratefully) continued to send mainly Conservatives to both the new provincial and federal parliaments; though within four years the fall of an initial party coalition ministry in Ontario ushered in a long reign of provincial Grit Liberalism at Toronto. In any event, the city's renewal as a seat of government effectively expanded its outreach as well. Now the easternmost areas of Ontario, along the upper St. Lawrence and Ottawa, had to look politically to Toronto, whether or not they remained economically close to Montreal. More than that, if businessmen in Brockville, Cornwall or Ottawa wanted legal measures, licences or grants that lay within the quite extensive realm of provincial authority, they henceforth had to deal with the new capital. Above all, since public lands and natural resources had been allotted to the provincial sphere, timber leases up the Ottawa, the potential development of mining or forest wealth in other northerly reaches of Ontario, thereafter depended on Toronto-based authority. In essence, the creation of the new province further promoted regional focusing upon its leading city.

Again the full consequences took time to be realized, and were far from plain by 1871, when the first Ontario ministry fell from office. But by then, Toronto was well embarked on a new wave of growth, to some extent borne on by the optimistic hopes that stemmed from the achievement of Confederation (which reached to the Pacific in that year) and the creation of the new provincial realm, but far more generally responding to the flourishing state of world trade. The end of the U.S. Civil War in 1865 had checked a booming wartime market. The loss of the Reciprocity Treaty the next year — terminated by an American Congress resentful of wartime border strains with Canada and increasingly dominated by tariff protectionists — had seemed still more threatening to the city. But a new world trade revival rapidly overcame these setbacks. Toronto continued to deal actively southward, as well as eastward to Montreal; and good prices and ready markets outweighed new burdens of American tariffs on its traffic across the Great Lakes or onward to New York. Hence, along with more railway-building, another lively era of city-building developed, in full swing before the Sixties closed.

Toronto had joyfully celebrated the inauguration of Canadian federal union on 1 July 1867 — with public bonfires, ox-roasting, military drills, lake excursions, and at evening, fireworks, while Chinese lanterns lit the trees of Queen's Park in softly glowing colours.[91] Most of the city's traders and political figures of either party had pushed zealously for Confederation. The mass of its citizens were eager to believe with them that a bright new age had opened for their country and community. They also remembered less happy events in the previous summer of 1866, when raiding forces had struck into Canada across the Niagara River, the Fenians, largely composed of Irish-American Civil War veterans who thus sought to bring Ireland's wrongs home to British territory. Toronto volunteer militia had gone to meet the Fenian invaders at the little Battle of Ridgeway in June 1866; some to die there.[92] A monument to the dead, who included young University of Toronto students, would rise in Queen's Park. It seemed almost the War of 1812 again; the city's anti-American feelings were swiftly revived. But soon these feelings were caught up in a rising hope for Canadian nationalism, in pride at Confederation and aspirations for its future. This spirit was to be particularly expressed by a new group

Review of the Queen's Own Rifles Volunteers at the Normal School grounds, 1863. The Confederation years saw much military activity in Canadian cities — markedly Toronto — in days of border threats during the American Civil War, potential worries over national defence, and afterwards in the Fenian Raids and the Red River Rising. Volunteer drills and reviews like this one were typical. The new Queen's Own would serve against the Fenians and through world wars to come.

Bloor's Brewery in Rosedale ravine, as painted by Paul Kane. The recorder of western Indians did this local scene in the Yorkville area, with the Sherbourne Street blockhouse, dating from the Rebellion of 1837, on rising ground beyond.

of youthful authors who in 1868 began the Canada First Movement, chiefly centred in Toronto.

Their main literary influence would follow later, but already there had been considerable cultural development in the city through its mid-Victorian years. Increasingly Upper Canadian writers gathered there, as its publishing houses built up a long regional lead — thanks to top daily papers like the *Globe* and *Leader*, the widely read church, farm and business journals, including the *Monetary Times* from 1867. In art, Toronto-raised Paul Kane had first exhibited his graphic paintings of Plains Indians in the city in 1848, and settled his studio there from 1853, following further with canvases on the West, supported by his patron, G. W. Allan.[93] Other talented artists like George Theodore Berthon, or Frederick Verner after 1860, also established themselves in Toronto. In science, the Canadian Institute, organized in 1849 with Sandford Fleming as a leading spirit, met regularly to hear papers and foster inquiry; it was led also by University College's professor of chemistry, H. H. Croft. In the medical field, the Toronto School of Medicine, begun by Dr. John Rolph on his return from rebellion exile, became Victoria College's medical school in 1854, while Trinity College and the University further had their own schools.

In music, choral music societies were especially active, while Dr. John McCaul, president of King's College and then of University College, was tireless in organizing musical performances. Concerts at the Music Hall or at a variety of smaller halls and churches were well-patronized entertainments throughout the period. And the theatre also made a more substantial appearance at the Royal Lyceum, which had opened on King near Bay in 1848. Its success really came under John Nickinson, an English actor-manager who ran it from 1853 to 1859. He established the city's first resident stock company, and also booked touring attractions, offering everything from Shakespeare to minstrel shows. After him the Lyceum declined, but struggled on, until in 1867 it got an excellent new manager in George Holman, who brought it to a high point by the start of the Seventies, with full houses, some opera in English, and current plays from London and New York.[94]

Plainly, Toronto by 1871 was becoming much more of a cultural centre, at least in comparison with all other Ontario places. It was, besides, the home of three university institutions, of major schools in the provincial educational system; and thanks to its medical men and colleges, its senior jurists and Osgoode Hall, it offered the fullest range of professional expertise in the province. Through the city's metropolitan press, top business and political elites, leading churches and cultural associations, it was progressively tending to direct Ontario views and standards. In all these ways, Toronto had become much more than a railway hub, however important that was. It was a rising regional social determinant as well.

Toronto by 1880. On the left, Spadina Avenue runs back to Knox College (3), University College (4) appears further right in line with Knox, and the domed Northern Railway roundhouse (8) stands on the Esplanade by the harbour. Near the centre, the Northern's big grain elevator (23) dominates its wharf, the low mass of the Parliament Buildings (12) shows on Front Street above the Esplanade, with the Metropolitan Church (15), St. Patrick's (14) and others inland behind. To the right, the three-towered Union Station (16) has tall St. James's (17) behind it at one end, St. Lawrence Hall's cupola (18) beyond at the other (seen between two of the station's towers), while the Don opens at the picture's far right. Trees are still widely evident, but so is the smoke of rising industrialism.

Chapter Four
The Industrializing City, 1871–95

The later Victorian era shaped an industrial Toronto. Driven by steam-powered machinery, it featured both the economic gains of wealth-producing factories and the social problems of massing, crowding numbers. Before the period ended, the city also had electric light, telephones and electrical streetcars, while the new power of the electric motor was enlarging its productive base still further. This rising sweep of technological change stemmed out of mid-Victorian railway years; but it was only with the 1870s that its transforming influence grew sizeably evident, until, by the mid-Nineties, the results in industrialization were decisively clear.[1] Moreover, if Toronto was thereby experiencing a process widespread across later nineteenth-century Canada, it felt it with particular force and enhanced its own metropolitan role through adding large-scale manufacturing to already established commercial, transport and other functions. Population growth was one telling indication. As the city drew increasing concentrations of factory labour and service workers, its numbers rose from 56,000 in 1871 to 181,000 even by 1891[2] — and this during a long deflationary cycle in world trade and prices that lasted from 1873 through 1895 with only brief upturns. Part of Toronto's population increase was due to extensions of its civic boundaries, but these mainly annexed fringe communities that were already tied to the urban complex. In sum, if the city grew so vigorously during a lengthy period of world constraint, industrialization supplied a vital reason.

URBAN ECONOMY: THE RISE OF FACTORY INDUSTRY

Once immigration and land settlement had strongly impelled Toronto's economic growth, then came rail construction. Now it was industrialism's turn. Industrial activities rose to be a major, not a minor, aspect of the urban economy. In 1871 there were around 530 manufacturing enterprises in the city, 2,401 by 1891.[3] Their work force increased from 9,400 to 26,242 between these years; their capitalization grew over sevenfold and their annual product value more than quadrupled.[4] Beyond that, there were multiplier effects: spin-off ventures; expanding industrial demands on market, transport and financial facilities; new factory needs for fuel and producer goods; or the housing needs of a swelling labour segment. The process would go on much further after 1895, but here already was transforming change.

In examining it, one first might note that in-built advantages again applied. Manufacturing advances in the now thickly settled southern Ontario region partly centred at Toronto because of its larger amounts of capital and labour, its well-developed entrepôt structure and radiating transport network. But, as in the days of rail-building, the drive of its entrepreneurs was influential also. Even by the later 1860s their efforts to take advantage of a much widened transport hinterland had laid a basis for factory industry. In 1866, for instance, apart from the heavy Toronto Rolling Mills with 300 workers, the Jacques and Hay furniture company used 400 on largely mechanized, steam-powered production lines. The lucrative Gooderham and Worts flour mill and distillery employed 160; and there were boiler and machine foundries, sash-and-door works or shoe and clothing factories, not to mention William Davies's 300-strong packing plant — whose expanding bacon empire may well have inspired Toronto's later nickname "Hogtown."[5] Some of these firms, especially foundries, had grown out of earlier artisan workshops. Numerous small ventures still remained, and many parts of manufacturing processes as yet were carried out by handicraft, or by skilled tradesmen, rather than assembly-line labour. Moreover, little businesses particularly survived in footwear or clothing production, the latter often employing women and children under veritable sweatshop conditions. Nevertheless, even by 1871, 71 per cent of Toronto's industrial

George Gooderham, left, son of the founder of Gooderham and Worts, became its president, president of the Bank of Toronto (1882), vice-president of Manufacturers Life, and largely controlled the Toronto and Nipissing Railway. The Gooderham and Worts plant near the Don mouth, above, produced a third of the proof spirits made in Canada by the mid-Seventies. Besides milling and distilling, the firm had dairy and beef-fattening adjuncts (animals fed on mash residues), operated mills and stores in the Toronto vicinity, and held sizeable railway interests.

labour force was in factories with over 30 workers, while units with more than 50 accounted for 57 per cent of the industrial product value. Such larger units also showed the highest usage of steam power in the city's manufacturing sector.[6]

That sector continued to grow while good times lasted into the earlier Seventies, and it was only about 1874 that Toronto began to feel a spreading world recession. The growth largely followed paths already laid down in metal-working and machining, furniture and carriage production, factory-made clothing, leather goods and food-processing.[7] While woodworking plants continued active, the day of simple sawmilling was all but over at Toronto; and neither basic textile manufacturing nor basic iron-and-steel production made much new headway. Instead, the city of the Seventies exhibited a quite diversified range of relatively specialized enterprises, including machinery-building, publishing and piano-making, the last especially associated with Theodore Heintzman, an immigrant from Germany via New York whose successful factory became a leader in an enduring Toronto industry.[8]

Pianos, in truth, provide an instructive example. The manufacture of finished articles like these points to the fact that the city's industrialization was largely advancing by import replacement, not the working up of staple resource supplies.[9] Furthermore, some larger merchants spread into manufacturing to enhance their business, just as they had already taken to investing in banks and railways: in this latest case, to substitute cheaper, locally produced goods for lines they had hitherto imported. Various wholesalers branched into machinery, footwear or clothing production; the firm of Copp Clark, booksellers, became a prominent publishing house; while dry-goods handlers like Gordon Mackay and John McMurrich acquired textile mills, though not in Toronto. Exporters, such as the distillers Gooderham and Worts, grain and lumber dealers or meat-packers also made increasing investments in new industries, but it was the importers, the city's key business group, who chiefly took the lead. In any event, it would be wrong to believe that Toronto merchants did not become actively involved in manufacturing developments, even while they also kept up their interests in transport and finance.[10]

The large Gurney stove foundry established in the city in 1868, the Taylor safe works, the big printing plants of the *Globe* or its main rival, the *Leader*, all spelled additional strength for the urban economy in that its industrial eggs were not in one or a few baskets.

Toronto's range of wares could find more varied markets in spite of trade recessions than those of other centres with a narrower dependence on dominant staple industries. Its factory goods could compete across southern Ontario with similar British or American imports, through having lower transport or labour costs and already established trade connections. They even began to invade markets in Atlantic Canada, thanks to their growing scale of production, after the completion of the Intercolonial Railway in 1876 gave fuller linkage with this region.

The rising force of industrialism was also indicated in the Seventies by the spread of protectionist sentiment within Toronto's business community. A protective tariff to foster home manufactures was by no means a new idea in the city. It had been strongly urged back in 1858 by the Association for the Promotion of Canadian Industry, which that year launched its public campaign at St. Lawrence Hall, and won some noteworthy success in the increased tariff of 1859.[11] The association had again appeared on the eve of Confederation to contest — unsuccessfully this time — new lower tariff duties projected for the federal union. But while Toronto manufacturers might look to protection, the predominant business opinion in the city was not yet solidly behind it. That was evident at new gatherings of business representatives held in 1870 to discuss "united action" on tariff revision. Though prominent figures like Mackay or McMurrich favoured it, the still more weighty A. R. McMaster (William McMaster's nephew, who now ran that leading wholesale firm) wanted no burden of high duties laid on his imports; and the major capitalist J. G. Worts stood for unimpeded commerce, holding that Canada had plainly prospered under free-trade principles.[12]

A keen debate continued between high- and low-tariff advocates, argued in the city's press and in the special forum of its businessmen, the Board of Trade. The powerful *Globe*, true to George Brown's own economic liberal creed, condemned seeking an artificial prosperity for industry at the cost of consumers, primary producers and merchants alike. Yet its Conservative competitor, the *Leader*, spoke out for protection, perhaps because Conservative politicians had been considering a "national policy" of tariff protection to promote Canadian growth, but probably also because the *Leader*'s owner, James Beaty, was an important city leather manufacturer with other industrial interests as well. In any case, protectionism gained ground, particularly when world price falls after 1874 brought multiplying business failures in the city and urgent cries for government action to defend the dwindling Canadian market. By 1877, in fact, the Toronto Board of Trade had adopted protection outright, to become a determined lobby in that cause.[13] This marked a conclusive opinion shift. The weight of Toronto business went protectionist, fervent for the National Policy that was championed by the federal Conservatives in their victorious election campaign of 1878. Manufacturing interests thus triumphed in the city, and when the high tariff of 1879 was enacted, it undoubtedly stimulated many new factory ventures there. Yet increasing industrialism had moved Toronto to the National Policy — not the other way around.

All the same, factory expansion (and overexpansion) rose rapidly into the Eighties, what with the sheltering tariff rates, a world trade revival early in the decade, and hopes of broad new markets raised by the Canadian Pacific Railway, now building to open the North West. A significant aspect of Toronto's resulting industrial boom was the shifting of already established factory enterprises from smaller centres to its greater facilities and supplies. The John Inglis business came from Guelph, to set up a plant with 100 employees, particularly producing equipment for advanced steel-roller flour-milling. John Abell's implement firm arrived from Woodbridge, northwest of the city, in 1886.[14] Above all, Hart Massey moved his thriving agricultural machinery company from Newcastle, Ontario, in 1879. In 1881 he bought out the rival Toronto Mower and Reaper Company, and by 1884 occupied a four-storey factory out on King Street West, with 400 workers and heavy steam power.[15]

Transfers were further invited by municipal bonuses, tax remissions and grants in money, land or facilities. These civic aids to industrialism — widespread at the time — had been taken up in Toronto to attract new enterprises largely in the bad years of the late Seventies, when a number of foundries, engineering works and footwear firms had all gone under.[16] Never very consistent or clearly successful, and usually controversial, bonussing remained a dubious factor in the city's industrial growth. But at least the recruitment of the Massey company paid off. Its mechanical reapers and binders took repeated prizes — notably at the well-attended Toronto Industrial Exhibition, held in enlarged Exhibition Grounds on the old Garrison Reserve late each summer from 1879. The company soon widely entered farm markets across Canada, as well as in Europe, South America and Australia. Then in 1891 Massey combined with the Harris firm of Brantford, a strong competitor that had already shaped an aggressive policy of establishing machinery-distributing depots in the Canadian West. Down to 1895 Massey-Harris absorbed a number of other related Ontario firms, while its Toronto plant by then comprised the city's largest single factory.[17]

Toronto's industrial boom slowed in renewed years of trade downturn in the mid-Eighties, picked up in better times towards the Nineties, then faced still worse world slumps until the middle of that decade. Essentially, however, its manufacturing sector continued to grow in scale and wealth. There assuredly were recurrent setbacks, or failures in worse years, along with harsh phases of labour strife and layoffs. With some exceptions, the city's footwear industry never really recovered from depression in the late Seventies, overtaken by cheaper products from Quebec.[18] Yet by and large the components of clothing, engineering and publishing strongly advanced, those of furniture, piano-making and meat-packing only somewhat less so; while agricultural machinery production soared in importance, breweries became innovative and expansive, and the heavily capitalized Gooderham and Worts distillery more than held its own.[19] Further, newer enterprises of the continuing industrial revolution appeared. The Industrial Exhibition was lit by dazzling electric arc-lamps in 1882.[20] The Bell Electric Light Company moved from London to Toronto in 1883, soon to sell equipment across the continent.[21] And the next year the Toronto Electric Light Company began lighting central streets with steam-generated electricity, then obtained a city-wide franchise in 1889.[22]

Furnaces, rubber and paper goods, carriages, chemicals and corsets, barbwire, brass fittings and track bolts, all were additional factory products of late Victorian Toronto.[23] By the early Nineties, major firms employed between 100 and 300 workers, with some 700 for Massey and over 500 for the Ontario Bolt Company.[24] Mechanized mass production had clearly become preponderant in leading industries, even at Christie Brown's big bakery. Furthermore, Toronto had not just built up its own industrial complex, but was extending it by taking over complementary outside factories, a process well exemplified by Massey-Harris. As well, firms based in Toronto were establishing subsidiary plants at suitable hinterland locations. One instance was the Polson Iron Works, founded in

Hart Massey, left, was president of the Massey Manufacturing Company from 1870, and Massey-Harris from 1891. By 1895 he had shaped a near monopoly of the agricultural implements industry in southern Ontario, making himself the region's leading industrialist. The firm's various factories are assembled in the promotional picture above. The Toronto unit was the largest (occupying the main foreground except for the right-most block) and by itself still of impressive size. A Massey factory interior is seen at far left. Bowler hats usually denoted foremen.

The industrial Esplanade by the 1890s, towards its eastern end — a setting much changed from the view on page 70. Behind the Elias Rogers coalyard is part of the big Consumers' Gas complex. It included retort and furnace houses for producing coal gas, gas storage tanks, machine and pipe-work plants, offices, service-wagon sheds, stables, coke dumps, and still more to serve a gaslit industrial city.

1886, which operated a large marine engine and boiler factory on the Esplanade and a modern shipyard at Owen Sound on Georgian Bay. In short, Toronto had emerged as an industrial metropolis by the mid-Nineties, not only through developing its own factory base, but also by organizing increasing hinterland manufacturing under its control.

URBAN ECONOMY: DEVELOPMENTS IN COMMERCE, FINANCE AND TRANSPORT

Commercial growth accompanied industrialization, as Toronto merchants benefited from supplying city factories and distributing their products. Wholesalers still tied to old low-tariff patterns did feel the weight of protective duties after 1879; but most adjusted effectively, and on balance, demands kept up for overseas or American imports. Moreover, the railway, itself an adjunct of industrialism, spanned Canada by 1886, when the Canadian Pacific's trains ran to the West Coast, thus vastly expanding Toronto's potential trading area behind the national tariff screen. Actual settlement of the western expanses proceeded all too slowly in the continued doldrums of the waning nineteenth century. Nevertheless, Toronto as a commercial metropolis still held its valuable southern Ontario hinterland, was doing increasing wholesale business in the Maritimes, and was beginning to make sales inroads in the pioneer West.

Bad years brought mercantile failures as well to Toronto. Solidly planted major wholesalers, like A. R. McMaster, Gordon Mackay or W. H. and H. S. Howland, held their positions, however, in spite of credit strains. The efficient John Macdonald was especially successful in keeping Ontario country merchants ordering through Toronto, by adopting internally specialized departments, each with an expert buying staff, and by purchasing direct from overseas manufacturers.[25] Increasing scale and specialization were, in fact, the marks of endurance and success in wholesaling as well as industry. General wholesalers had disappeared even by 1870;[26] and many new specializations emerged thereafter, from tea or tobacco firms to fancy-goods and footwear houses.[27] By the Nineties these too were tending to consolidate in still-larger departmentalized units.

Across the period Toronto's basic import trade went on growing, despite all fluctuations. Its value of some $9 million in 1871 had doubled by 1885 (deemed a "healthy" time by the Board of Trade), and still stood close to $20 million in 1895 ("a year of quiet recovery").[28] Meanwhile, the city's export business consistently stayed smaller. This was due largely to the dwindling of both lumber exports and the old Upper Canada grain trade. By the 1880s forest frontiers had retreated far northward of Toronto, while rural southern Ontario had increasingly turned to mixed farming suited to domestic markets. Consequently, the city's commerce remained chiefly oriented to importing and distributing. And in the continued competition with Montreal for hinterland custom, it made important gains. Montreal houses had struck back in the 1860s by introducing a dread new weapon, the travelling salesman. But in the Seventies Toronto wholesalers were sending out their own host of salesmen, utilizing the railways to cover the Ontario region with "drummers" carrying samples and order forms. In the 1880s Toronto's commercial army was even invading Quebec as well as the Maritimes, and soon the West.[29] On the whole, a kind of trade apportionment developed out of the competition. Montreal remained dominant in bulky, less-differentiated goods still largely brought by ship: staple groceries, heavy iron stock and basic textiles. Toronto loomed large in higher-value commodities, in dry and fancy goods above all, and consumer products generally.[30] By the mid-Nineties Toronto business had increasingly held Montreal wholesaling to a conjunct rather than combative role in most of Ontario, while actively contending with it in regions beyond.

Retailing similarly grew in scope along with the city's massing internal market. Toronto already boasted large, well-furnished stores, the leaders lining the favoured shopping area of central King Street. Here, for instance, stood clothing and textile emporia like "The Mammoth" of Thomas Thompson or "The Golden Lion" of Walker and Son, said in the mid-Eighties to be "the finest retail clothing house in the Dominion," with nearly 100 employees.[31] Yet two newer retailers soared especially. Timothy Eaton, a Methodist Ulsterman, and Robert Simpson, a Presbyterian Scot, both moved to Toronto from storekeeping in small Ontario towns, and opened little dry-goods shops at the unfashionable corners of Queen and Yonge, in 1869 and 1872 respectively. Eaton obtained a strong line of credit from a fellow Methodist, John Macdonald — religious bonds still played an influential part in city business — and with this backing embarked on aggressive, up-to-date retailing.[32] His various steps, such as fixed prices, cash sales only, "goods satisfactory or

Timothy Eaton, "king of retail merchants," founded a retailing empire with marketing innovations such as the Eaton's mail-order catalogue. A typical page from the 1894 edition is shown at right.

Ladies' Dress Skirts.

Navy, black and brown serge, lined throughout, Empire style as cut, $3.00.
Same style in black cashmere, lined throughout, $3.50.
Same style in tweed, in brown, gray and fawn mixture, $3.50, 4.50.
Same style as cut in navy, black and brown serge, trimmed with three rows black military braid, $3.75.
Same style as cut in navy, black and brown serge, trimmed with two rows each, black military and tracing braid, $4.00.
Fine black henrietta cashmere skirts as cut, lined throughout, $5.00, 6.00.

Ladies' fine navy and black serge skirts, braid trimmed, as cut, $5.00.

When ordering costumes give bust and waist measure, also length of front of skirt.

From every part of this vast Dominion there keeps a-coming by mail orders for this thing and that. We supply thousands of families in just such a way. Why not you?

Ladies' Eton Suits.

Black and navy serge, similar style to cut, $5.50, 6.50, 7.50 and 8.50.
Also a similar style in brown, navy and black, $11.00.
White duck costumes, similar styles, $7.00, 8.00, 9.00, 10.00.

Ladies' Blazer Suits.

In black and navy serge, $7.00, 8.50, 10.00.
Linen costúmes, similar style, $8.00, 10.00, 12.00, 14.00.

1614. Striped cotton, washing material, colors navy and white, black and white, and cadet and white, $4.50.

Ladies' Bathing Suits.

This style in all-wool, navy blue estamine serge, trimmed with white braid, $3.00.
Same style in misses' size, $2.50.

money refunded," were not wholly new, but Eaton put them all together and was open to further changes. He particularly strove to please women customers, who bought most of the yard goods and clothing, and drew them so successfully that by 1875 his store had a staff of fourteen, including two female "sales assistants."[33] In 1883 Eaton's expanded into a new four-storey block, with elevators, on the north side of Queen.

Simpson wisely copied Eaton's procedures, while trying to improve on them: for example, by putting in a tea urn for the ladies (though Eaton's went one better with a children's nurse).[34] Simpson's store moved to larger quarters on the south side of Queen in 1881; it installed two telephones to take orders in 1885 — Eaton's only introduced one. Actually, neither suffered in this game of one-upmanship. There was plenty of trade for both, and the convenience of comparison shopping drew a flow of customers to each store, handily opposite the other at Queen and Yonge. As they grew, in fact, they increasingly became dual dominant leaders of Toronto retailing, since no competitor could hope to rival both of them.[35] Furthermore, they gradually spread out from dry goods and clothing to shoes, house furnishings, toiletries and so on, thereby developing the modern department store much further in Toronto.

Then in 1884 Eaton's launched a mail-order enterprise, followed by Simpson's on a limited scale the next year. The first thirty-two-page Eaton's catalogue was distributed free to out-of-town visitors at the Toronto Industrial Exhibition.[36] It was the start of a new commercial conquest of the hinterland by Toronto metropolitanism, ultimately to reach from Atlantic to Pacific. Relying on improved rail and postal communications, efficient service and attractive prices (now partly secured by buying direct from manufacturers), Eaton's mail-order business was able to undercut many local stores in lesser Ontario towns. Its catalogue of 1890 proclaimed, "There is absolutely nothing in the entire establishment that you cannot have precisely as if you stood in person before any counter, and at exactly the same price."[37] Such invitations to so large a stock won favour. Accordingly, in 1893 Simpson's launched an extensive mail-order campaign of its own, offering free samples.[38] The next year, after a fire, it erected a handsome new store on its site, only to lose it to another blaze in 1895. Robert Simpson promptly rebuilt in even finer style: a six-storey edifice with steel and concrete frame, electric light, elevators, and a pneumatic tube system that delivered cash and change.[39] The giant retail store had been realized in Toronto, not only for the concentrated urban market, but for an ever-growing hinterland beyond.

The city's financial sector kept pace with commercial and industrial developments that produced expanding needs for banking, insurance and investment services. In the good times of the early Seventies (and under the favourable Banking Act of 1871), new chartered banks supplemented the city's Bank of Commerce and Bank of Toronto: the Dominion in 1871, the Imperial in 1873, presided over respectively by James Austen, the grocer-capitalist who had bought Spadina, and Henry S. Howland, a leading hardware wholesaler. Their directorates and chief shareholders were once more drawn largely from the city's mercantile elite. Meanwhile Toronto's largest bank by far, the Commerce, reached beyond its chain of Ontario branches to establish offices in Montreal and Chicago, and in 1875, New York. The highly conservative Bank of Toronto opened fewer branches, but its caution left it paying good dividends in the bleak years of the later Seventies, guided by its president, William Gooderham, who was succeeded by his son George in 1882. The big Commerce took losses, as in the collapse of an over-eager Manitoba land boom in the early Eighties; but its substantial assets, including those of President William McMaster, saw it through. On the whole, sound resources and careful direction kept most of Toronto's banks solvent during the stringent stages of the later Victorian era.[40]

The Imperial Bank, however, also essayed a gradual expansion into the West, sure that Canada's financial horizons lay here. In 1881 it opened a branch in Winnipeg, in Calgary in 1886 and Edmonton in 1891 — then the most northerly bank office in the country. The Commerce did not reach Winnipeg till 1893, but meanwhile reorganized its central position under a capable new general manager, Byron Edmund Walker, and the shrewd financial guidance of George Albertus Cox, its president from 1890. The satisfactory growth of Toronto banks was indicated by their assets as reported for 1880 and 1890. The Dominion's rose from $5.4 million to $12.4 million, the Toronto's from $6.2 to $11.7, and the Imperial's from $3.8 to $9.6 million. The Commerce still kept a commanding lead, at $21.3 million, then $22.8.[41] As Canada's second bank, it was yet far behind the first, the Bank of Montreal, with $47.7 million in assets by 1890.[42] Nonetheless, banking in Toronto had solidly advanced during an age of recurrent financial disorders, through servicing a great deal of the city's business, much of the Ontario hinterland's, and some of the emerging West's as well.

This banking was still largely commercial, financing trading credits and industrial working expenses rather than long-term investments, apart from railways. But Toronto's loan and mortgage houses also expanded, weathering the New York crash of 1873 and the tight years that followed. The Canada Permanent Mortgage Corporation remained the largest of the Toronto credit companies; its assets rose from some $3 million in 1870 to nearly $12 million by 1890.[43] The Freehold Loan and Savings, a subsidiary of the Bank of Commerce, dealt in Ontario real estate, but also followed the CPR westward to establish agencies on the prairies.[44] Trust companies emerged besides, notably the Toronto General Trust in 1882 under directors such as William Gooderham and William McMaster. Like the city's banks, its investment business was virtually controlled by an interlocking group of resident capitalists.[45] So were its insurance firms, which similarly increased in number and range, from the Confederation Life, established in 1871, and Manufacturers Life, in 1887, to new enterprises in fire, marine and farm insurance, which mobilized still more capital.

As an instrument for allocating capital, the Toronto Stock Exchange moved well beyond its original main concern with wholesale commerce. Municipal debentures, railway bonds, bank stocks and those of loan and insurance corporations were regularly traded from the Seventies.[46] This reflected the very growth of incorporated enterprises over the period, although, as yet, public joint-stock companies with shares to offer were mainly found in the sectors of finance and transportation, since private firms and partnerships still dominated commercial and industrial areas. In any case, stock-broking became an influential activity in Toronto, featuring the rising names of E. B. Osler and Henry Pellatt in the Eighties, and the young house of A. E. Ames by the early Nineties — key figures in the coming age of full-fledged corporate business power.[47] All in all, the financial segment of the urban economy developed very significantly, if not spectacularly, throughout the period.

Transport developments were similarly significant, if not spectacular. Railway promotion had revived in the city late in the 1860s, strongly pushed by an enthusiastic entrepreneur, George Laidlaw. Laidlaw envisioned inexpensive light railways to fill in Toronto's existing fan of lines into Ontario. By 1869 he had two such rail-

roads building, with impressive directorates that included William Gooderham, William McMaster and H. S. Howland: the Toronto and Nipissing to the northeast and the Toronto, Grey and Bruce northwestward. The former stretched to Coboconk in 1872, Haliburton in 1878. (See Map 4, page 78.) The latter ran to Owen Sound on Georgian Bay by 1873. In addition, the Northern Railway probed on into the woodlands of Muskoka, reaching Gravenhurst in 1875. Meanwhile, Laidlaw, "the prince of bonus hunters," promoted a further line into western Ontario, the Credit Valley, open from Toronto to St. Thomas by 1883, with other branches besides.[48] Though returns varied, the city's transport grasp was both extended and consolidated in this its second railway-building stage.

It did not do as well in rivalry with Montreal for the great railway to the Pacific. In the early Seventies, efforts by a group of capitalists centred in Toronto to obtain the charter for the transcontinental line were defeated by a Montreal-based scheme, which then collapsed in the Pacific Scandal of 1873. After the suitably punished Conservatives had regained power in 1878 (from virtuous but depression-frozen Liberals), they proposed a new Pacific rail charter. But again Toronto entrepreneurs lost to the greater wealth of Montreal, where a syndicate backed by the mighty Bank of Montreal undertook the building of the CPR. As that railway went ahead at last, Toronto's strategy was necessarily restricted to securing contact with its main line, to tap into traffic to and from the West. This "Pacific Junction" was finally achieved in 1886, when an extension of the Northern from Gravenhurst reached the newly completed transcontinental track at a point near North Bay, Ontario.[49]

Two years later, the big Grand Trunk absorbed the Northern, as it already had the Great Western in 1882. Amalgamation was impelled by too many recession years when only large systems could endure repeated deficits. The Toronto and Nipissing also fell to the Grand Trunk. The Toronto, Grey and Bruce and the Credit Valley went to the Canadian Pacific, which had itself begun invading southern Ontario. The resulting contest between two rival rail empires benefited Toronto, however. The CPR brought tracks of its own from Montreal and Ottawa into the city, running down the Don Valley to the harbour, where an agreement of 1892 gave it a right-of-way along the Esplanade and access to the docks. Subsequently, the CPR also established communications southward to Toronto from its main line, and secured links from Toronto to

The Union Station. When opened in 1873 on the waterfront, it was Canada's largest. In the Nineties an addition was built on its north side (right to Front Street), and the whole served on through the 1920s till demolished when the present station (to eastward) finally came into use.

Buffalo that connected it on to New York. Thus, the Ontario capital's role as a focus of rail traffic was further reinforced.

Water traffic and the port of Toronto did not develop so beneficially. The railways carried a mounting share of freight, increasingly restricting the port to heavy, lower-value goods, like stone and other building materials, coal and industrial iron. The removal of tolls on the American Erie Canal in 1883 (but not from Canada's Welland) gave a final blow to lumber shipments from the harbour; thereafter they came down from the Upper Lakes direct to the Erie at Buffalo.[50] On the other hand, coal imports by lake (from Pennsylvania mines) rose strongly, not only for railway, factory and gaswork use but also for heating, as in the Eighties coal took over from wood as Toronto's dominant fuel. Hence, lumberyards were widely replaced by coal dealerships along the waterfront, among them the large Elias Rogers firm, which also owned coal boats as well as mine properties.[51]

There was still a sizeable Toronto shipping fleet; and the steady displacing of square-rigged sailing vessels by fore-and-aft-rigged schooners gave more efficient bulk water-carriage, since the latter craft could be manned by smaller crews and more easily unloaded. At the same time, steamboats handled a growing amount of the remaining higher-value traffic: those owned in the city increased anew, from about 37 per cent of its total fleet in 1878 to 60 per cent in 1887.[52] Yet its steamers were mostly limited to short-range passenger transport. City shipowners were not investing greatly in long-range steam freighters, leaving these to other, mainly American, centres, although the trade of small neighbouring Lake Ontario ports did largely fall to Toronto shipping during the later Victorian years.[53] The cloud of sails along Toronto Bay, the smoke and bustle of visiting steamboats, obscured, in fact, the relative decline of the port.

Under an indolent Harbour Trust dominated by businessmen who did not want to raise expenditures, and with the waterfront almost wholly in private hands, little was done to maintain, much less improve, port functions.[54] Wharves decayed; the piling up of waste and silt, the latter evidently flowing in the Eastern Gap that had broken through in 1858, persistently reduced the harbour's deep-water capacity. The main Western Channel became dangerously narrow; ships often had to be towed to dockside. The 1870s saw the low point in deterioration, but aside from repeated dredging, the 1880s achieved little beyond starting a set of breakwaters to protect the Island, and thus the harbour, from erosion. By the Nineties there was more piecemeal work under way to improve the main entry, and plans to drain off sludges of pollution. Chiefly, however, the harbour that originally had made Toronto possible was left to laissez-faire neglect. The industrializing city had too many other prospects to give its port the attention it deserved.

POPULATION PATTERNS AND CITY EXPANSION

This later Victorian Toronto more than tripled its numbers between 1871 and 1895. Where did they come from? Natural increase and the annexation of suburban communities were only parts of the answer. A lot still turned on the intake of new residents. In regard to immigration, it was not generally as powerful a demographic factor in later nineteenth-century Canada as it had been earlier. While a varying stream of migrants continued to reach Canadian shores over the period, many were simply in transit to American destinations, and in any case, their influx was more than equalled by an exodus of Canadians to the United States: from 1861 right to 1901 Canada thus suffered a net loss in migration. But Toronto itself did manage to attract a substantial share of those who entered the country and stayed, thanks largely to its conspicuous economic growth despite world slumps — growth that promised employment, not least in rising industries. As a result, the city continued to display a high ratio of immigrants, ranging from roughly half its residents in 1871 to still about a third by the early 1890s.[55]

Relatively few Americans or continental European migrants settled in Toronto over this time, though some of the first group brought important business expertise and capital access for economic expansion. The much more numerous British arrivals (again predominantly English) offered more of the same, but also a larger amount of factory labour. By 1891, apart from the city's now substantial Canadian-born majority, nearing 100,000, there were still around 23,000 English-born, to 13,000 Irish and 6,300 Scottish, together with some 5,000 of U.S. origins and 1,500 other "foreign-born" — largely of German, Italian and Slavic backgrounds, and including a number of the Jewish faith.[56] Late Victorian Toronto remained British-Canadian to an overwhelming extent, but its ethnic variety was beginning to broaden also.

Natural increase clearly explained much of the preponderant

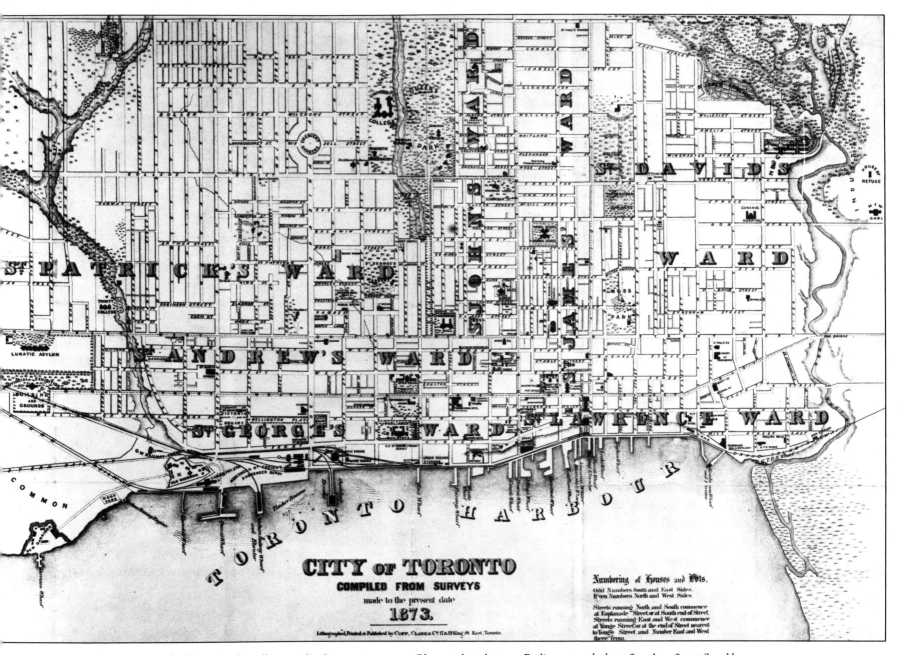

CITY OF TORONTO
COMPILED FROM SURVEYS
made to the present date
1873.

Lithographed, Printed & Published by COPP, CLARK & Co 17 & 19 King St. East, Toronto.

Numbering of Houses and Lots.

Odd Numbers South and East Sides.
Even Numbers North and West Sides.

Streets running North and South commence
at Esplanade Street or at South end of Street.
Streets running East and West commence
at Yonge Street or at the end of Street nearest
to Yonge Street, and Number East and West
there from.

This 1873 map displays a fairly well occupied urban territory up to Bloor, at least between Parliament and about Strachan Street (by old Garrison Creek on the west). East of Parliament, the area of Cabbagetown that reached to the Don was steadily filling — often with British immigrants — as a workers' residential district above the eastern industrial area. West of Strachan Street, the creek valleys north from about the Trinity College grounds slowed development. But this western quarter, too, saw growing settlement of workers employed in industries (like Massey) around the rail lines. Well-to-do residential areas were rising northward around Queen's Park, and up Sherbourne and Jarvis near the Horticultural (Allan) Gardens.

Canadian-born segment (of mostly British stock), but there was another demographic process that also enlarged the urban population: in-migration from the countryside. In an occupied southern Ontario, where agriculture was increasingly mechanized, land values high and few good farm lots left unopened, growing numbers were disposed to move: those with inadequate capital or on poor land, surplus labourers, small town hopefuls, sons without property to inherit, and young single women. Some of these might emigrate to the U.S, others reach the pioneering West. Yet still others sought nearer opportunities in Ontario urban centres, including, above all, the factories, stores and other employments of dominant Toronto. Moreover, thanks to that city's greater scale and complexity of activities, women could increasingly find jobs there — not only in traditional domestic services, shops or manufacturing, but also, for those more qualified, in teaching or office work, since female employment (at lower pay levels) was spreading in both these enlarging sectors.

Out-migration from Toronto went on as well as intake, and transiency undoubtedly remained a regular aspect of its urban demography. Nevertheless, the consistent rise in the city's numbers shows that it was obviously gaining far more than it might have lost through transiency. Taken together, natural increase, immigration and in-migration produced a fast-multiplying city unchecked by major epidemics, for by the 1880s effective civic health measures at last were being implemented.[57] But another significant feature of this whole demographic pattern lies not in numbers but in kind, in the qualitative nature of the expanding city populace.

Unlike many other industrializing North American centres of the day, Toronto did not draw its massing work force largely from "foreign" immigrants, but almost wholly from Anglo-Canadians, motherland English and Scots, and now acclimatized Irish, all English-speaking. Although religious differences would still affect this working body, far wider ethnic and linguistic separations were absent. There was no large pool of alien newcomers to be exploited through their language and cultural difficulties, or resented for taking jobs from "proper" citizens. This is not to say that Toronto did not display its own inherited ethnic prejudices and discords. British and Protestant feelings there could still readily turn to anti-American or anti-French phobias, and repeatedly reacted to supposed popish threats to liberty in French Catholic Canada. A belief that Canada was, and was meant to be, ascendantly British and Protestant ruled a large majority of Torontonians. They volunteered readily to put down the Red River Rising of 1870 and the North West Rebellion of 1885, blamed on French Catholic troublemaking, while Toronto newspapers rose in fury to demand that the arch-rebel, Louis Riel, hang for his sins in 1885.

Within the city, rowdy sectarian clashes between Orange Protestants and Irish Catholics continued; twenty-two occurred between 1867 and 1892, chiefly centring on March 17 and July 12.[58] There also were the more serious Jubilee Riots of 1875, when Catholic religious processions celebrating a papal anniversary were attacked in the streets by Orange mobs. Nonetheless, masses of police and militia were deployed in 1875 to ensure the Catholic's right to march — violence got little sympathy from orderly, respectable Toronto — and by the early Nineties most of the steam had gone out of Orange-Green feuding. It has been observed, besides, that over the period the Orange Order largely "institutionalized" sectarian strife within bounds that both sides recognized.[59] It almost became a ritual sport for group prestige, somewhat more bruising than football without pads. Besides, the Orange Order itself, well based in the working classes, virtually operated as part of the civic establishment, providing support for local politicians, thus ensuring city jobs for the duly accredited — rather like a company union.[60]

Beyond this declining sectarian discord, the later Victorian community, all but homogeneous in linguistic terms and largely so in ethnic, displayed a high degree of confident consensus. There was wide acceptance of a brand of evangelical righteousness, a pride in churches, church-going, temperance endeavours and earnest Sunday observance, which by the Nineties brought the community the not unwelcome title of "Toronto the Good."[61] Masses as well as classes widely espoused the ardent spirit of British imperialism that swelled in the later nineteenth century, hailing the glories of Anglo-Saxondom embodied in their great world empire.[62] By no means opposed to this was the citizens' faith in a Canadian national destiny, with their town at its forefront. Altogether, a broadly cohesive city reflected its own distinctive pattern of population growth.

That spreading growth also brought boundary enlargements. The last ward created within the existing city limits was St. Stephen's in 1875, on the northwest. But by then the city was pressing

The built-up downtown, around 1875, looking south from the Metropolitan Church tower. The south side of Queen is at the fore. Towards the rear, off-centre to right, is the new Post Office (back view) at King and Toronto streets, with its curving mansard roof.

on its margins, particularly north around Yonge to Bloor, beyond which lay Yorkville, a separate unit now in little but local authority, which was backed by its inhabitants' aversion to higher city taxes.[63] Toronto, however, equally wanted a wider tax base, especially as Yorkvillians largely worked in the city and used its facilities. Annexation, debated into the 1880s, really came to turn on Yorkville's need for a larger water supply, the result of its own growth. The city, which by that time had considerably improved its water system, refused to let the suburban community tap it.[64] Faced with horrors of drought, the embattled Yorkville burghers at last surrendered. In 1883 their town became St. Paul's Ward in the city. And this first annexation led to others, all enacted by Ontario's parliament. (Changing city and ward boundaries are shown on Maps 6 and 7.)

In 1884 the village of Brockton came in on the west, as the core of St. Mark's Ward. That year St. Matthew's was set up on the east, annexing Riverside (Riverdale) in an expansion over the Don. In 1887 St. Paul's Ward was extended both east and west above Bloor, as a part of suburban Rosedale and a locality today still called the "Annex" were acquired. In 1888 Seaton Village and Sunnyside were absorbed to westward; the next year the inclusion of the town of Parkdale, a well-to-do residential retreat, completed new St. Alban's Ward in this quarter.[65] By 1893, when a strip was added along the western lakeshore road, the city stretched virtually from the Humber mouth to Ashbridges Bay beyond the Don. While land speculators' hopes played a part, this series of annexations had mainly been effected to meet the facts of population increase and of the consequent demands for greater urban integration, services and revenues.[66] Hence, Toronto's territorial expansion was both effect and cause of swelling numbers — but, in any case, was a significant aspect of its whole demographic development.

URBAN SOCIETY: CLASSES, MASSES AND ORGANIZATION

The ruling elements of later Victorian Toronto firmly sustained a faith in Christian values, imperial loyalty, hard work, and due rewards of wealth. Nor is there any need to look for hypocrisies in their creed, especially when it seemed to work so well. They also believed in free enterprise (except for necessary state aids like the tariff), a free labour market and low taxation; in short, they took

their class interests seriously. Most of them took equally seriously the duty of Christian service to their church and community. It would be as wrong to deem them lacking in charity or social conscience as to overweigh their often quite practical compassion, or their readiness to take on service posts that brought desirable social distinction as well as a watch over expenditures. By and large, the Toronto elite acted like any other, in its own cause; but it did show involvement and responsibility, and subscribed to the general good in all rectitude.

This ruling elite clearly rested on personal business wealth. Though corporate forms of capitalism were present, they had not yet taken command. All the same, this was not just a crass plutocracy, where social ranking went by dollar count alone. New money needed time for mellowing; an Eaton or a Massey family would not win immediate upper-level acceptance. There were processes of social passage to be undergone, through giving the right parties (not too lavishly ostentatious) for the right guests, belonging to the right community organizations and churches (preferably Anglican or Presbyterian, though more urbane Methodism increasingly would do), displaying the right furnishings and "tasteful" art objects, and, especially, engaging in philanthropy. Moreover, shopkeepers and manufacturers, however large their operations, were not deemed as socially admirable as big wholesalers and financiers, unless, like the distillery-based Gooderhams, they had been present long enough and had acceptably diversified their business concerns.[67]

There was a continued strain of old-family gentility in upper-class society. If the proud York gentry were but a memory, Robinsons, Allans, Ridouts, Jarvises and others were still in evidence, although it helped if their scions were prominent in business or some public capacity as well. The long reign of Boultons at The Grange ended in 1875, when William Boulton's widow married Professor Goldwin Smith, formerly of Oxford and Cornell. Yet the magisterial Smith, "the Sage of The Grange," gained his own prominence as an English intellectual aristocrat, pronouncing trenchantly in journals and books on issues of the day. He represented, in fact, another leaven in the upper ranks provided by a growing intelligentsia of influential professional men. But again it helped if such city notables were manifestly successful doctors or lawyers like the legal star and leading federal Liberal, Edward Blake, or top academic statesmen like Professor Daniel Wilson, president

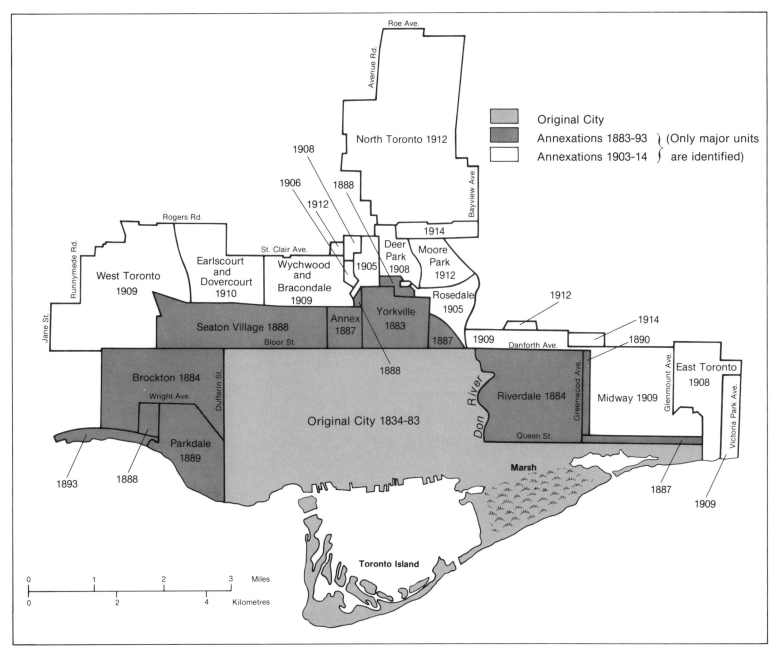

Roe Ave.

Avenue Rd.

North Toronto 1912

Bayview Ave.

Original City

Annexations 1883-93 } (Only major units

Annexations 1903-14 } are identified)

1908

1906

1888

1912

Rogers Rd.

St. Clair Ave.

Deer
Park
1908

Moore
Park
1912

West Toronto
1909

Earlscourt
and
Dovercourt
1910

Wychwood
and
Bracondale
1909

1905

Rosedale
1905

Runnymede Rd.

Jane St.

Seaton Village 1888

Annex
1887

Yorkville
1883

1887

1912

1914

1890

Bloor St.

1888

1909

Danforth Ave.

Glenmount Ave.

East Toronto
1908

Brockton 1884

Dufferin St.

Riverdale 1884

Midway 1909

Victoria Park Ave.

Wright Ave.

Original City 1834-83

Greenwood Ave.

Don River

Queen St.

Parkdale
1889

Marsh

1893

1888

1887

1909

Toronto Island

0   1   2   3   Miles

0   2   4   Kilometres

6 Toronto Annexations, 1834-1914

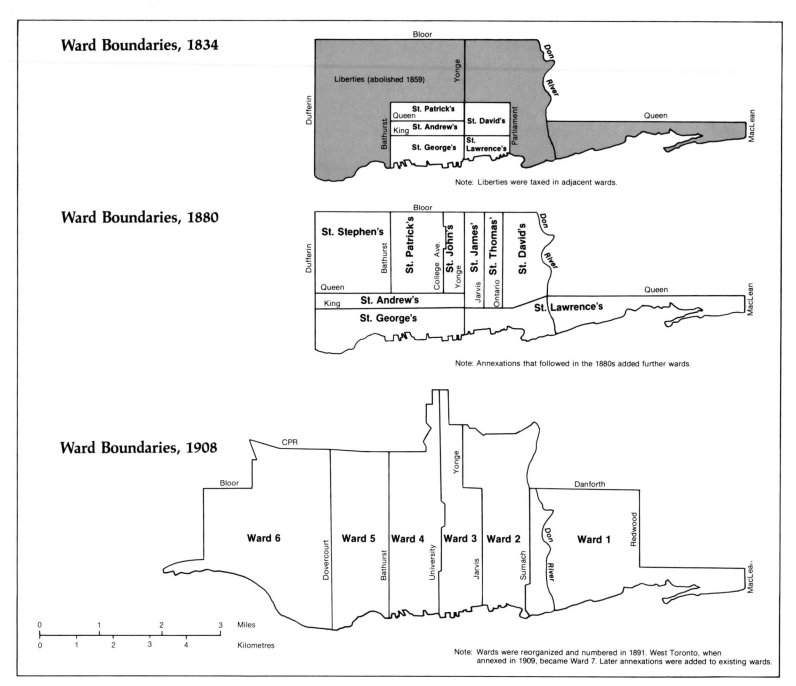

Ward Boundaries, 1834

Bloor

Liberties (abolished 1859)

Yonge

Don

River

Dufferin

Queen

Bathurst

St. Patrick's

St. David's

King

St. Andrew's

Parliament

St. George's

St. Lawrence's

Queen

MacLean

Note: Liberties were taxed in adjacent wards.

Ward Boundaries, 1880

Bloor

St. Stephen's

St. Patrick's

St. John's

St. James'

St. Thomas'

St. David's

Don

River

Dufferin

Bathurst

College Ave.

Yonge

Jarvis

Ontario

Queen

King

St. Andrew's

St. Lawrence's

Queen

MacLean

St. George's

Note: Annexations that followed in the 1880s added further wards.

Ward Boundaries, 1908

CPR

Yonge

Danforth

Bloor

Ward 6

Ward 5

Ward 4

Ward 3

Ward 2

Ward 1

Dovercourt

Bathurst

University

Jarvis

Sumach

Don River

Redwood

MacLea..

| 0 | 1 | 2 | 3 | Miles |
| 0 | 1 | 2 | 3 | 4 | Kilometres |

Note: Wards were reorganized and numbered in 1891. West Toronto, when
annexed in 1909, became Ward 7. Later annexations were added to existing wards.

7 Municipal Divisions: 1834, 1880, 1908

The British Victorian city celebrates the Queen's Diamond Jubilee, 1897. This scene on King at Yonge shows electric streetcars, which had replaced horse cars since 1894.

of University College and later of the whole university.

In any case, the urban elite was inherently business derived and oriented, led by merchant princes and banking magnates with railway entrepreneurs, big contractors and industrialists in strong association. As has been said, the economic interests of this leading element decidedly were interlocked. Socially they almost formed a new business Family Compact through intermarriages, linked investments, and church connections.[68] Of course, they were no closed circle, and their world was not that of old Compact officialdom. Still, a community does not escape its history. Though the later Victorian Toronto elite included both Liberals and Conservatives (far more of the latter) and dealt now not with a British governor but with Premier Oliver Mowat, the long-ruling Liberal master of Ontario, once a Toronto alderman in 1857, it staunchly upheld British ties, the established order and the duties of leadership in a way that would not have displeased Tory John Beverley Robinson.

The elite now was largely drawn from the generation of British immigrants that dated to the 1840s (or their children), persons who had mostly made it into the establishment from the middle classes, and there outlived many of the reforming impulses that some had felt — including the "Czar of King Street," George Brown, who appeared a fairly conservative Liberal by his death in 1880.[69] To the end of the nineteenth century and beyond, upper-rank Toronto essentially sustained a characteristic social conservatism, which is not to say that it became reactionary, opposed to further development, or to continued alterations by adjustment. The Gooderham dynasty, the McMasters, the Wortses, the Howlands and McMurrichs, and soon the Masseys and the Eatons, might maintain the predominant social tone; but they were builders as well of the much bigger industrializing city, and deeply involved in its growth and persistent change.

As for the middle classes, they remained the balance-weight of the community, largely sharing the social conservatism and values of those above them, looking, in fact, to join them, if they were sufficiently good. In the upper middle class were the households of well-to-do brokers, professionals and real estate dealers, lesser merchants and more factory owners. A few church or educational leaders, such as Chief Superintendent Ryerson, might have entry to top society, but most belonged in the level below. And in the lower middle class, smaller storekeepers and their families bulked large, as did minor contractors, craftsmen, office clerks and lower-rank teachers. Taken together, these middle classes represented sizeable economic power; politically, they were the core of the civic ratepayers' vote, and socially, the cohorts of temperance, Sabbath observance and public morality.

In social organizations, upper- and middle-class elements often readily combined: for instance, in the Mechanics Institute, in philanthropic agencies, and especially in church activities. Yet some significant insititutions were more largely upper class in emphasis, such as gentlemen's clubs, the Toronto Club being the oldest. The Albany Club became a social headquarters for affluent Conservatives; the National Club for Liberals. The distinguished Royal Canadian Yacht Club (chartered since 1854), the Toronto Cricket Club, Toronto Golf Club and Lawn Tennis Club served the social elite and upper middle-class aspirants at play. Besides these were the dining convivialities of the Board of Trade, the elevating scientific meetings of the Canadian Institute, or the various musical associations.

And finally, there were the church charitable, temperance, and mission-support groups, the Sunday schools and prayer meetings, which were a zealous part of this society and also provided valuable introductions and connections for the rising young. The Sherbourne Street Church, for example, emerged in the late Eighties and early Nineties as a very nesting-ground of wealthy Methodists, and was to be dubbed "the millionaires' church."[70] Still, dominant Anglicanism no doubt maintained a wider share of wealth behind it. And Roman Catholicism also acquired its own capitalist figures, such as Sir Frank Smith, an Irish produce merchant who became president of the Dominion Bank, the Northern Railway, the Toronto Street Railway and investment companies, as well as Conservative senator and cabinet minister.

Below the ruling classes and their allies, the masses of the city ranged from skilled tradesmen, factory or store workers, railway and port hands, carters and day labourers (plus all their families) to sweatshop denizens, the jobless, infirm and pauperized, the vagrant and disorderly. For the most disadvantaged elements, there were mainly just institutions imposed from above: church or public charities, moral uplift and temperance societies, and always poorhouses and jails. But the mass segment that was fairly regu-

The Queen's Hotel on Front Street, about 1884, with omnibus waiting. This first-class establishment drew many important visitors, among them Sir John A. Macdonald, who caucussed with Tory politicians in its Red Parlour. —which thus was deemed by honest Grits a den of party plots and patronage deals.

Well-to-do guests in the Queen's Hotel grounds, around 1880. Holland House is in the background, the "mediaeval"-styled residence built by Compact official H. J. Boulton back in 1831. Its locale, once of such fine gentry homes, was by now filling with wholesale firms close to the nearby railway stations, but the Queen's gardens remained a genteel oasis.

larly employed did have organizations that served its own needs: building and savings societies, benevolent or church associations — and, increasingly, labour unions.

Industrialization promoted unionism. In drawing lower-class family earners away from households and local workshops into mechanized, depersonalized employments, it also massed them in ever larger working units, where they could match their collective numbers against the employer's power over money and machinery. The degree of labour solidarity which thus emerged was limited by persistent traditions of individual or craft artisanry, sectarian or party ties that cut across class lines, and social conservative attitudes within the working class itself. Nevertheless, sufficient working-class consciousness did develop, together with enough determined union builders, to make Toronto a rising centre of labour organization with regional, national and international links beyond. Once more these developments did not start sharply within the 1870s. They had mid-century antecedents in recurrent collective efforts among the city's shoemakers, foundrymen and printers especially, and in the prosperous late Sixties unions seemed to be making growing headway in Toronto. Now as industrialism pushed onward in the early Seventies, so did the activities of city unions. They set up the Toronto Trades Assembly (TTA) in 1871, which the next year played a large part in sponsoring the Nine Hours Movement.[71]

This campaign to reduce the working day from ten hours to nine spread quite rapidly in urban Canada out of British and American labour backgrounds. In Toronto the printers took the lead: a well-established skilled trade in the city, whose own union there had been in continuous existence since 1844 and had become a member local of the American-based Typographical Union in 1866. In March 1872 the Toronto local struck for Nine Hours and higher wages, while the printing employers formed their own association to resist, dominated by the uncompromising, free-market Liberal, George Brown. The masters' front, however, was incomplete. James Beaty of the *Leader* adopted a pro-labour stand that was helped along by expediency: a chance to disable his old *Globe* rival, and to have his own now "run-down" paper stay open and reap circulation gains.[72] In their own cause, the printers also began the cooperative *Ontario Workman*, Toronto's first labour journal. The masters brought in non-union printers; the unionists strove to turn them away. There was fierce press talk on either side, and

charges by the masters of criminal coercion and conspiracy. At length they had striking printers arrested, whereupon the examining magistrate declared that under present law, unions were still in any case illegal combinations. It was an empty victory for Brown and his associates, for public sympathy swung strongly to the printers' union, held illegal merely for existing.

By now, mid-May, the strike nevertheless was ebbing, as was talk of a general strike for Nine Hours. The masters gave wage concessions; the printers eased their comprehensive nine-hours rule. More important, Prime Minister Sir John A. Macdonald shrewdly seized the advantage to put through a federal measure legalizing unions in conformity with existing British legislation. It did not add anything, merely confirmed what before had mainly been taken for granted; but it made Macdonald and the Conservatives self-proclaimed friends of the workingman.[73] In any event, the Nine Hours Movement had evinced the rising power of labour organization, produced a labour press and encouraged wider unionism — thanks considerably to working-class action in an industrializing Toronto.

Stirred by the mood of achievement, a key group of Toronto unionists (including J. S. Williams, editor of the *Workman*, and John Hewitt, founder of the Toronto Trades Assembly) led in erecting a national Canadian Labour Union (CLU) in 1873, which lobbied effectively for improved labour legislation. The economic recession after 1874, however, put severe strains on the union movement, and both the CLU and TTA collapsed in 1878-79. Then the recovery of the early Eighties brought a revival of labour activity in Toronto, displayed not only in fresh strikes, but also in the creation of the Toronto Trades Council in 1881 and a new national body, the Trades and Labour Congress (TLC), set up at a convention in the city in 1883. Furthermore, a powerful American organization, the Knights of Labor, entered Toronto in 1882. At its peak there, four years later, it had some fifty-three locals and nearly 5,000 members drawn from all across the labour spectrum.[74]

The Knights ideally preferred arbitration to the strike weapon, and espoused cloudily romantic rituals. But they sought to organize labour *en masse* to meet industrial capitalism, unskilled workers as well as skilled crafts. Consequently, their Toronto membership ranged from machinists, shoemakers and carpenters to streetcar drivers, dock hands and seamstresses.[75] Besides, they emphasized labour education through newspapers; their press was vigorous,

From 1879 an annual Exhibition at Toronto replaced earlier, shifting provincial fairs. It moved the Crystal Palace (enlarged) to broader grounds on the Garrison Common, and there celebrated technology as well as agriculture, exemplified by the "tower of electricity" on its prize list for 1885. By 1892, more buildings had been added, as portrayed on that year's prize list.

Street railway workers at the horse-car system's Yorkville depot, on Yonge above Bloor (till 1883, Yorkville's town hall). Men like these went through the hard-fought strike against the private streetcar company in 1886, and sought public ownership instead. The streetcar is one of the last horse-drawn vehicles, decorated to advertise the Elias Rogers company.

and talented journalists, most notably Phillips Thompson, emerged in its service. Through champions like Thompson, and printer-politician Daniel O'Donoghue, the Knights made evident progress in broadening working-class consciousness in the city. They also took to endorsing candidates acceptable to labour in civic politics. Still further, they waged a successful strike at the Massey factory in 1886, though the same year lost a bitter fight against Frank Smith's Toronto Street Railway Company.[76]

In time, the weaknesses in the Knights' own extended organization and their frequent reluctance to face confrontations led to their being supplanted by smaller, tighter, more-militant craft unions. But their legacy in expanded working-class horizons, labour writing and political action would remain highly significant in Toronto's transition to industrial society. Labour had plainly taken shape there as an enduring, influential force, a fact exemplified by strong city labour campaigns for endorsed candidates in federal, provincial and municipal elections during 1886–87.[77] Moreover, Labour Day was first celebrated in Toronto in 1886, when the Industrial Exhibition (with an eye to wider popular support) honoured the workers of the world, and a grand parade of union members marched out to the grounds to hail their mounting significance in the Canadian community.[78]

In renewed slumps of the late Eighties and early Nineties, there were few fresh working-class gains in the city. The Knights were fast fading; newer international, American-centred unions added Toronto locals only slowly. The election of E. F. (Ned) Clarke as mayor in 1888 — once a *Globe* printer arrested in 1872 — was hailed as a victory by labour, but this Orange politician who held office on through 1891 more truly symbolized a renewal of political links with Conservatism that dated back to John A. Macdonald as "the workingman's friend" of 1872. Moreover, while labour was an important component of the civic reforming groups who managed to end the unpopular old street railway monopoly in 1891, it did not succeed in its further effort to establish municipal ownership of the system.[79] Of more long-run significance, perhaps, were enlarging radical sentiments particularly among labour intellectuals, which carried some to varieties of socialism, and so to far more fundamental critiques of industrial life and relations.

Overall, when the later Victorian period drew towards a close, Toronto comprised a society controlled by a business elite and its values, increasingly stamped by industrial capitalism. Yet it was equally marked by active working-class responses and by sharper social divisions between propertied classes and wage-dependent masses, expressed as well in steadily growing residential separation.[80] Furthermore, education tended to maintain class differences, despite democratic ideals of mass schooling. Upper-class families had access to privileged schools like Upper Canada College. Middle-class children were thoroughly institutionalized into the public system, which still gave them advantages over lower-class youth. As for the latter, though education was officially compulsory, family needs and shifts often made it a come-and-go affair for them, so that poorer attendance and lower achievement continued to set them off. Nevertheless, for all this, rooted common traditions, long-fixed religious and cultural bonds, and the basic uniformities in Toronto's demography, kept the whole urban community rather less divided than those of many other major North American centres. The city on balance remained a coherent social unit, with firmly dominant patterns of outlook, standards and tastes. The results could be seen in the very urban landscape that evolved during the height of the Victorian age.

URBAN LANDSCAPE AND CULTURE: THE HIGH VICTORIAN CITY

Not just size and smoking factories distinguished Toronto's later nineteenth-century cityscape from that of earlier years. New building styles and techniques emerged as well, more concentrated central development, far better street transport and, especially, increasing land-use differences between residential, business and workplace districts. Moreover, in this expanding, changing environment, cultural life developed in keeping. The High Victorian city was both a physical fact and a state of living, each reflecting and interacting with the other.

As the Seventies began, good times saw Toronto in another building boom, which among other things produced more Italianate offices and residences, an enlarged Queen's Hotel, and a line of wholesale warehouses across the late Bishop Strachan's estate from York to Simcoe. The Metropolitan Church by Henry Langley, a stately Gothic cathedral of Methodism — which had come a long way from the frontier — went up at Queen and Church in 1872. The triple-towered Union Station opened on Front near York in 1873, and a commodious Grand Opera House in 1874 on Adelaide

The Board of Trade Building, 1889, at Yonge and Front. Important for its technology, not architecture, this was Toronto's first steel-framed building. Across from it stood the more attractive — but unrevolutionary — Bank of Montreal of 1885.

The Post Office, 1873, by R. C. Windeyer. This edifice heading Toronto Street well represents the opulent Second Empire style, with its dressy mansard roof and ornate facade. It was replaced by the decidedly less attractive Mackenzie Building after the Second World War.

Government House, erected by 1871 for the new Province of Ontario, on the site of its Upper Canada predecessor on Simcoe near King. It was the lieutenant-governor's residence till 1912.

George Gooderham's mansion, 1890, at St. George and Bloor. This prime example of Romanesque style was no less detailed in its rich interior woodwork.

Metropolitan Church, 1872, by Henry Langley. This picture of his "cathedral of Methodism," at Queen and Church, also shows the spire he added to St. Patrick's Cathedral up Bond Street in the background.

off Yonge. In design, these large edifices were free-handed Victorian versions of mediaeval or Renaissance forms; the latter further developed into the Second Empire style of Napoleon III's France. Thus the Opera House and the Post Office of 1873 were built in Second Empire manner, with ornamental mansard roofs, while Presbyterian Knox College and new St. Andrew's Church, both of 1875, took mediaeval shapes.[81]

Then in the later Seventies the spread of recession slowed developments. It was not till the recovery of the early Eighties that building in Toronto began a new advance, which this time virtually lasted to the end of the period. For in spite of various economic downturns, the industrializing city had now acquired so much momentum, population increase and accumulating wealth that major construction went forward with few breaks. Sure of their city and its future, Toronto builders did not let sporadic market constraints stop them long. Beyond this, new styles and another generation of designers took hold. The rising architect, E. J. Lennox, produced his Manning Arcade of 1884, a wide-windowed office block, and in 1885 Frank Darling co-designed the Bank of Montreal at Front and Yonge, an early example of French Beaux Arts classicism in the city.

Still more significant for High Victorian Toronto was the arrival of "Richardson Romanesque" from Chicago, where H. H. Richardson had adapted an early mediaeval Italian building style to feature great round arches on thick pillars, massive walls with much carved detail, and bold, asymmetrical roof-lines. This kind of Romanesque quickly rooted itself in Toronto. New provincial Parliament Buildings were erected in the centre of Queen's Park in heavy Romanesque blocks of red sandstone, begun in 1886 and completed in 1892. The big Confederation Life Building at Yonge and Richmond (1890) had Gothic touches, but stout walls and rounded arches indicated its Romanesque origin. That origin was much clearer in the pinnacled bulk of Victoria College, opened in 1892 on the edge of Queen's Park. And the new City Hall of E. J. Lennox (designed in 1890 though not finished till 1899) brought Romanesque's finest achievement in Toronto. Set at Queen and Bay on land exporpriated from Macaulaytown shacks, its clocktower soaring above the vista from the lake, this edifice was a testament in lavishly worked buff sandstone to the metropolitan dignity of the High Victorian city.

New technology also greatly affected major buildings, for instance, by introducing electric elevators, which offered far more range and speed than steam-powered or hydraulic lifts. In fact, they presaged the multi-storeyed office structure, the skyscraper — as well requiring new building techniques to give its height the necessary supporting strength. Here cast iron had pointed the way, from mid-Victorian times, supplying internal columns to uphold larger edifices, and even providing precast facades with moulded columns painted "stone" colour, as used on some remaining commercial blocks on Front. Cast iron led to stronger wrought-iron frameworks, then to the all-steel-framed building, whose outer walls were merely coverings, not ponderous supports.[82] This climactic last stage was reached in Toronto in the Board of Trade Building of 1889 at Yonge and Front. Externally, it was a seven-storeyed melange of Romanesque, Gothic and you-name-it, but its skeleton was steel. And F. M. Gouinlock's Temple Building of 1895 on Bay was a true skyscaper, ten floors high, if one still with iron framing and a largely Romanesque exterior (Map 8). Though tall buildings would not dominate the Toronto skyline till the next era, the High Victorian city had prepared their way.

Moreover, the vertical growth of offices and larger stores on expensive downtown real estate — made possible by metal framing and electric elevators even before skyscrapers fully emerged — maintained or enhanced the concentration of leading business activities within a compact core area. This central business district had sorted out its land use further by the early Nineties. While the main wholesale section remained close to the harbour and the railway stations, markedly along Front and Wellington, financial concerns were focusing around King and Bay, and the prime retail locality now centred on Yonge at Queen, where Eaton's and Simpson's ruled.[83] Electricity by then, moreover, could safely light big central buildings with incandescent "Edison" bulbs. Another achievement of electric technology also aided central concentration, once Toronto's first telephone exchange was installed in 1879. Spreading telephone lines gave downtown businesses ready access to customers, agents and dealers across wide distances, while they still could stay in close neighbourhood with related firms in their fields.

When electricity also brought much more efficient streetcar transport, it further promoted both central focusing and spatial outreach.[84] Little electric trolley cars had been in service at the annual Exhibition since 1885, carrying the public a short distance

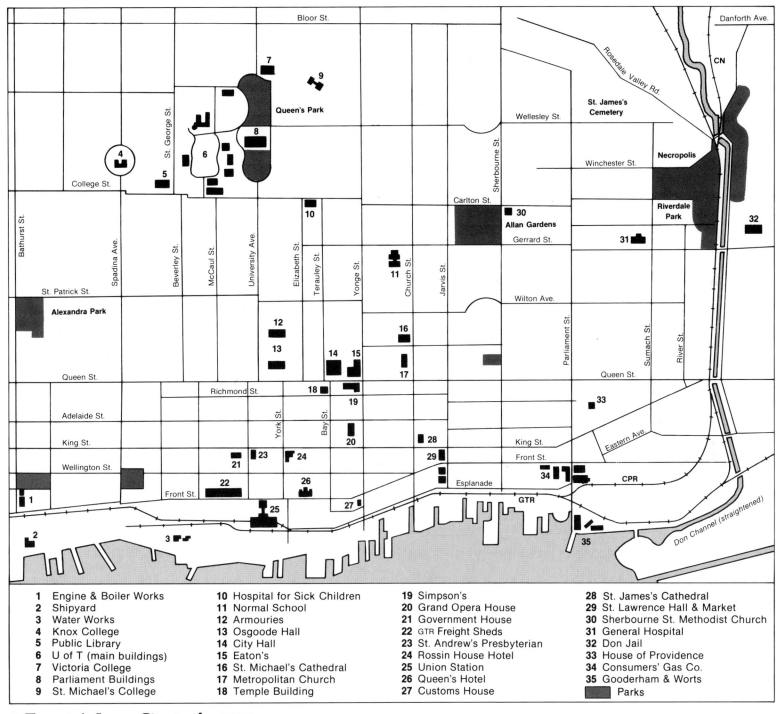

Bloor St.

Danforth Ave.

Rosedale Valley Rd.

CN

7

9

Queen's Park

St. James's
Cemetery

Wellesley St.

St. George St.

8

Winchester St.

Necropolis

6

4

5

College St.

Carlton St.

Allan Gardens

30

Riverdale
Park

31

32

Bathurst St.

Spadina Ave.

Beverley St.

McCaul St.

University Ave.

Elizabeth St.

Terauley St.

Yonge St.

Church St.

Jarvis St.

Sherbourne St.

Gerrard St.

10

St. Patrick St.

Alexandra Park

11

Wilton Ave.

Parliament St.

Sumach St.

River St.

12

16

13

14 15

Queen St.

17

Queen St.

Richmond St.

18

33

19

Adelaide St.

York St.

Bay St.

King St.

20

28

King St.

Eastern Ave.

Wellington St.

23   24

29

Front St.

21

CPR

22

26

34

Esplanade

27

GTR

Front St.

25

35

Don Channel (straightened)

1

2

3

1 Engine & Boiler Works	10 Hospital for Sick Children	19 Simpson's	28 St. James's Cathedral
2 Shipyard	11 Normal School	20 Grand Opera House	29 St. Lawrence Hall & Market
3 Water Works	12 Armouries	21 Government House	30 Sherbourne St. Methodist Church
4 Knox College	13 Osgoode Hall	22 GTR Freight Sheds	31 General Hospital
5 Public Library	14 City Hall	23 St. Andrew's Presbyterian	32 Don Jail
6 U of T (main buildings)	15 Eaton's	24 Rossin House Hotel	33 House of Providence
7 Victoria College	16 St. Michael's Cathedral	25 Union Station	34 Consumers' Gas Co.
8 Parliament Buildings	17 Metropolitan Church	26 Queen's Hotel	35 Gooderham & Worts
9 St. Michael's College	18 Temple Building	27 Customs House	▬ Parks

8 Toronto's Inner City to the 1900s

into the grounds.[85] Six years later, one of the terms on which a new company acquired Toronto's streetcar franchise was that it would electrify the existing horse-drawn system, and this was effected between 1892 and 1894. Since, however, the full impact of the electric streetcar obviously fell in a subsequent period, it is more important here to note that the horse-car system had already put a strong imprint upon Toronto's built environment — especially as its trackage had risen from a mere six miles in 1872 to over sixty-eight by 1891.[86] Extensions and new routes were mainly products of the expansive Eighties. By 1881 the main King cross-town car line ran from the Don to the Exhibition grounds; the track on Queen was extended west to Parkdale in 1886 and across the Don eastward as far as the outlying Woodbine racetrack in 1887. To the north, the Yonge Street route pushed on through newly annexed Yorkville in 1885, while among multiplying north-south routes, the Sherbourne line crossed Bloor in 1891 to enter Rosedale, now increasingly a favoured haven for the wealthy.[87]

Streetcar transport knitted up the differentiating city, moving workers and shoppers into the central core, carrying people outward to residential districts, and opening new fringes to suburban growth beyond the basic Shore Plain. Though the street railway linked homes to workplaces, it also made for their greater spatial separation, since considerably longer journeys to work were feasible in the streetcar city than in its walking predecessor. So residential areas spread out with car lines, and suburbs with wider living space developed, mainly for the more well-to-do who could afford the regular costs of longer trips. The result was a further sorting-out in land use. Middle-class residential districts grew towards the outskirts, along with upper-class enclaves and estates, while between these reaches and the in-town business or industrial areas, predominantly lower-class neighbourhoods took shape. They were often within short range or walking distance of factories, which themselves mainly clustered either down towards the eastern end of of the harbour, near the Don mouth, or out westward, south of King, close to railway lines. In these emerging working-class districts, keen-eyed developers and contractors from the Seventies on put up lines of mass housing on small plots: narrow brick houses usually attached or semi-detached. And this spatial allocation again related to the streetcar. It occurred between high-value centrally located property and the outlying districts with their transport-added costs. Enlarged, horse-drawn, High

Victorian Toronto developed land-use patterns of social segregation to a degree unknown in the smaller walking city.[88]

The poorest quarters were generally located in deteriorating stretches of the old inner city. Slum conditions were intensifying here, as in the back-lane cottages of near-central St. John's Ward, which included old Macaulaytown, or in areas close to railyards, noisome factories and packinghouses further out to east or west. Nevertheless, tenements, crowded, cheerless hives of poverty, still generally did not arise. The bulk of working-class families continued to live on ordered streets of rented small houses, houses that some of them came to own. These rows of nestled homes, displaying plump mansard Second Empire roofs or sharp Victorian Gothic gables, may look picturesque yet — certainly to modern-day redevelopers who "restore" them.

Middle-class areas had similar if more roomy brick residences, with a stained-glass window or two, verandahs, and decorative gingerbread fretwork. Wonderfully gingerbread wooden summer homes also spread on the Island — a special world in itself. But the upper middle class, and the upper class particularly, also responded to the Romanesque urge. They erected imposing mansions with characteristic broad arches on heavy pillars, embellished stone or brickwork, and perhaps a rounded tower. George Gooderham's residence of 1890 on Bloor at St. George (now the York Club) remains an outstanding example; yet such elite homes appeared along St. George near the University, through the highly regarded Annex, along upper Jarvis and Sherbourne, and on into Rosedale.[89]

And cultural as well as material expansion went on in this physically changing city. Its upper levels acclaimed literature, art and science even when they did not understand them, for they were dutifully Improving Victorians. Besides, Toronto's enlarging wealth and audience, its already strong professional and educational components, and its advancing control of means of communication, all clearly stimulated literary, informational and artistic developments. Thus, the early Seventies in the city saw the literary upsurge of a group of young national idealists, prominent among them George Taylor Denison, already a veteran of the Fenian Raid of 1866, and William Foster, a Toronto lawyer whose pamphlet of 1871, *Canada First*, gave the movement its name. Linked with the aspiring Liberal politician, Edward Blake, and backed by Professor Goldwin Smith, the Canada Firsters founded an able journal, the *Nation*, in 1874. Thereafter, bright enthusiasm faded in the gloom of economic recession. Yet Canada First was a real expression of Toronto's own nation-building hopes, and the authors and poets it engendered left strong marks on Canadian writing.

Furthermore, this nationalist movement inspired new periodicals in the city, such as the *Canadian Monthly*, established in 1872, with Goldwin Smith as a keen contributor. This was replaced by the *Week* in 1883, which lasted till 1896 as an eminent journal of "politics, society and literature." Smith also produced his own pungent *Bystander*, voicing his scathing appraisals of sordid Canadian politics and his mounting doubts that Canada even deserved to be a nation. The citizens of Toronto read their Sage's charges while flatly rejecting his final answer, union with the United States; some, like George Denison, took up the goal of a British imperial federal union instead. More widely to the residents' tastes, however, was the work of Henry Scadding, son of Simcoe's estate manager and long the Anglican rector of Holy Trinity, whose *Toronto of Old* (1873) was a valuable record of the city's early life. His writings evoked both Toronto's pride in its past and belief in its present — feelings warmly displayed in the celebration of the fiftieth anniversary of cityhood in 1884, a glorious moment of parades and civic festival.[90]

On other levels of popular culture, John Ross Robertson's *Evening Telegram*, launched in 1876, brought mass journalism to the people. Its imperialism, sensationalism and Orange Order news marked it as a city institution for generations to come, but so did its stress on the complex local affairs of a now large community. Along with a breezily independent *Telegram*, the daily press included the Liberal *Globe* still; the *Mail*, founded as a Conservative organ in 1872 to replace a dying *Leader*; the *Empire*, another Conservative party paper, begun in 1887 but absorbed by the *Mail* in 1895; and three more independents, the *World*, started in 1880, the *News*, 1881, and the *Star*, 1893. These plentiful dailies kept up the power of the city's printing offices; their staffs produced more authors for the realm of literature. The allied domain of publishing grew also with leading firms like Copp Clark, Gage, Hunter Rose, and the Methodist Publishing Company. An illustrated press emerged besides, well exemplified in *Grip*, a light-hearted weekly of comment under J. S. Bengough from 1873 to 1892. His deft, blather-puncturing political cartoons in *Grip* were among Toronto's best achievements as a centre of opinion-making in later Victorian times.

Concern for the availability of literature led to a free Public Library.[91] By the Eighties in Toronto, the private Mechanics Institute that had provided limited reading rooms and some adult education was all but out of date. Institute lectures and exhibits had lost popular appeal. The YMCA since the 1860s had offered young men alternative interests, and the public schools supplied night classes from 1880. Yet the institute still held its large building and book collection. Urged on by Alderman John Hallam, champion of free libraries, and funded under provincial legislation, a municipal Public Library took over, opening in 1884. The central library unit was enlarged, while within four years branches were added to west, east and north. The Mechanics Institute gave way to a major civic cultural and educational institution, another lasting attainment of High Victorian Toronto.

Formal education grew also. More public and separate schools went up; kindergartens were pioneered (1883); compulsory schooling was extended; and in secondary education, Parkdale (1889) and Harbord (1892) were added to Jarvis as high schools or "collegiate institutes."[92] In 1891 august Upper Canada College moved to spacious new suburban quarters at the head of Avenue Road above St. Clair. On the university level, William McMaster gave funds for Baptist McMaster Hall, opened in 1881 on Bloor near Avenue Road, while Wycliffe College (evangelical Anglican) appeared beside Queen's Park in 1882. Wycliffe, Catholic St. Michael's and Presbyterian Knox College subsequently affiliated with the University of Toronto, while Methodist Victoria agreed to federate in 1887, but did not transfer from Cobourg for five years more. The School of Practical Science, a provincial technological institute established on the campus in 1878, was also linked with the University in 1887. Toronto's metropolitan centring of higher education was manifestly strengthened.

In a surge of post-Confederation Canadianism, the Ontario Society of Artists (OSA) was established in Toronto in 1872, the first enduring professional art association in the country. Its leaders included the distinguished watercolourist John Fraser, then Toronto partner in the well-known Notman and Fraser photographic firm of Montreal, and Lucius O'Brien, who romantically depicted rugged Canadian land masses. Toronto artists, in fact, took on national scope, evidenced in the western mountain paintings of O'Brien, Fraser and T. Mower Martin, prairie scenes by Frederick Verner, and in the whole group's role in the founding of the Royal Canadian Academy (RCA) at Ottawa in 1880. And the

Professor Goldwin Smith at about forty. From the 1870s nearly till his death in 1910, he was a literary mover and shaker in Toronto: ardently liberal in doctrine, but foe of set party cliques; a strenuous critic but strong backer of public causes, from workers' and farmers' rights to civic reform, from welfare needs to the advancement of the University of Toronto.

THE BEAUTIES OF A ROYAL COMMISSION.

"WHEN SHALL WE THREE MEET AGAIN?"

This typical Grip cartoon of 1873 concerns the Pacific Scandal of the day, when John A. Macdonald's government was accused of taking bribes (as election funds) in awarding the charter for the Canadian Pacific Railway. Here J. S. Bengough spears the government's resultant inquiry into itself, as three John A.'s congenially deal with one another.

Toronto Art Students League of 1886 fostered rising talents like Charles Jefferys, often found in young commercial artists' ranks. Indeed, newspaper, book-publishing and advertising work in the industrializing city attracted a growing number of draughtsmen and designers, such as Charlotte Schreiber, painter, one of the first women illustrators in Canada, and a founding member of the RCA. Furthermore, initiated by the OSA and headed by T. M. Martin in 1877, a little, provincially aided Art School in Toronto rose with the city's cultural growth to become by the Nineties the chief art-education institute in Ontario.

Developments in music were similarly linked to the High Victorian city's swelling affluence and audience, its increasingly cultivated tastes, and the professionalism all these encouraged. The Toronto Philharmonic Society was revived in 1872, after earlier sporadic existences. Under F. H. Torrington, the organist of Metroplitan Methodist Church, the Society's symphonic orchestra and its chorus of well over a hundred became very successful, so much so that Hart Massey decided to give Toronto a proper modern concert hall. Massey Hall was opened in 1894 off downtown Yonge Street: a large, austere, red-brick mass externally, but internally marked by exotic Moorish touches, and more important, excellent acoustics. The period saw as well the founding of the Toronto Choral Society, the Mendelssohn Choir and three music schools, including the predecessor of the Royal Conservatory of Music.[93]

Musical drama did not develop as significantly. Grand opera was usually imported; light opera also came from touring companies, or local amateurs. Yet theatre in general flourished, in spite of continued condemnation by Methodists and other stricter elements. "Good" theatre, in fact, had become much more desirable to upper-class society, providing as it did suitable cultural amusements and occasions to be seen. For the non-elite, while taverns still filled traditional roles in recreation, many also found escape from office and factory drabness, crowded homes and urban pressures, in the exciting glitter of theatre. Minstrel shows remained constant favourites on this popular stage, as did flimsy musical farces. Superior offerings were quite regularly available, however, from Shakespeare to recent London and New York hits. They mostly went to the Grand Opera House of 1874, a well-equipped structure seating 1,300 (and later enlarged) that supplanted a smaller, failing Royal Lyceum.[94] There were other, mainly lower-grade, rival houses, but the Grand dominated the whole period. And the upshot was that Toronto rose to be a leading theatre town on provincial and trans-border circuits.

Organized sports also developed rapidly in a built-up, regimented city craving leisure-time releases. Its needs and numbers further promoted mass spectator sport and sports business. Racetracks became big enterprises, notably the Woodbine, which from 1883 yearly ran the top-level Queen's Plate race. American baseball fast overtook English cricket; amateur and professional leagues set up from the Seventies drew heavy crowds. Still, Canadian lacrosse was even more popular. A Canadian version of rugby football took hold in the Eighties, and huge cycling meets became a virtual craze by the early Nineties. In winter, there was curling, ice-boating on the bay, or skating on large rinks, which attracted far more than hockey as yet, though intercity contests for the Stanley Cup dated from 1893. In summer, yachting and, above all, rowing reigned. The latter, marked by the prowess of the Argonaut Club founded in 1872, was crowned when Toronto's Ned Hanlan won American and British professional singles championships from 1876, and held the world title from 1880 to 1884. Victor in some 150 races, an international star, Hanlan remained a hero of High Victorian Toronto: in sports culture also, "no mean city" of its time.

URBAN POLITICS AND SERVICES

Municipal affairs were deeply affected by industrial and demographic growth, which extended the city's tasks as well as its territory, increasing calls on services and heightening problems of finance. Civic taxation rose from some $239,000 in 1861 to $937,000 by 1881; and the tax rate, since 1861 around fifteen mills on the dollar, climbed to twenty in 1878.[95] Beyond that, new political factors were entering: working-class activism, demands for efficient "business" management to restrain rising city budgets, moves to put utility monopolies in public hands, and moral designs for humanitarian progress through civic assaults on vice. All these produced concerns for municipal reform and popular action such as mid-Victorian Toronto had seldom known. Yet the later Victorian city faced public needs on a scale equally unknown in its past.

One thing, however, did not change: Toronto's lasting political preference for the Conservative party. Perhaps the federal Conservatives' commitment to the National Policy renewed that preference, but it equally appeared in provincial politics where tariff

The Metropolitan Church Bicycle Club on an outing in the 1890s. The replacement of the "penny-farthing" cycle by the equal-wheel "safety" bicycle made cycling popular for recreation as well as for sport.

The Red Jacket Rink of the Toronto Curling Club on the frozen Don in the 1870s. A carefully assembled "composite" picture of the day, when photography could not yet handle real outdoor action shots.

The touring "Gentlemen of England" play the Toronto Cricket Club, 1872, at the club grounds (now part of the University campus). In background at right appears University College, and to the left of the club pavilion, the home of Frederic Cumberland.

policy did not apply. In six federal elections between 1872 and 1896, Torontonians returned sixteen Conservatives to four Liberals; in seven Ontario contests from 1871 to 1894 they chose fifteen Conservatives to three. Municipal politics, of course, were ostensibly non-partisan; still, here too, if labels were not worn except by some resolute Labourites, Conservative ties and Orange links were widely apparent among civic politicians, whether or not some might take up civic reform.

To say the expected, any reforming thrusts took time to develop. During the Seventies, the regimes at City Hall stayed much as they had been, led by largely part-time mayors, lawyers and business worthies properly apprenticed as former aldermen, who with veteran City Council comrades kept the municipal system running reasonably well on established, restricted lines. In 1874 the mayoralty did revert to direct popular election, but this caused little change in old-guard council management,[96] not till the 1880s brought new protagonists and an altered context at last. The city by that time was feeling its problems of scale. Revived, if often uncertain, prosperity also roused a hopeful, restive climate; the Knights of Labor began shaping a working-class political front, and the urgings of moral humanitarians rose in fervour. The latter were centred in a church-based temperance movement that went back to the Forties, but by now they were more generally seeking the purification of the whole civic community. The resulting urban crusade was clearly much affected by the contemporary drive for "clean" municipal government in far more corrupt, boss-ridden American city administrations; yet if Torontonians remained acutely suspicious of U.S. power, they had often accepted American ideas. Moreover, a provincial act of 1884 gave the civic vote to widows and unmarried women with due property requirements, which likely added further weight to Toronto's moral reformism.[97]

Its first plain political manifestation came in 1884, when Alderman J. J. Withrow, a Liberal, ran for mayor and was beaten by the old-guard candidate, A. R. Boswell, by only 3 votes. Withrow tried again the next year, to lose by 145 to Alexander Manning, a rich builder-developer and ex-mayor.[98] But this still close loss only fired the forces of reform. The Manning side was charged with every sort of municipal vice: as being tools of the liquor trade (certainly well tied to Conservative local interests), promoters of brothels and depravity, dealers in bribery and graft. It was all very surprising to Manning and company, just filling their same old role, and it was even more surprising when, in the elections of 1886, a "citizens' candidate" and political novice, William Holmes Howland, triumphed.[99] A minor insurance company president, if member of a leading family, Howland had once been a Canada Firster and a campaigner for the National Policy, but his chief claims to the mayor's office consisted of his devoted labours among the city's poor, his fervent evangelical beliefs and vigorous teetotalism.

In office Mayor Howland faced a council still dominated by old-guard forces. He failed in his temperance designs to reduce liquor outlets, failed to carry out a much-needed program of public works, and his investigations of a price-fixing coal ring and other jobbery bogged down. Nevertheless, the mayor's championing of the unsuccessful strike of 1886 by unionists against the heartily disliked monopoly of the Street Railway Company kept up public sympathy. He was viewed more as a victim of evil forces than as a failure, and hence worthy of another chance. With strong labour support as well as that of temperance faithful and civic uplifters, Howland was decisively re-elected in 1887, and this time took with him a much more favourable council. In consequence, liquor licences were cut, roads widely improved, and the city administration strengthened, while a new morality officer warred on bawdy-houses and illegal drinking-places. The authoritative mayor, however, retired at the end of the year, under personal financial and health strains; he died in 1893, not yet fifty. His successor in the mayoralty was not the reformers' candidate, Elias Rogers, the big coal merchant — whose temperance rectitude was blasted at the last moment by revelations of his involvement in a coal ring.[100] Instead, Conservative Ned Clarke won, deputy grand master of the Orange Order and publisher of the Orange *Sentinel*.[101] Still, Clarke had clear trade-union origins, and initially backed by a labour-Tory alliance, held Toronto successfully through four terms in all.

In view of this outcome, reforming Howland, emblematic as he was of High Victorian Toronto's moral fervour, might seem of merely passing note in city politics. But he was far more significant. He was a positive, directing mayor, as Clarke was also, taking the lead away from the old collegial council, which never wholly regained its clubby power. The changes Howland promoted in enlarging civic activity would only continue, as would lively issues of reform. In 1891 the streetcar franchise was wrested from the hated old company, though transferred on supposedly good terms to a hopefully better one.[102] In 1893 a spreading slump raised fresh

William Holmes Howland. His mayoralty of 1886-87 represented the first real breakthrough by forces of urban reform in the industrializing city, pointing the way to greater changes in the following generation.

cries for strong, efficient city government to end the aldermanic deals of real estate "boodlers." In 1894–95 new charges of incompetence and graft in the council brought on a major inquiry into municipal operations, which spurred demands for technical expertise and trained officials, and a remaking of the city's governing structure. The results were to follow in the next period — yet to all this Howland represented an essential transition. In short, the moral and humanitarian reformer had marked the passage to a new stage in municipal political life, embodying on one side positive civic leadership with wide popular backing, and on the other, full-time executive control of urban government services. The City Efficient was challenging laissez-faire assumptions in the industrializing municipality.

A prime question of services in the Howland years (and before and after) concerned the civic water system. Even by the 1870s the city had plainly outgrown the inadequate, polluted supply provided by the franchised water company, now retained on a contract basis while long-projected city water works were further considered.[103] In this regard, practical needs and technical or financial aspects were uppermost, not public ownership as a principle — but needs no less produced a major civic enterprise. In 1872 a Water Works Commission was voted in, to design a new system and take over the old one; in 1873 the private company accepted a purchase offer. By 1877, when the completed public utility was transferred directly to the city, homes with piped water had already increased to some 4,100 from a mere 1,375 in 1874.[104] They reached nearly 16,000 by 1883, as residents took steadily to a more ample and reliable city system, which featured new pumping equipment, more sewers, a holding reservoir north of town, and far greater fire-fighting capacities.[105] Yet the quality of the water remained in doubt: "drinkable sewage," the *Globe* called it in 1882.[106] Basic to the problem was the need for a large trunk sewer to drain the expanding system properly, together with the fact that sewage still poured into the harbour within range of the water intake. Thus, the Howland regime sought to construct a sewer east to Ashbridges Bay, only to have the voters reject its costs. A longer intake pipe to the open lake at least was built, but when this sprang leaks within the harbour in 1892, it caused brief returns to water carters and typhoid dangers.[107]

While health-science exponents made scant headway on the water purity issue, they saw other decisive gains in the field of public health. Until the Eighties there were few significant changes, but then both federal and provincial incentives, as well as Toronto's own realization of the sanitary dangers in an exploding urban environment, brought the establishment of a permanent medical health officer, whose work became a vital part of civic administration. In 1883 Dr. William Canniff took up this post, a well-qualified city physician and an enthusiastic sanitary reformer. He dealt with infectious diseases, effectively checking smallpox outbreaks, though he had less success controlling diptheria. He and his staff regularly inspected schools and factories, went after bad private housing, foul privies and refuse dumps, and spread their preventive care to meat, milk and ice suppliers also.[108] They lacked much coercive power, however, and had to operate with purse-pinching aldermen who still showed laissez-faire reluctance to infringe on rights of private property. Canniff, in fact, retired from his job in 1890, frustrated by setbacks, especially regarding pure water supply.[109] Nonetheless, under him and his successor, Dr. Charles Sheard, public health services were institutionalized for a far cleaner Toronto. That the city death rate fell from 21.3 per 1,000 in 1883 to 15.18 by 1896 suggested their continuing value.[110]

For all this, hospitals in Toronto still largely functioned as refuges for the sick poor, not as key centres of medical treatment. The varying provincial or municipal grants they received came to them as charitable agencies, in which private philanthropy or religious purpose also played large roles. The large Toronto General Hospital, tight for money, was indeed reproached by the provincial inspector in 1877 for not admitting sufficient poor sufferers, but fund drives pushed by board member William Howland eased its situation.[111] Charitable motives produced the Hospital for Sick Children in 1875, founded by a group of upper-class women led by Mrs. Samuel McMaster, wife of a nephew of William McMaster.[112] In the Eighties this venture of high future importance was strongly aided by John Ross Robertson, the wealthy owner of the *Telegram*, who also raised donations through his paper for the hospital's fine new Romanesque building, opened in 1891. St. Michael's, a Catholic foundation though available to all, began in 1892, and still more small hospitals appeared and grew.

Other areas of social service saw similar growth in grant-assisted philanthropic institutions. The industrializing city responded to the human problems massed by its material development through the Houses of Industry and Providence, Boys' and Girls' Homes,

Police Constable William Leonard, 1887. A stalwart member of Toronto's police force of the period — with handcuffs at the ready.

The new electric streetcar, in summer form. Closed bodies replaced "toast-racks" of this sort for winter use. This one probably ran on the Carlton-College cross-town route west to Dovercourt Road.

and city missions, adding to them Protestant and Catholic orphanages, the Toronto Relief Society, and still more, including a city relief officer — although Goldwin Smith had to undertake to pay his salary in 1883.[113] Yet the need was great, even in good times. Roaming tramps seemed to defy social regulation. Inadequate housing was a continual bane, winter unemployment a repeated scourge. Job losses in bad years caused far more misery than any strikes — so much so that the poor might put their children in orphanages, to redeem them in better days from veritable human pawnshops.[114] Baby farming, broken families and battered wives, drunkenness, vagrancy and violent assault were still other vicious aspects of poverty on the dark side of Toronto the Good.

Towards the end of the late Victorian era, real wages did rise, while the possessing classes went on doing their uneven best with public backing to alleviate, if not eliminate, the worst features of suffering. Yet under these circumstances it seems remarkable that public order was so well sustained, in spite of brief exceptions like the Jubilee Riots of 1875. Major crime in the city was far less prevalent than sensational press reports made it appear; drunk and disorderly charges climbed sharply between 1883 and 1887 (influencing the temperance reformism of the Howland years), but then steadily declined.[115] Probably Toronto's cultural uniformities and God-fearing social controls had some bearing here, as did the Salvation Army, present from 1882. So, quite likely, did an augmented police force, watched over by a rigorous George Taylor Denison, who served as the senior police magistrate right from 1877 to 1923.

Other kinds of urban services also developed further. New parks were created in the city's extending domains, a purpose also pushed by Howland. On its western margins, John Howard, the architect, conveyed his beautifully treed and hilly estate, High Park, to Toronto in 1873, though held back part until his death in 1890; while east up the Don, broad Riverdale Park (and Zoo) was developed by the mid-Nineties. Road improvements made progress as well. The laying of cedar-block paving on major streets proceeded from the early Seventies. Macadamized gravel or merely graded earth roads stayed more numerous; but by 1884, out of 163 miles of city streets, over 44 had been cedar-surfaced, to some 52 more cheaply macadamized; and cedar paving covered Yonge Street from King to Bloor, as it did the main downtown thoroughfares.[116] This wooden pavement, much superior to rutted gravel or plain mud-

holes, remained popular till about 1893, but still split and heaved, and its cracks collected noxious dirt. It was gradually to be replaced by asphalt, introduced from Trinidad in 1887, a crucial change for increasingly heavy central city traffic.[117]

The coming of the electric streetcar under the newly franchised Toronto Railway Company of 1891 also much facilitated traffic movements. With power initially from the Toronto Light Company, and then from its own steam plant on the Esplanade, the system's extending lines coped (for the time at least) with rush-hour crowds downtown, speeded street flows in most weather, and became an ever more important urban service to burgeoning Toronto. By 1895, in any event, the High Victorian city was merging into its still bigger twentieth-century successor. Policemen stood on traffic duty with stop-and-go signals as trolley cars ground by. Crossings were lit by brilliant electric arc lights, incandescent bulbs as well as gas mantles glowed from windows. Electric signs adorned theatres, and Eaton's and Simpson's advertised their latest tremendous sales to residents. Many people deplored the wearing urban pace and congestion, and those who could afford it left for summer vacations by quiet watersides, away from the clamour of the "Queen City."[118] In varied ways, a Toronto still with us had taken shape.

King Street east of Yonge in 1912, with the King Edward Hotel rising in the background.

Chapter Five

The Nearly National Metropolis, 1895–1918

Between the mid-Nineties and the First World War, Toronto neared the rank of a national metropolis, as its advancing financial power in particular confirmed a hold on hinterlands that now ranged Canada-wide. Closely involved with this advance was a new era of expanding trade, resurgent immigration, rapid western settlement, and much-enlarged resource frontiers. Linked as well were mounting supplies of cheap electric energy, continued industrial growth within the city, and far more investment in its built environment, from downtown core to radiating suburbs. Throughout the whole period Toronto, as before, was sharing developments broadly experienced in Canada. Yet once more its reponses had results of their own. After a spell of slower progress in the still-depressed mid-Nineties, its population began a new climb, reaching 208,040 in 1901, 376,538 in 1911 (with further annexations under way), then 521,893 by 1921.[1] Though its metropolitan role remained surpassed by Montreal's and was challenged somewhat within the West by the fast-rising regional metropolises of Winnipeg and Vancouver, Toronto came second only to Montreal in national scope and influence during the prewar decades. The wartime years brought it further headway, and marked, in fact, both a rounding-out of the city's past phases of evolution and an opening up towards the four-times larger Metropolitan Toronto conglomerate that was to emerge by the 1980s. Accordingly, as both conclusion and transition, the war years provide an appropriate sequel to the vigorous upthrust of the young metropolis during the early stages of the twentieth century.

URBAN ECONOMY: BUILDING FINANCIAL AND CORPORATE DOMINANCE

The years 1895–96 stayed mainly slow, but then world-trade recovery waxed into a great boom that essentially ran on till 1913.

This pervasive boom and the spread of western Canadian settlement, and thus of national markets for industrialism, were undoubtedly basic factors in Toronto's economic growth down to the First World War. Nevertheless, the leading feature of that growth was the expansion of the city's financial interests, which powerfully reinforced its metropolitan functions by adding far greater investment and policy control to its dominance over hinterlands. The agencies of Toronto finance extended operations from Atlantic to Pacific, channelling funds into western farmlands and transport, northern lumbering and mining, city utilities and urban real estate. And what this really represented was the city's massing corporate business power, rising to a national scale.

The day of the big business corporation arrived in Toronto.[2] Company boards and salaried management were supplanting personal proprietors and partners in command of major firms. Money magnates teamed with brokers and top lawyers to design heavily capitalized projects, acquire controlling stock or carry mergers, as these became more promising routes to wealth and power than manufacturing or marketing a better mousetrap. Certainly, high finance and the managerial revolution still had some distance to go in Toronto before the First World War, but their forward sweep was evident. It showed in the swelling size of the city's banks, bank clearings, loan and insurance companies, in the incorporation of big industrial, power and resource ventures, and in much proliferating stock-exchange activities. In fact, two new exchanges emerged in the city after 1896 (combined as the Standard Stock and Mining Exchange in 1899) to deal in the fruitful new field of mine investment, and there was plenty of company share trading for the older Toronto Stock Exchange as well. The very rise of corporate business towers on the downtown skyline betokened the ascent of finance.

Why this ascent? In part, it was one more exemplification of the "them as has, gits" rule. The city had already evolved leading regional financial institutions, ever since the early appearance of the Bank of Upper Canada, and particularly since mid-Victorian times. With structure, assets and expertise substantially in place, it was altogether likely that this whole funding system would rapidly expand in the new national prosperity, when credit demands soared high and investment prospects looked so inviting. Then too, Toronto's attainments in commerce, industry and transport had gathered it both capital and connections. These could be worked into a financial net that spanned the continent, its strands not only rail and postal routes, or telegraph and telephone lines, but well-established credit lines besides.

Yet there were other factors. One was the continuing initiative of Toronto business leaders; aggressive readiness to grasp opportunities was not new in an otherwise conservative community. And there was the city's ability to attract American capital, also not new. American investment as well as Yankee technology had reached Toronto business across the Lakes at least from the 1830s. But now the scale of input became decidedly new, as big U.S. corporations and entrepreneurs set up branch plants behind the Canadian tariff wall or turned increasingly to exploit untapped Canadian resources. Toronto, moreover, was both a recognized reception point on an investment path that stemmed largely from New York, and, as capital of Ontario, a crucial centre where development rights to vast provincial resource riches could be negotiated and implemented. And so American interests were drawn to this trans-border investment focus. Ties from the old days of Erie Canal traffic or the railway-building Fifties were now reconstituted in a far more weighty New York–Toronto financial axis.

There was British investment too, and with Canadian, American and overseas capital accessible for national or regional fields of development, Toronto's financial empire advanced on practically all fronts. It was most plainly evidenced in banking. Here the city's big Bank of Commerce kept to the fore, still presided over by George Albertus Cox (named a senator in 1896), with Byron Edmund Walker as general manager till Cox retired in 1907 and Walker succeeded him — to be knighted "Sir Edmund" in 1910. Both honours, incidentally, were not unrelated to the bank's close comradeship with the Liberal party, in national office from 1896 to 1911. Cox and Walker together shaped a program of expansion, tripling the Commerce's assets between 1895 and 1906.[3] In 1898 it

opened the first bank in the Yukon, during the Klondike gold rush. It dotted branches across the populating western plains, and the purchase of the Bank of British Columbia in 1901 added 7 more in that province, plus offices in San Francisco and Portland. Eastward, in 1903, the takeover of the august Halifax Banking Company brought in 20 Maritime branches, that of the Eastern Townships Bank in 1912 a large block in Quebec, while Newfoundland was invaded with an office in St. John's.[4] By the war years the Commerce was strongly represented in all the Canadian regions. It had 379 branches in 1915; notably, 181 of these were in the West, to 169 in central Canada.[5] At this time its old rival, the Bank of Montreal, had only 181 branch offices in all, though it led by far in total assets, having some $334 million worth to the Commerce's $250 million.[6]

Nonetheless, Toronto's chief bank had clearly made itself a national institution. In lesser degree the city's other chartered banks did likewise.[7] The Imperial Bank had put 48 of its 125 branches in the West by 1915. It also advanced into northern resource frontiers, to the Cobalt silver field in 1905, and to subsequent opening mine or lumber realms. The Dominion Bank, guided from 1901 to 1924 by Edmund Boyd Osler (later Sir), stayed more largely in Ontario; yet it had outspread western branches too, and greater assets than the Imperial. As for the cautious, soundly paying Bank of Toronto — still ruled over by George Gooderham down to 1905 and soon by another William Gooderham — it located one-third of its branches in the West. Moreover, in 1900 the Bank of Nova Scotia moved its general managership from Halifax to Toronto to gain a more central headquarters for expansion. This bank, second in size only to the Commerce in Toronto, added many more eastern Canadian links to the city's financial operations, and with them an extensive Caribbean business. Overall then, Toronto banking grew far beyond regional dimensions. By the First World War, it controlled 34 per cent of all banking offices in western Canada, to 33 per cent for Montreal-based houses, while its bank clearings also rose at a higher rate.[8]

Similar developments occurred in insurance and investment enterprises. Toronto indeed became the unrivalled capital of the Canadian insurance business. In 1910, for example, its fire and life insurance companies together held policies in force worth $609 million, to not quite $130 million for Montreal firms. The Canada Life Assurance Company was Toronto's leader, while Confedera-

These portraits are from **Torontonians As We See 'Em**, *a project of the Canada Newspaper Cartoonists' Association, published in 1905. They show (across the top, left to right): George Albertus Cox, the canny leader of Toronto corporate finance, power behind the Bank of Commerce, Canada Life, and other investment enterprises in or far beyond the city; Edmund Boyd Osler, head of the Dominion Bank, director of the CPR and Toronto MP, 1896-1917; and Henry Pellatt, the builder of Casa Loma, knight of the brokers' ticket tape, colonel of the Queen's Own, and president of the Electrical Development Company. At left is John Craig Eaton, retail potentate, in his new car. The buildings are the firm's Toronto headquarters and Winnipeg store.*

tion Life, Manufacturers Life and North American Life also stood high; and Imperial Life, established there in 1897, was rising fast. Canada Life had actually begun in Hamilton in 1847, but in 1899 moved its base to Toronto through the determined drive of the redoubtable Senator George Cox. The next year he became its president — adding to his Bank of Commerce headship — and launched the firm on widespread national expansion that reached into American and overseas markets as well.

Imperial Life, a new Cox creation, was another in a set of powerful concerns dominated by the senator and his chief associates.[9] They included the Central Canada Savings and Loan Company, which invested extensively in real estate, the wealthy National Trust, which fattened nicely on western mortgages, and Dominion Securities, which within four years of its foundation in 1901 was the biggest bond dealer in Canada. There were other major Toronto financial houses besides, but the scale and interweaving of the Cox group made them especially strong exemplars of the city's corporate finance. Cox ruled Canada Life till his death in 1914, when his son Edward replaced him. Imperial Life soon got Cox's stockbroker son-in-law, Alfred Ernest Ames, as vice-president, and son Frederick Cox as general manager — who, with his brother Herbert, was also ensconced in Central Canada Savings. A close Cox friend and fellow Methodist, Joseph Flavelle, the able manager-director and later president of the big William Davies pork-packing house, served variously on the boards of Canada Life, Imperial Life, Central Canada and the Bank of Commerce. He also presided over National Trust, which had A. E. Ames as its vice-president and by 1904 offices in Montreal, Winnipeg and Edmonton. And a Cox protégé, E. R. Wood, headed Dominion Securities and managed Central Canada Savings.

Nor were these the limits of the Cox Toronto-centred empire.[10] It stretched at least from the Crow's Nest Pass Coal Company in the Canadian West to the Sao Paulo Tramway Light and Power Company in Brazil, from which developed Brascan. It spread to other power, transport and industrial ventures. As early as 1892, Cox and the Bank of Commerce had jointly acquired over a million dollars in bonds of the Toronto Railway Company, then enfranchised to electrify the city's streetcar system. This led to growing links with William Mackenzie, the railway promoter who headed the new Toronto transit monopoly. Mackenzie himself spiralled as a utility magnate, with streetcar and electric projects from Winnipeg, Niagara and Saint John to Detroit, Havana and Barcelona, considerably underwritten by the Cox companies. The Commerce and the Central Canada also backed the financing of a western rail system being strung together by Mackenzie and his partner, Donald Mann, in competition with the nation-wide CPR. In 1901 this Canadian Northern line announced its intent to become a transcontinental railway, and in 1903 yet another was chartered, the Grand Trunk Pacific, on whose board Cox sat as a founding member — where Flavelle would also join him. Meanwhile, within Toronto, this time in manufacturing, the Cox coterie had linked with Massey interests to form the large Canada Cycle and Motor Company in 1899: Cox vice-president, Flavelle a director. Their CCM merged a series of bicycle firms, but by 1906 was successfully producing automobiles as well.[11]

Accordingly, if in the young century the flamboyant American-born Sir William Van Horne, engineer-builder of the CPR, was the reigning financial figure in Montreal, so Senator Cox, the astute, calm entrepreneur from Peterborough, Ontario, was the ruling embodiment of Toronto finance capital. And while Cox was still old-style in looking to personal and family aspects of control, he was new-style in building up his wealth through corporate investment, utilities and real estate, not primarily commerce or manufacturing. For money tycoons, not merchant princes or captains of industry, now led the way in Toronto. True, Joseph Flavelle, a millionaire himself by 1900,[12] had risen out of produce-dealing, but he increasingly entered into major financial undertakings, of which the National Trust was only one.

Other members of the city's new corporate elite were no less closely associated with investment control over large units of production or service: men like Edmund Walker of the Commerce, financier *par excellence*; Edmund Osler of the Dominion Bank, who emerged from stockbroking; Frederic Nicholls, managing director of the combine Canadian General Electric (CGE); or Henry Pellatt, another leading stockbroker, who had earlier got into utilities through the Toronto Electric Light Company that held the city's street-lighting franchise.[13] Finally, among still more, Zebulon Lash, Toronto's most prominent solicitor, was influential on the board of National Trust and other companies, reflecting the new significance of corporation lawyers in the city.[14] The capitalist generalship of men like these played a large part in Toronto's rise as a financial metropolis in the years before the First World War.

Assembling bicycles for Canada Cycle and Motor Co. (CCM), a Cox-Massey combine of 1899.

OTHER ECONOMIC DEVELOPMENTS

The prewar boom was finally curbed by depression in 1913, till war demands renewed the pace. And throughout the flush times, the enlargement of Toronto's commerce and industry closely accompanied that of its finance. As for commerce, retailing growth was now more apparent than wholesaling, in a city that itself constituted a rich central market for big retail firms. These largely bought direct from suppliers, not through city wholesalers, and sold direct to hinterland customers by mail order, as did Eaton's and Simpson's, or through chain store outlets of their own.[15] Moreover, the old measures of wholesale trade, the values of the city's exports and imports, had lost some of their meaning as Toronto entered increasingly into an expanding national economy.[16] Much of its merchandise fed Canadian home markets, not export fields; many of its wares now came from within the country, or if imported, arrived by rail rather than via its harbour. Yet the city's wholesale trade generally remained healthily profitable, given the much larger total volume of commerce. Furthermore, the spread of mining and mill towns in northern Ontario, from Sudbury and Sault Ste. Marie in the Nineties to Cobalt and Timmins between 1905 and 1912, produced valuable new markets for Toronto wholesaling to enter.

Nevertheless, if the city's wholesalers still did well in absolute terms, they and the merchants' traditional organ, the Board of Trade, had relatively lost weight in a financial-industrial metropolis. More noteworthy now than the Board of Trade was the Canadian Manufacturers' Association headquartered in the city, dating from 1871 but incorporated in 1902, and by then growing prodigiously.[17] Insofar as big merchandising still held high rank, its best representatives had surely become Eaton's and Simpson's. Eaton's established mail-order offices and department stores well beyond Ontario, and in 1909 set up a separate mail-order division, which got a headquarters building and factory of its own on a much enlarged Toronto store property.[18] Simpson's, reorganized after the death of its founder in 1897, also vigorously expanded with new funding and direction. Significantly, however, two of Simpson's three controlling partners were now Joseph Flavelle and A. E. Ames, and working capital came from the Bank of Commerce.[19] While Eaton's stayed under family rule, Timothy Eaton being succeeded on his death in 1907 by his son John Craig, its main rival had become another gilt-edged holding in the hands of financiers and managers.

The same trend appeared in industrial development, from CCM to CGE, a trend to strongly capitalized major units, often amalgamations, with considerably more mechanization and complexity in their operations. The effects on Toronto industry were displayed in census statistics for the period. The reported number of its manufacturing plants fell from 2,401 in 1891 to 847 in 1901, but this was rather a sign of greater concentration in larger-scale enterprises, since the number of their employees expanded across the same period from about 26,000 to more than 42,000.[20] Then in the remarkably prosperous decade from 1901 to 1911, the city's industrial units multiplied to 1,100, while their work force rose above 65,000 — and over the whole twenty-year span, their capitalization grew nearly fivefold, to reach some $145 million.[21] Moreover, the total value of Toronto's manufacturing output advanced by 243 per cent between 1890 and 1910, Montreal's by 145 per cent.[22] And a signal rise in the average productivity of Toronto plants confirmed that their increased capitalization was paying off.

In any event, manufacturing became by far the largest employer in Toronto in the prewar years, displaying its 65,000 engaged in 1911, to nearly 40,000 in commerce and finance, around 20,000 in building trades, 18,000 in domestic and personal services, with transport, the professions and government work well below in declining order.[23] Among the city industries, clothing establishments had the most employees (and a sizeable female majority).[24] Metals and machinery stood next, while printing, food processing, woodworking and furniture, leather and rubber goods, musical instruments and vehicle-making exhibited successively fewer numbers. In sum, Toronto's industrial pattern had now greatly altered in character since the preceding period that established it, although it had markedly expanded and added newer components like electrical supplies, elevators and automobiles. More important was the fact that the city's manufacturing sector was still further outdistancing those of other Ontario centres. By 1911 Toronto employed 27 per cent of the province's industrial force, compared to 10 per cent back in 1881,[25] since to its older advantages as a transport and commercial entrepôt had now been added its primacy in financing large corporate enterprises.

Important, too, was advancing electrical technology in factories, applying adaptable electric motors to do away with the restrictive clutter of belt-driven steam machinery. But the growing demands for efficient, mass electric power for manufacturing, lighting and street railways required the developing of some great new energy source, such as the hydroelectric potential of Niagara Falls. In 1903 the Electrical Development Company, set up by Mackenzie, Nicholls and Pellatt, secured extensive Niagara power and transmission rights from the Ontario Liberal government. They constructed a magnificent generating plant at the Falls, which by 1907 was delivering power to Toronto.[26] Their projected total electric monopoly, however, met hot opposition in the City Council and from a "cheap public power" movement, strong across southern Ontario.[27] Accordingly, a new Conservative provincial regime in 1906 erected a public power-transmission authority, an Ontario Hydro-Electric Power Commission that would construct its own lines and sell low-cost hydroelectricity to municipalities. In Toronto the City Council contracted with the commission for delivery in 1908, organizing the Toronto Hydro-Electric System to build its own civic utility.[28] Commission power finally reached the city in May 1911. Though the Mackenzie interests still held a large part in power generation at Niagara, the low public transmission rates, providing electric energy from a seemingly unlimited supply, became one more impelling factor in the city's economic expansion.

In transport, Toronto's railroad services continued to expand as well. Mackenzie and Mann moved their Canadian Northern headquarters there in 1899, to work on extending their prairie rail system eastward, and later, westward to the Pacific. By 1906 Canadian Northern track ran from Toronto past Parry Sound. The remaining gap to the Lakehead was closed by 1914; the next year this Toronto-based railway was open to Vancouver. The CPR in 1908 also completed a direct link between Toronto and Sudbury on its main line. By 1915 the Ontario capital not only had these routes to the lands above it (plus the original Northern line up to North Bay) but access to the Grand Trunk Pacific besides, completed that year as a transcontinental. Still further, the provincial government's own colonization railway, the Temiskaming and Northern Ontario (TNO) begun in 1902, pushed on into northeastern Ontario from North Bay, opening up new resource areas to Toronto. Thus, in the Cobalt silver boom of 1905–10, prospectors and suppli-

ers could reach the mining camps by direct train from the city. The TNO built on to Cochrane in 1908 to intersect with the National Transcontinental coming from Quebec, the eastern half of the new Grand Trunk Pacific route. In consequence, Toronto's ability to tap the North was further enlarged. Even by 1909 over 90 per cent of northern Ontario's trade flowed mainly to that centre, to less than 10 per cent for Montreal.[29] And these land transport gains abetted more investment northward.

Toronto's water-borne transport, however, faced incessant problems: inadequate financing, the competition both from railways and other major lake ports, a restricted, ineffective harbour board, and beyond that, undirected private control of almost all the waterfront. Certainly, the port kept busy over the period, but even much of its basic coal trade had now diverted to rail.[30] Moreover, Toronto shipowners remained slow to invest in expensive, specialized, steel lake freighters. They left them largely to outside lines, and clung to older, cheaper vessels crammed indiscriminately with freight. As for port improvements, they went on only piecemeal: breakwaters to check erosion of the Island, piers to protect the eastern entrance, undertaken in 1901, and a deeper western entrance dredged south of the old channel, finally completed between 1908 and 1911 thanks to federal government funds.[31]

At length, by 1910, the growing realization that only well-funded public management could reverse laissez-faire neglect and spur port development roused a campaign for a comprehensive civic harbour authority. Pushed by the Board of Trade and the press (as the *Telegram* decried "docks that cannot be reached and a 1,300-acre swamp"),[32] the City Council won the voters' approval for a Toronto Harbour Commission, established by federal act in 1911. The new commission, with unrestricted borrowing rights and the power to expropriate, sell or lease waterfront lands, set up its plans in 1912, and within two years owned 95 per cent of the harbourside property.[33] It took up rebuilding and increasing dock facilities, deepening and protecting the harbour, and rationalizing shore land-uses. Depression, then war, slowed down its work, which was still far from removing the drab, depressing tangle around the port. But at least an impressive start was made, as public interest at last gained ground after a century of private exploitation and abuse of Mrs. Simcoe's "beautiful clear" bay.

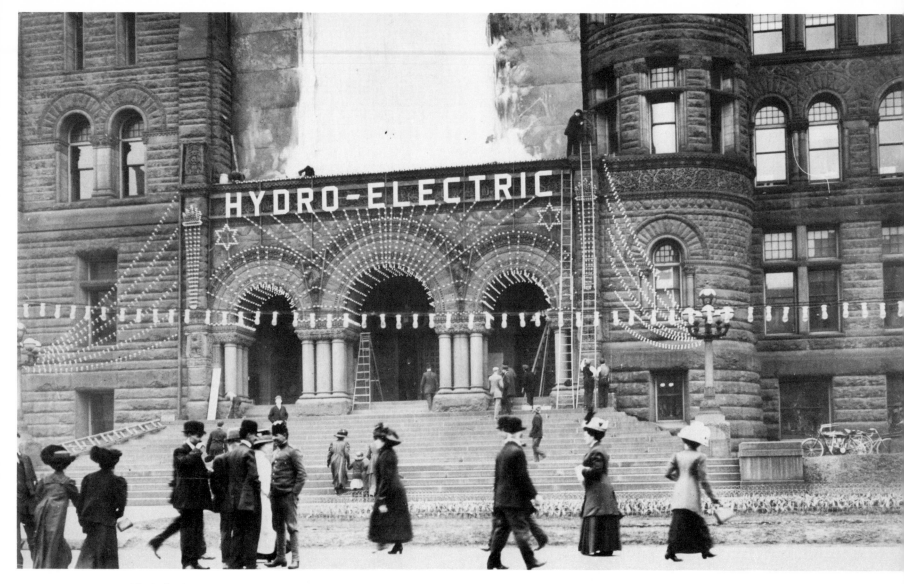

Public hydroelectric power reaches Toronto, 1911, and "Niagara Falls" cascades down City Hall for the celebration.

POPULATION TRENDS: ETHNIC GROWTH
AND CIVIC ENLARGEMENT

Still more impressive was the impact of immigration on the prewar city. In the good times from the late Nineties onward, immigrants again flowed abundantly into Canada, to farm the "last, best West," work on resource frontiers or build up urban centres. The years 1901-11 especially showed a large net balance of population intake over exodus, the decade before having been burdened by depression in its first half, while that following soon brought world war to check immigration. Accordingly, the first twentieth-century decade saw Toronto's own growth particularly affected by the incoming tide: indirectly, through the overall expansion of Canadian numbers and activities; directly, through the substantial addition of new producers and consumers to the city itself. At the same time, the surging young metropolis attracted a continued influx from Ontario rural areas and lesser towns; in fact, in-migration, natural increase and boundary extensions all played parts as well as immigration in Toronto's rapid prewar population rise. Yet the upsweep in transatlantic migration had a special significance, since this now produced a mounting element of non-English-speaking ethnic residents in the city's midst — no longer sparse handfuls, but forming a whole new feature in its demographic pattern.

The main mass of immigrants who entered the community in this era were still drawn from the British Isles, again preponderantly from England.[34] But streams of continental European newcomers, long running to the United States, by 1900 had begun to find more Canadian destinations as well — among them, the workplaces and construction jobs of thriving Toronto. This growing foreign presence in the city was reflected in the decline of its overwhelming Anglo-Celtic majority from 91.7 per cent in 1901 to 86.4 in 1911.[35] By 1921 this was down to 85.3 per cent, to fall through successive decades as other immigrant groups arrived. Hence, though the prewar years scarcely upset the predominant pattern, they did mark an advancing, different demographic trend: away from the homogeneity of the nineteenth-century British Canadian city towards the ethnic pluralism of the modern metropolitan community.

Even by 1911, the census for that year indicated there were over 30,000 foreign-born in Toronto,[36] the bulk of them readily apparent from language and cultural differences, and their residential clustering in low-rent, near-central neighbourhoods. A smaller segment of the non-British newcomers, Americans by birth, were far less perceivable by trait or residence, and quickly assimilable, too; while any Asian-born then constituted a mere 0.3 per cent of the total urban populace.[37] But the main, continental European segment of the "strangers within our gates" (so termed in a classic study of 1909 by J. S. Woodsworth) included Austro-Hungarian and Italian nationals, and diverse former subjects of Imperial Russia. Many of the last were Jews, as were others drawn from Central Europe. The Jewish community in Toronto, in sum, now stood at more than 18,000, having grown sixfold since 1901.[38] The Italian community thus far was much smaller, at about 4,000; yet it had also multiplied over four times across the decade.[39] Moreover, the Germanic and various Slavic communities together were not inconsiderable, though far more fractionalized. In that regard, even the Jewish and Italian groups were not at all as homogeneous as appeared from outside.

The established community saw problems of public welfare and cultural dislocation stemming from these strangers, who were largely poor, unskilled villagers in origin. They had alien customs, conversed together incomprehensibly, crowded into run-down inner areas, most notably "the Ward" (in once St. John's Ward) west of Yonge and above Queen. (See Map 9, page 181.) They collected in its low-rent housing both from economic necessity and desire for familiar neighbours: approximately 10,000 foreigners lived in the Ward even by 1907.[40] There the established order might feel an unassimilable slum ghetto was developing, generating immorality and crime as well as fiscal and sanitary ills. High-coloured articles on Ward conditions became a staple of the city press. City churches set up missions to these handy heathens. In part the missions provided needed welfare and help in adjustment to a new country, but they also sought to convert Jews and foreign Christians to acceptable (majority) Christian faiths — with no great success.[41]

The foreigners themselves, however, sought chiefly to survive in their own identities, and to make economic headway in a difficult but materially promising environment.[42] They did both. While learning the language and ways of Toronto, they worked as they could: women quite generally in garment sweatshops, needle trades and laundries; men often in road work, building construction or door-to-door peddling. From peddling some rose to operate little family stores, usually in their own ethnic communities, where immigrant boardinghouses and eating places also brought income. Some newcomers with artisan or entrepreneurial skills built up their own modest businesses; others bossed ethnic labour gangs; and still others put hard-gleaned earnings into small house properties as landlords, or dealt in shipping more home-country migrants out to jobs or back to the old land. By the First World War, in consequence, not only a middle class, but ethnic notables of some influence and affluence, were becoming evident inside this new society. Without in the main losing their own cultural and religious patterns, the strangers had rooted themselves, become far less strange in the process, and laid a basis for the subsequent growth of their communities within Toronto.

Despite the long-term importance of this emerging ethnic variety, the British arrivals did much more to make prewar Toronto again an immigrant city, although they did not loom as anything so visibly different. Most of the British migrants, who arrived from about 1897 on, came from a highly urbanized and industrialized homeland.[43] They moved with little noticeable disruption into factories, stores, services and dwellings across the city, although many did tend to settle in newer-developing neighbourhoods, such as around Gerrard or Danforth east of the Don, or in other extending districts beyond the older built-up core. Some working-class newcomers helped add radical sentiments brought from their British trade-union backgrounds, but much more widely Toronto's strong imperialist feelings were reinforced. The city warmly upheld the unity of the Empire in the South African War of 1899–1902, recruiting volunteer troops to fight and die on distant sunburnt plains. Again in 1914 Toronto went determinedly into the Great War overseas, with recent British arrivals forming a high proportion of the early units that were raised locally. Red-coated public school cadet corps, black mourning banners at the death of the revered Victoria, profuse Union Jacks for the coronations of Edward VII and George V, were further public testimony to the paramount British heritage of the prewar community.

In any event, the British migrants served to make Toronto — in the short run — less Canadian than it had been. The 1911 census, for example, showed that since 1901 the city's proportion of native-born inhabitants had fallen to 63 per cent, or around 205,100; the British-born risen to 28 per cent, or about 91,000.[44] Among this latter group, there were twice as many English as Scots and Irish combined, while there now were fewer citizens of Irish birth than

The Wolfishes, a Jewish family, outside their Elizabeth Street store, 1913.

Winter in the Ward. The rear of Centre Avenue, 1912.

A Macedonian boarding house on King East, 1911.

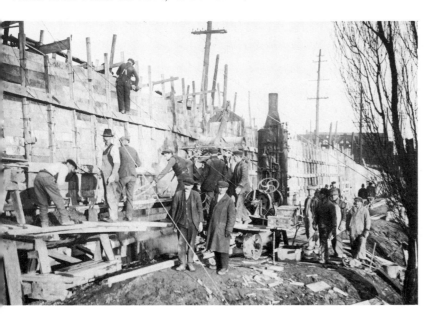

Italian labourers at work on a retaining wall on Dundas. Often such migrants went into construction gangs, intending to stay in Canada only temporarily. Yet many of these "sojourners" in time became residents.

Arriving British immigrant families cross a footbridge at Union Station around 1910. Less distinctive as newcomers, the British were by far the most numerous entrants to settle in Toronto in the prewar period.

Parliament Buildings in Queen's Park decorated to welcome "Heroes of Paardeberg" returning from South Africa. The battle of Paardeberg, 1900, was the "first major overseas engagement ever fought by Canadian troops serving officially as such."

Turnout at Yonge below Richmond for a parade of troops in 1900, during the South African War. The troops are behind this zealous crowd.

residents of Jewish origin in Toronto. The religious census of 1911 showed corresponding patterns. The Anglican church came first, in rounded numbers having some 101,000 adherents, while Roman Catholicism had fallen to fourth place, with 43,000. Presbyterians and Methodists stood second and third with 65,000 and 63,000. Interesting again, though, the Jewish faith was now sixth largest, coming behind the Baptists.[45]

Census figures revealed still more about the city's demographic growth over the young century years. In sex ratios, for example, there was a total female preponderance over male of about one per cent in the population of 1911, a margin that had actually fallen from some 3 per cent in 1891, since immigration, as usual, had initially brought in higher proportions of male venturers.[46] But breaking the sex ratios down for the main component demographic groups revealed something else. While the British-born immigrants by 1911 displayed a male preponderance of 8 per cent, and the foreign of 12 (indicating the larger number of young male transients or temporary "sojourners" among them), the Canadian-born majority element itself showed a female predominance of over 7 per cent.[47] This last fact surely reflected the continuing feminization of employment amid the established community — increased jobs for women in offices, stores, modernized factories, telephone service or education — and was no doubt related to in-migration from the countryside as well. Wartime industrial needs would later enlarge the working roles of women in Toronto much further.

And in general, after registering only around a 15 per cent increase between 1891 and 1901, the city's total population shot up by over 80 per cent from 1901 to 1911, to go on climbing till the depression of 1913 and the coming of war.[48] These swelling numbers consequently sent Toronto flooding beyond its existing limits, and led to a big new set of suburban annexations. They began in 1903 with minor additions both north of Yorkville and bordering Humber Bay. (See Map 6, page 125.) Then in 1905 the bulk of Rosedale and lands northward up Avenue Road to above St. Clair Avenue were taken in. To this, the rest of the old Annex west of Avenue Road was added the next year, while 1908 saw the Deer Park estate included, again thrusting Toronto centrally north around Yonge beyond St. Clair. To the east, in 1908-9 Midway, East Toronto and Balmy Beach entered as the city advanced out the Danforth and Queen routes, carrying it far past the Don and Riverdale to the eastern lake beaches. To the west, in 1909-10 the annexing of Wychwood, Bracondale, Earlscourt, Dovercourt and West Toronto pushed the civic borders to the village of Swansea and the Humber Valley, where once the Toronto Trail had run. Still further, in 1912, the inclusion of Moore Park, a northward offshoot of Rosedale, and North Toronto, by now a sizeable municipality in its own right, produced a total new area more than half the size of the original city limits of 1834.[49]

Two other small annexations in 1914 completed the process. It left a civic territory that stretched between Jane Street on the west, Victoria Park Avenue on the east, and Roe on the north. The whole area roughly formed an inverted "T", in which the cross bar reached from the lake to well above St. Clair in its western half, above Danforth in its eastern, while the stem ran on north past Eglinton, past the vanished Montgomery's Tavern of 1837, and on up main-route Yonge Street to the incipient residential districts of Lawrence Park and the Bedford Estate. This much-expanded domain had now spread far beyond the original Shore Plain to the higher grounds above; and outside it still newer suburban communities of "Greater Toronto" were steadily rising by the First World War. Altogether, here was a powerful demonstration, and consequence, of the city's rapid demographic growth in the prewar years.

SOCIAL PATTERNS IN A HIGH-FLYING METROPOLIS

The elite of this fast-growing society differed more in degree than kind from their Victorian predecessors. They had more money; their scope and expectations were greater. In the previous era, for all the city's advances, a sluggish world economy had still restricted its horizons, and it had known gruelling phases, too. But after 1895 the good times that rolled to 1913 were only briefly marked by downturns. Prime Minister Laurier had proclaimed the new twentieth century would belong to Canada; if so, Toronto's leaders meant to have their share of it. However much western boosters might tout the marvels of their Winnipegs or Vancouvers, Toronto's opulent saw how much they themselves controlled and might hope to control. Beyond that, the taxes on their fortunes were still minimal; the graduated income tax would not be introduced as a

Heading north on Queen's Park Circle in the family cutter during the 1900s. A coachman is at the reins.

"temporary" (!) emergency measure till the First World War. Economically secure and socially unthreatened, the city's elite were soaring in a golden age.

At the same time, there were some changes in their make-up. The powerful financial element quite naturally advanced in prominence: the multi-company overlords, utility and investment magnates, key stockbrokers and corporation strategists. They joined the bankers, big industrialists and merchants in high social estate, though not many wholesale merchants were still as eminent. Henry Pellatt was a prime example of the newly conspicuous financier. Knighted in 1905, he supported his own militia regiment, the Queen's Own Rifles, taking it at his expense to England in 1910 for imperial manouevres at Aldershot — as a true knight might do.[50] By 1914 Sir Henry had reared Casa Loma, his huge baronial castle on the hill, close by the old Baldwin, later Austin, property. From landed gentleman to merchant-banker to millionaire stockbroker, so runs this record of hillcrest dominance, nicely suggesting the evolution of Toronto's upper class. Other city financial figures were not as ostentatious in their use of fortunes, but also maintained fine homes, along with country places or Muskoka summer retreats.

By now the prestigious families that dated back to Compact days at Little York had largely departed social leadership. Aside from surviving Jarvises, Ridouts and Denisons, such lineages as Gooderhams, Cawthras and Howlands had grown sufficiently well-aged to fill their place. But newer wealth was fully reputable when held by financial masters such as Osler, Walker or Pellatt, especially if knighthood gave a confirming accolade. Masseys and Eatons yet faced some doubts, being closer to shirt-sleeved shop work, but were plainly beyond rejection. Generally speaking, however, the Toronto elite was becoming still more North American–plutocratic in nature, in spite of its imperialist devotions and infusions of counting-house knights. Against this should nevertheless be put traits inherited from earlier times. Colonial gentry survivals (though the reign of The Grange ended when Goldwin Smith died in 1910), concern for obligations of rank, and enduring British customs or assumptions, continued to mark this urban upper crust. It did not cease to disdain brash dollar vulgarity, preferring more dignified display. Its considerably materialist members duly sought approved culture, at least in music, suitable art and "good" theatre — the last still not accepted by firm Methodists. The rich also made substantial contributions to major public philanthropies as well as to churches. But equally they purchased expensive motor cars in the opening automobile age, kept elegant sailing craft at the Royal Canadian Yacht Club, supported golf and tennis clubs or thoroughbred stables, toured abroad, and held shining formal balls and dinners. In short, they had a high time, breathlessly reported in the social columns of the city press.

Upper-class women lived a rather narrow life, largely restricted to supervising the stately home, doing good works, assuring worthy marriages, and policing the social code. Their daughters' scopes were similarly limited to being debutantes, then marrying well; but their sons and husbands had the world as their oyster, so long as they avoided the sins of waste and bankruptcy or being caught in immorality. Private education for the young was all but vital, less for its academic quality than for instilling manly Christianity and clanship in boys, and feminine refinement for their sisters. Upper-class boys acquired associations for their later careers at Upper Canada College and similar boarding schools outside town, each athletic and Anglican, or at a Presbyterian counterpart, St. Andrew's, founded in Toronto in 1899. The girls prepared for social duties and the marriage mart at Anglican Havergal and Bishop Strachan schools or at Branksome Hall (1904), the last more middle-class and non-denominational but strict on Bible study. Some of the young esquires went on to university and professions; most went directly into business and old-school relationships there.

The middle classes again ranged from the near-rich and nearly-in down to numerous families of storekeepers, craftsmen-proprietors and clerical workers. The professionals and intelligentsia in the upper ranks were usually as involved with church and charitable work as the thoroughly rich, and far more so with cultural activities, while municipal affairs chiefly stayed in middle-class hands. Once more, upper- and middle-class interests and outlook showed no great divergences between them. Still, there were differences. The worthy middle might yet question excessive pretensions and undemocratic arrogance among the top layer. The mass public school system was essentially the urban middle-class's own bulwark and generational mould. Their youth really got a broader education from it in this era than the young gentry trained in games and godliness at private schools, and thus perhaps became more culturally active. But more than this, through improving

Joseph Wesley Flavelle's Holwood House, adjoining Queen's Park Circle, was built 1901-2, and is now part of the University of Toronto. Millionaire meat-packer and financier, part-owner of the Robert Simpson Co., Methodist philanthropist and university governor, Flavelle ultimately was named chairman of the wartime Imperial Munitions Board, for which service he was made baronet.

Benvenuto, William Mackenzie's home on the Avenue Road rise, was erected in 1890 for a large-scale real estate promoter, S. H. Janes, but was purchased by Mackenzie when he settled in Toronto after building western rail lines. Apart from being president of the Canadian Northern and Toronto Railway Co., Mackenzie was a financier and utilities magnate. He was knighted in 1911.

levels of education, some middle-class women were enabled to realize considerably greater potentials than the upper-class sisterhood, so affluently yet tellingly confined by their own lifestyle.

In the light of later feminism, these possibilities might yet look pretty meagre. Nevertheless, an increasingly complex metropolis did offer more opportunities for middle-class woman to make new ways, for those with the ability — and courage — to pioneer them.[51] Not just women store and office employees, librarians and teachers, had found city roles, but women journalists, artists, social and medical workers as well. A nurses training school was developed at the Toronto General Hospital under Mary Snively, its superintendent from 1884 to 1910.[52] Women had been admitted at the University of Toronto from 1886, when nine registered; by 1898 there were 155, and co-education was becoming an accomplished fact.[53] Still further, Emily (Jennings) Stowe of Toronto, American-trained as a physician, had won an arduous struggle in 1880 that made her the first Canadian woman authorized to practise medicine. Her no less able daughter, Dr. Augusta Stowe-Gullen, became the first woman faculty member of the city's Medical College for Women, which lasted from 1883 to 1906, by which time the effective acceptance of co-education at the University rendered a separate female medical school unnecessary.[54] In 1895, besides, Clara Brett Martin of Toronto led in the admission of women lawyers to the courts.[55]

Beyond that, Toronto women were now pressing for equal voting rights, for federal, provincial, and full municipal suffrage. Again this was pre-eminently a middle-class campaign, headed by Dr. Stowe, who presided over a Women's Enfranchisement Association from 1893 till her death in 1903, and then by her daughter as president till 1911. Flora McDonald Denison, a successful city businesswomen and editor, also keenly pushed the cause, as did the powerful Women's Christian Temperance Union. Yet repeated suffragist efforts were baulked by male intransigence and the doubletalk of politicians down to the First World War. Nevertheless, the growing self-awareness and public participation of middle-class women both shaped a democratic movement and expressed the changes proceeding in urban female life.[56]

Middle-class family life still mainly revolved about home and church. Family structure adjusted (as it usually does) to reputable women working outside the household. But the bulk of them by far still centred there, engaged in cares of house and children; and the care of adolescents was lengthening thanks to later school-leaving. The average family size in Toronto, 5.3 in 1891, was still just over 5 in 1911.[57] This was simply the household unit — there might be extensive kin beyond it, certainly among families well rooted in the city. Next to the home, and well ahead of the school, the church remained the firmest middle-class social institution. It was not only a place of worship and of Sunday school, of mission and charitable endeavours, but a recreational resort as well, for church guilds, choirs, bazaars and magic-lantern shows. Older evangelical fervours may have been declining as churches laid less stress on individual salvation and more on the social gospel of collective human betterment; yet Toronto could claim to be the City of Churches still. A volume of 1902 on *Landmarks of Toronto* described 193 alone.[58] Prominent among these for Anglicanism was St. James's, still socially the most distinguished, wealthy St. Paul's on fashionable Bloor Street below Rosedale, and St. Alban's serving the Annex. Methodism featured the Metropolitan, Sherbourne Street and St. Paul's (Avenue Road) churches; Presbyterians gathered to St. Andrew's, Knox or Bloor Street churches; while St. Michael's crowned a Catholic hierarchy of worship. The list could be vastly widened — not forgetting rising Jewish synagogues.

The lower classes continued to share extensively in Toronto's religious life, even though church authority worried about the growing numbers of secularized and unconnected among them. Their home life, too, had much in common with that of the better-off, if far more likely to be pinched and crowded; while ideals of upward mobility also persisted in working-class families — no doubt fostered by the public educational system that preached literacy, learning and diligence as sure means to success. Quite evidently, the large majority of Toronto's workers still maintained individual family homes. In 1901, for instance, there were approximately 41,000 families in the total community to some 39,100 houses; and 66,100 in 1911 to about 60,500.[59] This ratio does not take count of multiple occupation in many poorer, rented dwellings or the state of some of those so-called houses. Still, it indicates that despite a growing residential shortfall (partly reflected in immigrant boarding) the bulk of Torontonians had still avoided tenement dwelling. Most ordinary citizens could yet approve another claim: that theirs was a City of Homes as well.

Before the turn of the century, moreover, the city's working-class young had been considerably inculcated into public schooling.

Middle-class and professional women were plainly taking on more public roles in Toronto in this era. This presence might take the form of community works like the women's drill team of the St. John's Ambulance Corps, seen above at Hanlan's Point stadium in 1909. More exceptional was the achievement of Emily Jennings Stowe, left, a pioneer champion of women's rights, the first licensed Canadian woman physician, and head of the Women's Enfranchisement Association till 1903.

Children lined up to buy household fuel at the Consumers' Gas Works on Eastern Avenue about 1908. Coke could be obtained for five cents a bushel, meeting a vital need for poorer families.

Baseball at the Elizabeth Street playground in the Ward.

A stronger truancy law helped from 1891, requiring all children eight to fourteen to attend full time annually; henceforth attendance rates began to climb.[60] Free textbooks after 1892, a boys' industrial school, another for girls, both flourishing from the mid-Nineties, and generally more emphasis on practical subjects were further aspects of the process. Boys took manual training in the Toronto schools by 1901, for example, and girls could get bookkeeping and stenography. Classes in commerce, industrial design and basic scientific technology had also been offered at night since 1891 and in the day from 1900 in a regular Technical School that expanded into a large new "Central Tech" by 1915. Yet as late as 1914 only 373 children of unskilled-labour origins went on to the non-compulsory public secondary schools, compared with 2,086 drawn from various middle-class mercantile and professional backgrounds.[61] On the other hand, much the largest single element then present there was 1,662 sons and daughters of the skilled-trades sector, implying that the school system indeed was carrying onward a significant segment from the working class.

Nonetheless, schools, homes and churches could hardly be deemed distinctively lower-class features of Toronto's society. Labour developments and unionism were. Underlying economic conditions were vitally important in this connection. Despite more jobs and larger nominal wages, the city's workers got little out of the great boom that rose from 1896. While the rich winged high, and the middle classes flapped hopefully after them, the lower classes found that about all that spiralled ever upward in their case was prices. Impeding the working masses' way to better real wages and more union rights were governments wedded to "free" labour contracts, businessmen fearful that increased labour costs would harm their competitive position, and even immigrants who at times could only compete for less than going rates — say, of a dollar a day for a sixty-hour week.[62]

Under these pressures Toronto workers reacted increasingly. Union locals nearly doubled in number between 1900 and 1906.[63] There were fresh series of strikes — 1902–3 and 1912–13 were times of particular strife. Some efforts like the Bell Telephone strike of 1907 were successful; here the public's sympathy for overworked girl operators and its dislike of a monopoly utility carried weight. The street railwaymen's strike of 1902, however, brought rioting and militia patrols, while the garment workers' and tailors' strikes of 1912, preluded by a brave struggle of largely Jewish women cloakmakers against the might of Eaton's, virtually faded into futility.[64] Building tradesmen and metal workers at times made ground, as did those craft aristocrats, the printers. But generally the gains were limited, for labour failed to develop much wider solidarity. Even so, employers joined in close resistance, organizing the Toronto Employers' Association in 1902, sanctified by economic doctrines apparently proven in the very success of uninhibited capitalism.

The relative failure of labour organization to win major advances in Toronto cannot simply be ascribed, however, to the power of the interests sternly aligned in opposition. Continued social conservatism, circumscribed craft viewpoints among the city's working class, and fractionalization of left-wing groups were also involved. Still further, the national mainstream organization of Canadian unionism, the Trades and Labour Congress, which might have coordinated local activities better, was subjoined to the American Federation of Labor in 1902. This brought the TLC strong transborder links and practical emphasis on bargaining within the existing business system, but a satellite Canadian labour movement did not overcome its own internal separations thereby.[65] Consequently, in Toronto, unionism did not much alter its discrete craft patterns or make any great new outreach to the unskilled body.

All the same, in the prewar city, organized labour headed and consistently marked lower-class society, adding to its self-consciousness. The new Labour Temple, set up in 1904 as a headquarters and forum of local unionism, was influential here.[66] More than that, labour figures increasingly took part in shaping the city itself, in the press, in social roles and in civic governance. Leaving aside left-wing socialist writers like Phillips Thompson, or veteran unionists like Robert Glockling, the best single example was that of James Simpson, redoubtable workers' champion, prominent civic official — and ultimately mayor in 1935.[67] An English-born artisan immigrant of the 1880s, an earnest social-gospel Methodist, Jimmy Simpson served as a printer, then reporter; rose as leader of the Typographical Union, the Toronto Labour Council and later the TLC; joined the Technical School Board in 1902 (in which labour was deeply interested); and was elected to the comprehensive Board of Education in 1905, advancing to chairman in 1910. In 1914 he won the top seat on the city's Board of Control. He was elected far less as the socialist he had become than as an urban reformer of proven ability appealing to all classes; but he did not forget his

Manual training classes like this one at Lansdowne School in 1915 were an indication of increased stress on "practical" subjects in mass education.

For working-class women, factory work had become a large-scale occupation. Factories of the garment trade, like this one seen in 1908, had a particularly high concentration of female workers.

concerns for the masses. Even by 1914 lower-class Toronto had made plain inroads on the rule of its betters, as Simpson himself well illustrated.

Below the established working families, there still were those of casual labour, the foreign immigrants scarcely integrated (though some were already joining unions), and the deeply impoverished, outcast or brutalized. The immigrants of the Ward quite rapidly produced their own internal social institutions of religious bodies and ethnic clubs; the lowest underclass had not much more than street gangs. Otherwise, they all were variously served by the Salvation Army, the Associated Charities (an organization of middle-class philanthropies), church missions, welfare agencies and a vigilant police force — as ready to strike down breaches of the Toronto Sunday or too open wine-drinking among foreigners as to rout out slum vice and crime. Here, in fact, was another Toronto, turbulent and disreputable to the older community, a witness to declining cultural uniformities, fast-mounting urban scale and effective social segregation. It was depicted in lurid terms of degradation in C. S. Clark's graphic exposé of 1898, *Of Toronto the Good*, but for most of the solid citizens, the alien Ward was the nub of the question, the core of moral and physical infection.[68] Actually, scarlet immorality was not a concentrated presence in the hardworking Ward. Brothels and disorderly houses, for instance, were largely found in poor, English-speaking inner districts, and by 1910 around Nelson, Adelaide and Richmond Streets West, all outside the Ward.[69] Yet prejudice could easily attribute Toronto's seamy side to lowly newcomers in its society.

CHANGES IN CULTURAL AND BUILT ENVIRONMENTS

Apart from those who had to crawl, and struggle to do so, Torontonians flying high in nation-wide prosperity saw their own aspirations reflected in cultural developments. Imperialist they might be, but also assertively national in their belief in Canada. And their community, Ontario-shaped and British-bonded, still became a larger focus of cultural nationalism, in Anglo-Canadian writing, learning and the arts. Evidencing such nationalism, the Toronto author-editor Castell Hopkins produced *Canada an Encyclopaedia* in six volumes (1897-1902), then the *Canadian Annual Review* (1902-22). G. N. Morang published the major biographical series *The Makers of Canada* in twenty books from 1903 to 1908, while further signs of the national surge in Toronto's publications were the twenty-three volumes of the sterling collective work *Canada and Its Provinces* (1914-17) and the often colourful *Chronicles of Canada*, thirty-two in number (1914-16).

Significant also were the historical documentary volumes of the enduring Champlain Society, founded in 1905 under Edmund Walker of the Bank of Commerce, James Bain, Toronto public librarian, and Professor G. M. Wrong, head of history at the University of Toronto. Men such as these shared in developing the city's broader intellectual role, as did Professor James Mavor, a political economist outspoken on public issues, or Dr. James Loudon, president of the University from 1892 to 1906. In science (Sir) John McLennan, University head of physics from 1907, led in studying radioactivity and low-temperature phenomena; the biochemist A. B. Macallum pioneered in scientific medicine; and astronomy won a prominent Toronto place — all greatly owing to the presence of the country's largest university.

Moreover, the wealthy elite gave time and money to the city's cultural institutions, if often largely from concern for social duty and civic prestige. The Royal Ontario Museum, founded in 1912, and the Art Gallery of Toronto, set up in 1900, had Edmund Walker as their major progenitor; he was, however, a connoisseur in his own right. And Hart Massey's estate provided Hart House for the University, a splendid Gothic structure begun in 1913 as a cultural and athletic centre for students — men students only for many years ahead. The University, too, gained much from Joseph Flavelle as chairman of the commission in 1905 that examined its affairs. The commissioners, including Goldwin Smith, Walker and University representatives, recommended measures almost wholly accepted in the provincial act of 1906: a new pattern of university government at arm's length from political interference, larger funding, expansion of technical education and research, but also maintenance of the "liberal culture" of academia, an aim assuredly upheld by Flavelle and Walker, who were no anti-intellectuals.[70] Under a new president, Robert Falconer, with more grants and big buildings added, the University entered a fresh era of growth. Trinity College had already joined federation in 1904, though kept its Queen Street campus for some twenty years more. The School of Practical Science was incorporated as an engineering faculty in 1906, while faculties of education and forestry were set up the next year, and one for music in 1918.

Socio-cultural leaders: the Royal Commission on the University of Toronto, 1905. From left to right, they are: Rev. Bruce Macdonald, principal of St. Andrew's private boys' school; Rev. H. J. Cody, rising Anglican clergyman and scholar; Sir William Meredith, chief justice and chancellor of the University; Joseph Flavelle, commission chairman; A. H. V. Colquhoun, the secretary, and editor of the Toronto News; *Goldwin Smith, long interested in university affairs; and Edmund Walker (later Sir), general manager and soon president of the Bank of Commerce.*

Art flourished also. In 1911 The Grange became the home of the Toronto Art Gallery, a bequest initially suggested to the Goldwin Smiths by Walker.[71] More important, a new phase of painting emerged in Toronto. Charles Jefferys preached "the pine and spruce as themes fit for a painter,"[72] and others like J. E. H. MacDonald and Arthur Lismer began developing a distinctive vision of the native Canadian landscape as found in the northern immensity of the Precambrian Shield. Above all, a young Toronto commercial artist, Tom Thomson, was led to paint the lake and forest vastness of Algonquin Park, brilliantly rendering its wilderness sweep and colour. His example was pursued by MacDonald and Lismer, Lawren Harris, Frederick Varley, and by A. Y. Jackson from 1913. These Toronto-based artists, who in due course went on to Algoma, Lake Superior and Canadian realms beyond, veritably transferred to art the outthrust of the metropolis into northern hinterlands. Though Thomson died all too early in 1917, the "Algonquin School" of painters was already fully recognizable by the First World War. In 1919 it grew on into the Group of Seven, destined to shape a long-dominant approach in Canada painting. Yet clearly, it had sprung out of the nationalist seedbed of prewar Toronto.

The city no less maintained its place as a music centre, deemed "the choral capital of North America" around 1900.[73] Its Mendelssohn Choir widely toured the United States, conservatories flourished, and the Toronto Symphony Orchestra took form between 1906 and 1908.[74] In drama, there was again much less indigenous growth. Amateur theatre did rise in quantity and quality in the new century, and began trying modern pieces of social realism scarcely ventured yet in the "play-safe" commercial houses. Still, Toronto's professional fare continued to be imported mainly from American-operated stage circuits — standard classics, current London and New York plays, popular melodrama and musical comedy. Vaudeville, too, grew highly popular, although the cause of its eventual doom, the cinema, had already appeared late in the 1890s in little flickering movie houses, and by the war played in sizeable theatres. The rule of the Grand Opera House was also ending, as newer rivals appeared; not just the Princess Theatre or Shea's Vaudeville, but also an Edwardian Beaux Arts jewel, the Royal Alexandra, completed on King in 1907, and the large and lavish Winter Garden opened on Yonge in 1914. Tied to outside circuits, Toronto by the war was nevertheless Canada's best-provided theatrical town.

The city's periodicals circulated widely across Canada, such as

"Old Houses, Toronto, Winter," by Lawren Harris, a major member of the Group of Seven. This celebrated painting, first exhibited in 1919, most likely depicts houses in the Ward.

Maclean's Magazine, started in 1896, and the more analytical and critical weekly, *Saturday Night*. The daily press still displayed the intense partyism of the Conservative *Mail and Empire* or Liberal *Globe*, but it also included the populist *Telegram* or *Star* and the higher-calibre *News* or *World* — none of them less opinionated for being independent. There were powerful journalists directing them, the most noteworthy being (Sir) John Willison, editor of the *Globe* from 1890 to 1902, and of the *News* till 1910, who made the latter a truly effective non-partisan paper, owned in 1903-8 by Joseph Flavelle.[75] Yet the king of the owners was still John Ross Robertson of the *Telegram*. He used his newspaper wealth handsomely to endow the Sick Children's Hospital and foster historical works, while keeping his journal strong on the empire, Orangeism and civic politics.

Popular culture was further expressed in booming organized sport. Baseball games attracted thousands, especially to the main stadium at Hanlan's Point on the Island by 1911.[76] Cycling, however, declined as a sport activity around 1900, becoming a largely plebian means of urban transport instead. Rowing similarly was losing public appeal, or rather, other spectator sports were taking over. Intercollegiate league football, organized in 1897, brought epic contests between Toronto's Varsity, Montreal's McGill and Queen's of Kingston. The "Big Four" public football league set up in 1907 and comprising top Toronto, Ottawa, Montreal and Hamilton teams, produced still larger epics, fed on by sports journalists, who fed sports fervour in turn. Lacrosse matches, track events, racing at the Woodbine, drew other large followings, although tennis, golf and cricket remained narrower preserves of the upper classes. In particular, hockey now ruled the winter. In public arenas or at outdoor rinks in parks, young players and older watchers alike shared roaring enthusiasm for another national development, Canada's number-one popular game.

Arenas and theatres, the *Globe's* new edifice of 1896, the *Telegram's* of 1900 (both on Melinda Street, below King off Bay), the Royal Ontario Museum erected in 1913 on Bloor near Avenue Road — these were some of the cultural agencies embodied over the period in the city's built environment. But urban construction in this boom-time covered a great deal more: offices and residences, hotels and banks, roads, sewers, and harbour works. As city expanded into metropolis, it felt a new architectural impulse as well, arising from the Chicago Exposition of 1893 but only making its main impact on Toronto from about 1898 on. The great Chicago fair had produced a City Beautiful of exhibition structures, with grand Roman colonnades, dignity and spaciousness. This show of academic classicism, tying in with the related Beaux Arts movement out of France, inspired an architecture that was imposing, ordered and cultivated, but less venturesome and adaptive than that of earlier eras.[77] As a result, young twentieth-century Toronto got prime buildings that could look nobly classical, but often smacked of imitated antique models planked down in the local scene.

An eminent example was the new Bank of Toronto headquarters of 1911, designed by a leading New York firm. It graced the financial core at King and Bay with a facade of lofty columns, much marble and bronze within, to give banking wealth the trappings of imperial Rome. Other bank projects enabled the Toronto firm of Darling and Pearson to erect their own classical designs: a bank was scarcely a bank henceforth if it was not the Temple of Jupiter. Then Montreal architects with Toronto's John P. Lyle achieved the crowning grandeur of a new Union Station between 1914 and 1919.[78] This huge, colonnaded Beaux Arts monument (which is not only imposing, but works) fortunately survives on Front Street, as one of the last great terminuses of the railway age modelled on the magnificent baths of Roman emperors.

Earlier, the opulent King Edward Hotel of 1903 by E. J. Lennox, architect of the City Hall, also displayed much classical detail and an interior with massive Roman pillars. More than that, classically clad steel skyscrapers were spreading in the downtown. In the central business district along King, down Yonge and up around Queen, the period produced ten-storey structures like the Kent and Lumsden buildings — tall slabs, flat-topped with projecting classic cornices — the fifteen-storey Canadian Pacific Railway Building of 1913, and a twenty-storey Royal Bank, completed two years later. There were other large structures, like the big Eaton's complex that occupied most of two city blocks with sales floors, warehouses, delivery stables, a factory and a wireless station on its twelfth-storey roof.[79] The Toronto cityscape thus massed vertically as well as centrally between the Nineties and the war. From the lake, church spires or public edifices no longer commanded the scene, but the climbing steel of big finance, transport and merchandising. Our own urban setting had demonstrably appeared.

Other expansive building spread new offices, schools and factories out across the city, but only residences can be touched here. At first, on through the Nineties, the "Queen Anne" American

Toronto's yearly Exhibition (here in 1909) drew huge crowds. The glass-domed Horticultural Building (1907) on the site of the earlier Crystal Palace still stands. The city invested heavily in such structures for its late-summer fair, loftily renamed "The Canadian National Exhibition" in the 1900s.

High Park mineral baths, about 1911. Out west off Bloor, High Park had become a popular recreation area.

Island hotel, regatta course and bathers at Hanlan's Point, 1907. Hanlan's, named after the family of the great rower, who had a hotel here, was once the area of Gibraltar Point, and now a resort focus. Summer cottages and yacht clubs (plus other hotels) spread out over the rest of the Island; yet so did grass, trees, sand beaches and lagoons.

Lacrosse at Hanlan's Point, 1909. Not only Canada's own summer game drew masses of fans to this stadium, but baseball — and Tom Longboat running. The amusement park (behind) brought others by Island ferryboats to its roller-coaster, "aerial swing cars" and roller-skating arena.

Women's hockey before the First World War at the University of Toronto, with Hart House, the Massey benefaction, partly completed in the background.

style had a hold on wealthy and not-so-wealthy home construction: an amalgam of bulging towerlets, sweeping verandahs and lavish shingling that would have astounded that eighteenth-century English monarch — later Victorianism gone picturesquely wild. But properly classical Edwardian homes then took over, more British than American in origin — for example, Joseph Flavelle's stately Holwood House of 1902 beside Queen's Park. There still were unlikely outbreaks, such as Lennox's extravagant Gothic castle fantasy, Casa Loma, for Sir Henry Pellatt. But most new Rosedale, Avenue Road or St. Clair homes for the well-heeled were solid versions of English gentry mansions, even when underwritten by northern Ontario mining wealth, or utility and western railway fortunes (Map 9).

In any case, the prewar era was a noonday for the building speculators and real estate developers of Toronto, when money was plentiful, by-laws weak, and gaining licence from jobbing civic officials imposed few hindrances.[80] Land prices zoomed as did trading in vacant lots. But at the same time construction leaped ahead, in dollar value across the whole period well outdistancing other Canadian cities, including vibrant Vancouver, wonderful Winnipeg and, in general, Montreal besides. From an annual construction worth $1.3 million in 1895, Toronto's yearly building permits by 1901 totalled $3.5 million, $14.2 in 1907, $18 million in 1909, and peaked at $27.4 in 1912. The next year brought depression, but permits fell only slightly, and stood at $20.8 million in 1914, still in leading position.[81] Aside from major projects, much of the construction effort went into private housing. This, in part, produced newly modish apartment houses for the fairly well-to-do, on better residential streets then still not too far from downtown. Wider developments, however, took place in more-outlying neighbourhoods of new middle-class homes, from West Toronto to the eastern Beach section, and north beyond St. Clair — comfortable brick dwellings with broad front dormers above pillared verandahs becoming a set Toronto builders' style. And by the war years, new superior locales were being promoted to the north, in Moore Park or Forest Hill, for instance, since Rosedale, Avenue Road and the Annex were running out of building space — as Riverdale, Parkdale or upper Jarvis already had.[82]

Lower-class residential construction also proceeded, some of it along side streets in older one-time suburbs, but a good deal also in newer fringe areas: as in less-favoured parts of North Toronto, out

west about Bloor towards St. Clair, and also east of the Don, around Gerrard Street and Danforth Avenue. The full development of the Danforth district was nevertheless impeded by poor communication across the wide, wet Don flats until a giant bridge spanned them, connecting Bloor with Danforth as a through crosstown route. Yet this Don Viaduct, planned since 1903, was only begun in 1915 and finished in 1918. Furthermore, private developers typically put more money and effort into higher-profit housing. Though lines of working-class homes arose, immigrant crowding or industrial expansion in older districts deteriorated and depleted the housing stocks for wage earners, and new building (at inflated costs) could not meet their needs sufficiently. Rents, in fact, had shot up by 95 per cent between 1897 and 1907, while 1912–13 showed a clear excess of new families forming over house completions in the city.[83]

In response to fears of spreading slums and radicalized workers unable to meet rents, Toronto turned civic attention to its residential shortages. A first Housing Commission was named in 1907, and Dr. Charles Hastings, the energetic medical health officer, urged "garden suburbs" as the answer to urban overcrowding.[84] In 1913 the Toronto Housing Company appeared to build low-cost publicly assisted housing — largely a combination of philanthropy with business interests concerned by mounting wage demands. It did not achieve much, since depression and war intervened, but it signified some public recognition of responsibility for housing development; and its Riverdale Court east of the Don and Spruce Court west of the river were well-designed, small examples of high-density accommodation on a soundly human scale.[85] At any rate, the question of public housing had now crossed the city's threshold, although it would be long years before it was more effectively taken up.

Building development, which amassed money and provided jobs, also sprawled Toronto well beyond its original lakeside site, and raised recurrent problems of supplying more public transport. In 1892 a Belt Line steam railway had been opened to surround the main city and give access from all quarters. But when it closed after two years of operating at a loss, the field was left to electric streetcars. So-called radial electric lines were built from the city outskirts into the neighbouring hinterland. That on north Yonge ran to Richmond Hill by 1896, and reached Lake Simcoe in 1907, much improving on Governor Simcoe's old passage northward.[86]

The Royal Alexandra Theatre, 1907, on King west of Simcoe. Effective design kept the audience intimate with the stage — and still does today, after an excellent restoration.

The Bank of Toronto, built in 1911, at King and Bay. This grandly classical edifice expressed the wealth of the city's financial institutions.

Similarly, the CPR Building, erected in 1913 at King and Yonge, marked the big rail line's necessary presence in the Toronto metropolis. It is still standing today.

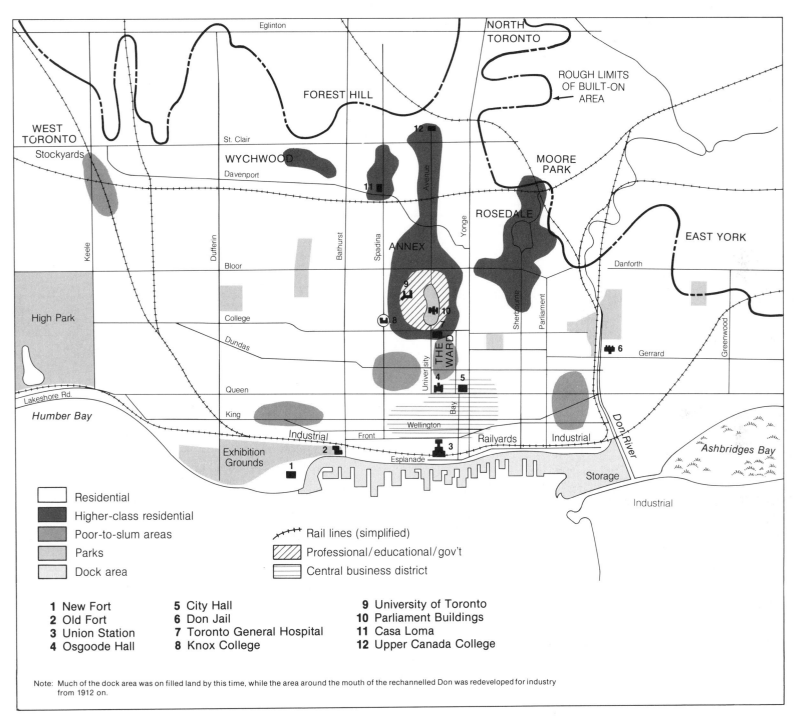

WEST TORONTO

Stockyards

NORTH TORONTO

ROUGH LIMITS OF BUILT-ON AREA

Eglinton

FOREST HILL

St. Clair

WYCHWOOD

Davenport

MOORE PARK

ROSEDALE

EAST YORK

Keele

Dufferin

Bathurst

Spadina

ANNEX

Yonge

Sherbourne

Parliament

Danforth

Greenwood

Bloor

High Park

College

Dundas

THE WARD

University

Bay

Gerrard

Humber Bay

Lakeshore Rd.

Queen

King

Industrial

Wellington

Front

Railyards

Industrial

Don River

Ashbridges Bay

Exhibition Grounds

Esplanade

Storage

Industrial

Residential

Higher-class residential

Poor-to-slum areas

Parks

Dock area

Rail lines (simplified)

Professional/educational/gov't

Central business district

1 New Fort	**5** City Hall	**9** University of Toronto
2 Old Fort	**6** Don Jail	**10** Parliament Buildings
3 Union Station	**7** Toronto General Hospital	**11** Casa Loma
4 Osgoode Hall	**8** Knox College	**12** Upper Canada College

Note: Much of the dock area was on filled land by this time, while the area around the mouth of the rechannelled Don was redeveloped for industry from 1912 on.

9 Toronto by 1915: Land Use

The radial terminus at the city's northern limits, from which Richmond Hill, Aurora, Newmarket and Lake Simcoe could be reached. This Yonge Street electric route was finally done away with after the Second World War — in a move to save electricity by taking to oil-powered buses.

Among others, a suburban radial line went east along Kingston Road to Scarborough by 1904, and one westward from Sunnyside to Port Credit by 1905. They were swift and sure, compared to primitive "automobiling" on the unpaved rural roads of the prewar era. And while growing in number, automobiles then largely remained rich men's symbols, though some became express delivery vehicles within the city. For internal transport, however, the electric streetcar was the key to public movement. The cars grew in size and had trailers added. They ran out to new amusement grounds at easternmost Scarborough Beach and to the western beaches at Sunnyside; their traffic more than tripled between 1900 and 1910.[87] Streetcars, moreover, served Toronto's sports facilities, theatres, museums, libraries and colleges. The city's cultural as well as material environment owed much to them.

POLITICAL ASPECTS: URBAN SERVICES, REFORM AND PLANNING

The very importance of streetcar service also thrust it into civic political life. One episode was close to comedy: the great fight to gain Sunday streetcars that climaxed in a city plebiscite of 1897.[88] Yet the issue hit at a firm-set institution, Toronto's closed and righteous Sabbath. The franchised Toronto Railway Company (TRC) led by William Mackenzie was more than willing to have its cars used seven days a week, while many politicians and businessmen were quite ready to see Sunday activities enlarged. A mass of bicyclists desired good Sunday access to parks and sportsgrounds by the TRC; and labour, too, widely wanted to get the most of its one full day for recreation. Some workers, however, feared that efforts for shorter hours would be set back by a more open Sunday. More forceful still was opposition to Sabbath desecration — especially among Methodists — which brought clergymen and capitalists to join with labour figures such as Jimmy Simpson in passionate resistance. At a grand rally in Allan Gardens, they sang out, "Rally to the Standard, boys, against our City's foe! For the cause of Sabbath rest we'll strike another blow."[89] Nevertheless, the ensuing plebiscite voted narrowly in favour of Sunday cars. Moral reformers deplored the victory of secularism and sin, but more likely the outcome was at base a response to urbanism, to the leisure needs of a new large city. Nor was Toronto Sabbatarianism finished. In 1912, spurred by a militant Lord's Day Alliance, it at least succeeded in closing winter toboggan slides in the city parks on Sundays.[90]

The opening decades of the twentieth century raised other streetcar issues, on which the TRC found scant support.[91] Service problems — delayed and crowded cars, or too many uncomfortable old ones — were inevitable complaints as the company struggled to keep up with ever-growing traffic. Yet its profits did not fail to keep up, and it was known as a hard employer, prone to strikes and remorseless strikebreaking. The TRC did build more cars and improved downtown routes to relieve congestion. The City Council, however, chiefly wanted "new lines," extensions out to the widening urban limits. On this the company stood by its franchise of 1891, good for thirty years, insisting that it need only serve to the city limits of that date. Mackenzie himself got into the developing suburban radials, but this meant extra fares where (and if) these lines met with city tracks.[92] The city fathers repeatedly took the company to court for inadequate service. Some of them talked of expropriation, and citizen meetings urged public ownership. In 1907 the civic case for new lines even went to the judges of the imperial Privy Council, where its ultimate defeat contributed to a decision of 1910 to build city-owned routes to extend streetcar service.[93] In 1912 the first of these Civic Car Lines was opened on Gerrard East; on St. Clair and on Danforth the next year. An actual attempt to buy out the TRC in 1914 was then halted by the outbreak of the war: the commitment seemed too large. But it was pretty clear that the company franchise would not be renewed on its expiry in 1921. And meanwhile, the city was learning how to operate its own transport utility. Already by 1914 some 21 per cent of its population lived beyond the limits of the old private service.[94] Significantly, too, a report of 1915 indicated that working-class districts now provided the "greater proportion" of streetcar users of the expanded transit system.[95]

Fire and water service also made significant progress, thanks largely to a disaster, the Great Fire of April 1904, that devastated nearly twenty acres in the downtown warehouse district at a cost of over $10 million.[96] No lives or dwellings were lost in this night conflagration, but more than 5,000 workers were left temporarily jobless. Breaking out in a neckware manufactory (perhaps from defective wiring), the fire centred around Bay Street between Wellington and Front. Though the buildings here were of solid masonry, their inflammable stores, wooden inner construction and

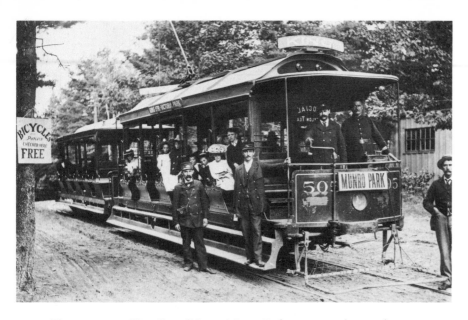

The streetcar out King Street West to Munro Park, 1900, another popular recreation ground.

Workers laying a streetcar intersection on Queen Street West at Roncesvalles, about 1910.

A group of streetcar-track workers operating out of the Front Street shops, photographed in 1905.

Rush-hour crowding on Queen: the kind of congestion which did not help the franchised company's reputation.

Yonge St. north from King

The streetcar city in full flower. Yonge Street north from King, 1910. "Autos" and carts are evident, but the trolleycar clearly dominates — as do overhead wires.

Ruins after the fire of 1904 on Wellington west of Bay, in the heart of the wholesale district.

unprotected elevator shafts produced exploding blazes that leaped streets under a driving wind. At their fullest extent, flames raced from Melinda near King down to the tracks on the Esplanade, east nearly to the Customs House on Yonge, west almost to the Queen's Hotel on Front. Toronto's now well-organized, full-time fire department put some 200 firemen, steam pumpers, water tower and ladder trucks to use, plus men and equipment arriving by train from as far as London and Buffalo. But all too typically, water pressure proved as inadequate as were fire-proofing measures. At length, a wind shift and some better-protected buildings enabled the firemen to stop the spread. Afterwards — in the good times — recovery and rebuilding moved on remarkably fast. Yet the city also adopted far broader building regulations; much reconstruction was done in steel-reinforced concrete; and a new high-pressure water system was approved by public vote for the downtown area, finished in 1909.

Along with the high pressure system, other improvements in water supply were effected by 1910 through a major scheme originally designed in 1896.[97] Water was now taken well out in a still-pure lake, passed through a modern filtration plant on the Island, then pumped by tunnel under the bay to enlarged reservoir facilities. A sewage disposal plant was opened by the Scarborough Bluffs, remote from the city intake line. The trunk sewer thus was achieved; only storm drains henceforth flowed into the harbour. By 1912, accordingly, the typhoid death rate in Toronto was below 0.2 per thousand, less than any comparable North American centre.[98] Moreover, under an active health administration, well exemplified by Dr. Charles Hastings as medical officer, the city took up extensive powers over privy pits, unhealthy boardinghouses, and indeed any premises from 1916.[99] Sanitary reform was far from all-embracing, but public controls were steadily extended over once-sacrosanct private property rights. If Toronto sanitation was not perfect, an annual death rate that continued to fall from 15.18 per thousand in 1896 to 11.2 in 1914 said something of obvious value.[100]

Hospitals played their part also. There were six general hospitals by the First World War, ten specialized ones.[101] In particular, the Toronto General Hospital moved in 1913 from its overcrowded old quarters into fine new buildings by Darling and Pearson at the corner of University and College, replacing a tract of "Ward" slums.

The city met the price of the site, and the province promised substantially larger grants from 1905. But a great part of the funds for the ultimate 670-bed complex costing $3,450,000 came from wealthy Toronto philanthropists. Joseph Flavelle, who had joined the hospital's board in 1902, vigorously directed the fund-raising. Among others, the Massey, Eaton and Gooderham families, Cox, Walker, Osler and Lash made major contributions, and at the end Flavelle added to his own in paying off a $250,000 deficit.[102] The citizens gained a first-rate health facility, the University a teaching hospital soon of world quality, and the metropolis a further centring of scientific expertise and professional training. In sum total, Toronto hospitals by the war had truly evolved from charitable shelters to curative institutions for all, supported by paying patients, and provincial and municipal aid, yet still with care for needy cases.

What this indicates is a real advance in public betterment, but by no means the attainment of some just welfare society. As late as 1900, a number of homeless elderly were still being committed to jail in Toronto, their crimes consisting of infirmity and absence of family support; the true crime being the lack of sufficient space in refuge agencies.[103] One of three new wings opened in 1898 at the House of Industry did provide more room for aged inmates, yet it was soon filled to capacity. The shelter and relief needs of working-age people were no doubt eased by the prosperous times of the new century. Yet, leaving aside the damage still done by seasonal layoffs, it has been estimated that most male manual workers in Toronto then earned less than enough to support a family adequately, requiring wives and children to work as well, with effects upon the household unit that could readily show up in city welfare problems.[104] Excessive infant mortality was a further woe, at length reduced through the institution of public health nurses in 1908 and the compulsory pasteurization of milk in 1914. Another initiative in welfare, however, was taken in combatting juvenile deliquency and child abuse through Toronto's municipally assisted Children's Aid Society.

Reflecting conservative concerns for social order, humane sentiments of the social gospel, and newer ideas on childhood as a life stage of its own, the Children's Aid Society (begun in 1891) became an influential welfare instrument in Toronto from the mid-Nineties onward, with J. J. Kelso as its guiding spirit.[105] It sought to

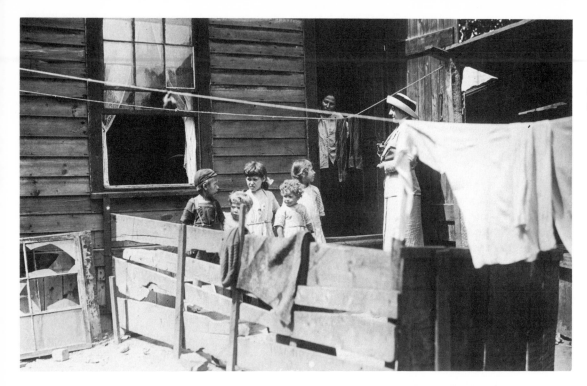

The visit of the public health nurse, in 1913 here, was an indication of the "attack on slums."

Sewers come to the Ward — another reflection of improving public health standards. This excavation is on Elizabeth Street, 1910.

109,042.

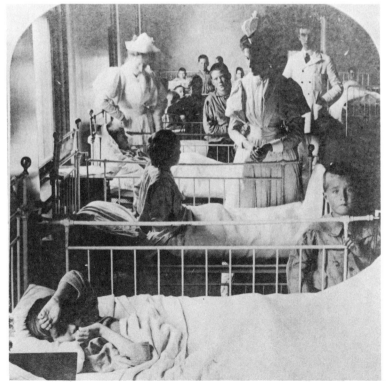

The most obvious sign of the broadening of medical facilities in this era was the opening in 1913 of the Toronto General Hospital, above — one of the prewar city's finest achievements. Fronting on College Street, with University Avenue (old College Avenue) at the right, it marked the development of a growing hospital complex in the area. At left is the convalescent ward of the Sick Children's Hospital in 1902, within its building just to the east on College Street.

sustain the family unit, seen as the very basis of society, by improving the home environment; but in dealing with neglect and cruelty, it widely took to foster homes. The Society's own shelter, besides, housed both dependent children and delinquents. As a typical result of covering so much, these quarters became overcrowded, so that the city cut its grants in 1901 because of undesirably congested conditions! Nevertheless, the Society held to its claim, "It is wiser and less expensive to save children than to punish criminals."[106] This stress on child saving as sound policy as well as social compassion led on to a separate juvenile court in Toronto by 1912, probation officers, family visitors, and volunteer aides, the Big Brothers and Big Sisters, given some training at the University's new Department of Social Services.[107] Apart from other accomplishments, the city's social service thus grew more professionalized, largely thanks to the impetus of the child welfare movement ardently espoused by Kelso.

From waterworks to welfare, these urban services demanded far more in city finance and administration, as did asphalting roads, running civic power lines, enlarging park facilities and the police force, or expanding the annual Exhibition that drew close to a million visitors by 1912.[108] Toronto's government was now big business; the city's debt, steady at about $12 million through the 1890s, was $60 million by 1914.[109] Municipal expenditure seemed almost out of hand, given its restricted revenue base in property taxes, while politicians' promises of retrenchment looked empty, given constantly increasing commitments. Consequently, rate-burdened businessmen raised stronger calls for management on "business principles." But this was only one of the springs of the urban reform movement that welled up anew.[110] Another, flowing chiefly from the intelligentsia, had both aesthetic and social-engineering aims. It sought to realize the City Beautiful concept, which looked to planned arteries adorned by handsome buildings and parks, to erase degenerate slums, and to establish an effective urban physical plant under an expert bureaucracy. The plush Guild of Civic Art, dating from 1897, stressed spatial plans, with many "garden-city" features. The University social scientist S. Morley Wickett also led from 1902 in urging municipal control of the city's "utility base" under trained professional administrators.[111]

Nor was this all. Older moral reformism swelled again to cleanse Toronto of boodling politicians allegedly mired in dirty deals or sold to liquor interests. Labour leaders still fought private monopolies and urged democratic public ownership. Newspapers like the *World* championed the ordinary citizen against big interests, and John Ross Robertson of the *Telegram* invoked true civic spirit against urban vice and blight.[112] This medley of causes often overlapped and at times evinced cross-purposes. But generally it represented responses to problems of power in an increasingly collectivized urban polity. Whether or not idealist rhetoric had much meaning for the practical running of a complicated urban political mechanism, manifest results were to be left on the civic power structure: governmental changes that sought to combine efficiency and democracy, the inception of planning controls on unbridled laissez-faire development, a quite professional municipal civil service, and potent public enterprises like the Toronto Hydro, Civic Car Lines and Harbour Commission. The collectivist state was taking over in Canada and its provinces, and not least in Toronto itself.

This trend in the city was displayed even as the period opened, when stark evidence of aldermanic bribe-taking from a judicial inquiry late in 1894 roused demands for stronger executive authority.[113] Both an elitist citizens' reform committee and union leaders pressed for a city-wide Board of Control above council; politicians agreed, if it were elected by the council from its own numbers. In 1896 this board of four was implemented, the first in Canada. In 1904 the controllers became directly elected by citizenry, viewed as a further step in democratic urban reform. Otherwise, beneath the executive of mayor and Board of Control, the older pattern of a council of aldermen elected by wards persisted. Wards had been numbered and considerably amalgamated since 1891, and these bigger wards were largely just extended northward during the series of annexations made in the new century.[114] (See Map 7, page 126.) The design was partly to sustain "good government" efficiency by keeping general interests paramount over local ward issues and parochial ward politicos, but it also assured broader mixes of ward residents, thereby effectively reducing the weight of the working-class municipal voters.

Despite these structural changes and the preachings of reformers, urban politics in prewar Toronto kept much of its former character. There still were political in-groups linked with Conservative and Orange machinery, lawyers and contractors steering land-lot schemes, merchants and manufacturers keenly

The state of a residential road: Muddy York still in 1912. Such roadways, however, were no longer evident in paved downtown Toronto, only towards the fringes. Moreover, the first paved highway outward, to Hamilton, was in process within two years.

The city police had its mounted constables, like the one
above left, posed around 1900, and its men on foot wore
similar British "bobby" uniforms. Then in 1912 the first
motorcycle squad was formed. As shown above, its
members did not receive uniforms till the experiment was
judged a success. The first motorized police (at left)
came in 1912 — but the first parking ticket in 1907.
And the first motor fire truck entered service in 1911.

guarding business interests — and not very many labour representatives. Ward Three (now containing "the Ward") also witnessed the colourful reign of the machine politician, Dr. Beatty Nesbitt, as boss of its rising immigrant ethnic vote.[115] The mayors of the period generally remained safely substantial worthies with regular backgrounds as aldermen and most often strong Conservative ties. The majority of them were prosperous lawyers, though they included "the People's Bob," Robert Fleming, a Liberal real estate broker (mayor in 1896-97, as he had been in 1892-93), Joseph Oliver (1908-9), a lumber dealer, and Horatio Hocken (1912-14), once a printer-unionist, who had risen to control his own press company but stayed sensitive to reform issues.[116]

In provincial and federal politics, moreover, prewar Toronto by no means lost its Conservative identification. The Ontario Conservative Whitney regime of 1905-14, with its cheap hydroelectric program, new grants to the General Hospital and University, proved in many ways much more favourably disposed to the city's interests than previous Liberal provincial governments had been. And while in federal affairs the long rule of Sir Wilfrid Laurier at Ottawa had enhanced Liberal links in Toronto, Laurier's pursuit of a new reciprocity agreement with the United States in 1911 caused an outright revolt among some of his leading party supporters in the city. The National Policy of protection had become an enduring article of faith for its Board of Trade and Canadian Manufacturers' Association, but far more than city industrialists took alarm at the thought of American goods flooding the Canadian market through reciprocity. In particular, the "Toronto Eighteen," a pre-eminent group of Liberals, came out with a manifesto against the proposal; their number including Walker of the Commerce, E. R. Wood of Dominion Securities, J. C. Eaton, president of Eaton's, W.T. White, managing director of National Trust, and Zebulon Lash, now vice-president of the Canadian Northern. When the Conservative government of Robert Borden took over in Ottawa that year, Toronto's dominant interests snuggled to it in reinforced devotion.

Nonetheless, whatever the enduring aspects of the city's political life, the collectivist changes across the period decidedly had impact. Even by lip service, civic politicians had to acknowledge urban reform, and many not only endorsed, but pushed, the practical extensions of civic authority — that is, the growth of public enterprises so obviously wanted by the voters.[117] The municipal rulers spent funds on large projects directly authorized by ballot, and some that were not; they accepted executive management and interventions into private rights to degrees that would have startled their forebears. But most of all, they helped revive public planning through establishing some real designs for land-use, absent almost since the colonial days of Little York.

The move towards planning and spatial control was first effectively expressed in "non-residential restrictions," provincially enacted at the city's request in 1904, to enable it to specify location and land use for stores, manufactories, laundries and so forth; and thereafter extended to cover a wide range of other items, from hospitals to dance halls, gas stations to stables and junk shops.[118] This was a highly practical response to the problems of congested urban living, but it soon covered large areas of the city, and led onward to restrictions for residential areas as well. By 1912, accordingly, Toronto was prohibiting tenement or apartment houses in most of the latter areas; in fact, zoning was taking form, though not yet explicity.[119] At the same time, more widely general planning schemes emerged, largely deriving from the aesthetic reformism of the Guild of Civic Art. In 1909 they produced a full-size city plan, with new diagonal main arteries, an enlarged park system and waterfront amenities. This was followed by a plan from the council's Civic Improvement Committee in 1911, a municipal scheme which stressed efficient routes for streetcars, railways and private traffic, but also proposed developing parks, waterfront and a civic centre.[120]

Neither plan saw action, though they did produce University Avenue (the former College Avenue) as a grand roadway. Besides, they led to the City and Suburbs Act of 1912, which required further subdivisions within five miles of the city to be publicly approved, and established a City Surveyor's Office to administer the measure. In consequence, the city gained planning control over land and new street layouts for the first time.[121] And official planning in Toronto took off from here. The urban tract in general was still marked by arrays of poles and overhead electric wires, uneven route development and cluttered locales. But a major civic break had been made into the future. Until depression — and much beyond that, war — rose abruptly in the way.

THE WAR YEARS: SEQUEL AND TRANSITION

From 1914 to 1918 Toronto deeply experienced the carnage of world war, even though remote from battlegrounds. Some 70,000 of its men — a seventh of national enlistments — went into the forces, the weight of its younger male adult population.[122] One in seven did not return, and of those that did, many were so badly wounded that their lives were shattered. The strains on families at home were bitter as well. Never had the city faced human loss and heartbreak on such a scale, or for so long. When it was over, there was pride no less than mourning, and perhaps the assurance of having come through a cruel testing. But the breezy, unlimited optimism of the bright new century was gone forever. An age had closed for a now-maturing metropolitan city.

The outbreak of war with Germany in August 1914 was assuredly greeted with patriotic fervour and renewed optimism. Young men thronged to volunteer at the University Avenue Armouries and other recruiting stations, to get in on a heroic venture overseas before it ended, or at least to escape from the unemployment of the depression since 1913. From 1915, however, when Canadian troops were increasingly committed to the trenches of Europe, the full demands of a murderous, stalemated conflict hit home to Toronto. Not just the casualty lists steadily mounted, but numbers of returning wounded: the old General Hospital and the former Bishop Strachan's School were taken over on a growing list of military hospitals.[123] More columns of soldiers marched to Union Station, the Exhibition held troop depots, the University officers in training. And flying fields were established around the suburbs to provide men for the new warfare of the air, making Toronto the chief aviation centre in Canada.[124] Army recruiting drew increasingly on family men rather than the original young single floaters of 1914, but over 1916 the supply of volunteers began to run short. Hence, the next year most Torontonians grimly approved the national government's adoption of conscription, to share the real costs of patriotism equitably. But the troops departing, the casualty lists arriving, paced their very life. At least they found a popular, responsive wartime civic leader in "Tommy" Church, mayor from 1915 right through 1921. He was there whenever the soldiers left; he knew the men and their next-of-kin to an amazing degree.[125] At last an end came. In November 1918 the signing of an armistice was heralded in the city by factory whistles, church bells, bonfires, and sheer release of emotion. The four-year agony was over.

War had meant a draining emigration, not to be stopped till the troops poured home. Meanwhile, immigration into Toronto had come to a virtual standstill, though in-migration to its war factories rose, and women, above all, entered urban employment in greater numbers. They replaced men in many former jobs, but also filled new places in munition plants, equipment factories and much more. Yet demands for labour still increased, and in due course impelled workers generally to larger and more active union organization.[126] All this did not occur at once; large-scale war production took time to be required and organized, while there was unused capacity left by prewar depression first to be taken up. In fact, a slump lasted well on into 1915, and only by 1916 had the turn-around clearly taken place.

In the subsequent wartime boom, propelled by demands for munitions, the urban economy grew rapidly again and jobs became plentiful. But at the same time, inflation sent living costs upwards over 50 per cent between 1915 and 1919, while food alone climbed by nearly 75 per cent.[127] Housing was heavily overcrowded, thanks to high rents and little new building.[128] Labour strife rose as well, as did outcries against rapacious war profiteers, or demands for government controls on food and basic goods, instituted to some extent in 1917–18 (but following Prohibition, in 1916). Toronto grew feverish, displaying hot suspicions of conspiring foreigners and "socialists" no less than exploiting capitalists or unpatriotic squanderers. Optimism was dead indeed.

Nevertheless, significant economic gains did come out of the city's wartime years. Its investment interests advanced in size and scope. For example, the assets of the Bank of Commerce stood at $467 million by 1919, compared with $537 million for the Bank of Montreal, further reducing the older rival's lead.[129] Toronto's retail trading empires similarly extended, while its transport system was used to the utmost — even though the Canadian Northern Railway, financially strained in the 1913–14 depression and hit by high construction costs, went into crisis, and in 1917 was taken over by the federal government. Yet Toronto manufacturing was especially stimulated. An aircraft industry emerged, mainly in air frames but with engine components; and overall, war production considerably expanded factories, shipyards and power facilities.

New war plants themselves would be mostly as short-lived as the munitions they turned out. Still, the large factories required to fill huge shell contracts, the precision skills demanded, fostered both broader industrial organization and higher technical capacity in

Toronto was a major recruiting and initial training centre during the Great War. Military tents dotted the University campus in 1915 — which then settled down as an officers' school.

Troop train leaving Union Station, 1916. Altogether 70,000 Torontonians served.

On the home front, some Toronto women took up rifle practice, though those who went overseas mainly did so as nurses and nursing aides.

Far more women went into the city's war factories, as here milling shell caps at the Russell Motor Car works.

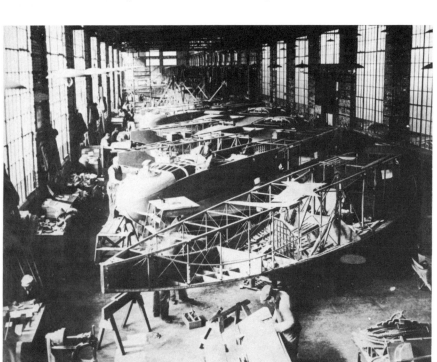

War plants poured out aircraft also. This assembly line at the Canadian Aeroplane Co. produced seaplanes.

War demands raised heavier industries as well, exemplified in this pouring of steel at British Forgings Ltd., near the waterfront.

Toronto's citizens could let loose at the Armistice, 11 November 1918, in happy hordes like these on King Street.

Toronto. A strong case in point is that of the Imperial Munitions Board (IMB), set up in Canada in 1915 to supply the British government and headed by Joseph Flavelle. He created a network of shell, machining and aircraft plants, with contracts out across the country, but with expertise and management centred in Toronto: "the biggest business that had ever existed in Canada, indeed by mid-1917 the biggest business in North America."[130] Though Flavelle would be more remembered as a pork packer who purveyed bad bacon to soldiers — a sensational press story amply discredited — he was a powerful force in wartime Toronto.[131] If anyone then earned his title it was portly Sir Joseph of the IMB.

By the close of 1918, when the blood-letting had passed, though war's disruptions had not, the chief desire was a swift return to normal. It would not happen, even though many other older patterns of life resumed, and former issues put by in the great ordeal were brushed off for the postwar era. For what was normal — 1913, or 1910, or 1900? Too much had gone on changing, both because of and in spite of the war. For Toronto, it had assuredly meant transition from a bygone youth. Ahead lay a metropolis that counted its residents in millions, not thousands, and was interconnected with a widespread complex of suburban towns. Automobiles would sweepingly refashion its built environment; aircraft, electronic media and new modes of service industry extend still broader hinterland links; social welfare needs and massive civic investment heavily pattern its municipal policies. And the collectivized community, increasingly regulated and regulating, would face far bigger issues of reconciling the claims of mass urban democracy with those of local neighbourhoods or growing ethnic pluralisms.

None of this, of course, was wholly new by the end of 1918. Toronto's population then was nearing the half million mark, and the nucleus of ethnic variety was set firmly in its midst. Its automotive traffic was now expanding fast; the war had engendered the development of aircraft and technological service industries; and the problems of big urban government's relations with citizen-responsive rule had plainly come into view. The war years had been prologue no less than epilogue, as the metropolis moved on towards national primacy. From Simcoe to Jimmy Simpson, Berczy to Joseph Flavelle, was a very long way. Yet 1918 still marked only an end to the beginnings of what human action would do to transform a Lake Ontario locality into a world-scale city.

Looking up the financial mainline, Bay Street, in 1912. At the top of the picture are the Temple Building, Toronto's first real skyscraper, by this date already outclassed, and the City Hall's Romanesque tower, itself being hemmed in by other rising structures.

Aerial view of the heart of the city about 1917. In the foreground, at the foot of the central Yonge Street artery, is the Board of Trade Building's curved front; to the left, across Yonge, the Bank of Montreal. Up Yonge, the major skyscapers rise, including the tallest, the Royal Bank. Just north of it on the east side is the Confederation Life Building. At the top towards the left is the City Hall tower; just below the City Hall, the Temple Building on Bay, and to the right of the City Hall the mass of Eaton's and Simpson's. Down Bay from the Temple Building are banks, insurance headquarters and newspaper offices.

Appendix
Statistical Tables

TABLE I
The Growth of Manufacturing in Toronto, 1871-1921

Year	Population	Number of Firms	Number of Employees	Yearly Payroll ($)	Value of Articles Produced ($)
1871	56,092	530[1]	9,400	2,690,993	13,686,093
1881	86,415	932	13,245	3,876,909	19,562,981
1891	181,216	2,401	26,242	9,638,537	44,963,922
1901	208,040	847	42,515	15,505,466	58,415,498
1911	376,538	1,100	65,274	36,064,815	154,306,948
1921	521,893	—	185,443	205,486,690	—

[1] Table LIV, which provided aggregates for cities, did not provide a category for number of firms in 1871. This figure was arrived at, therefore, by extracting for Toronto individual industries listed by city in Tables XXVIII-LIII of vol. 3 of published *Census* for 1871. Note also that after 1891 the census only counted employees in firms with more than five workers. This might explain somewhat the drop in units at 1901 — but was no less part of the rise of larger-scale plants, as growth in work force numbers makes plain. See Spelt, *Urban Development*, pp. 155-59. See also chapter 4, note 3, p. 208.

Source: *Census of Canada*, 1871-1921.

TABLE IV
Population Growth in Central Canadian Cities, 1851-1921

Year	Toronto	Hamilton	Ottawa	London	Kingston	Montreal City
1851	30,775	14,112	7,760	7,035	11,627	57,715
1861	44,821	19,096	14,669	11,555	13,743	90,323
1871	56,092	26,880	24,141	18,000	12,407	115,000
1881	86,415	36,661	31,307	26,266	14,091	155,238
1891	181,215	48,959	44,154	31,977	19,263	219,616
1901	208,040	52,634	59,928	37,976	17,961	267,730
1911	376,538	81,969	87,062	46,300	18,874	470,480
1921	521,893	114,151	93,740	53,838	24,104	618,506

Note: *Census of 1911*, vol. 1, p. 554, Table XIV, provides figures for 1871-1911 period sometimes at variance with totals provided in other volumes. With the exception of Kingston, 1911 compilations cite larger population totals, but Toronto's here are consistent with those in Tables I and III.

Source: *Census of Canada*, 1851-1921.

TABLE II
Males/Females in Toronto's Population, 1831-1921

Year	Males	Females	Total Population
1831	2,362	1,607	3,969
1841	6,941	7,308	14,249
1851	15,176	15,599	30,775
1861	21,677	23,144	44,821
1871	27,539	28,553	56,092
1881	41,917	44,498	86,415
1891	69,521	74,502	144,023[1]
1901	72,864	83,234	156,098[2]
1911	161,842	165,911	327,753[3]
1921	250,944	270,949	521,893

[1] This was revised to 181,216 in 1901 and subsequent censuses. See chapter 4, note 3, p. 208.
[2] Obviously incomplete figure; total too low for entire city.
[3] The same as above — incomplete. Better ratios shown on p. 426 in vol. 2, *Census of 1911*.

Source: *Census of Canada*, 1871-1921.

TABLE III
Toronto as a Percentage of Ontario Population, 1831-1921

Year	Toronto Population	Ontario Population	Percentage
1831	3,939	236,702	1.6
1841	14,249	455,668	3
1851	30,775	952,004	3
1861	44,821	1,396,091	3
1871	56,092	1,620,851	3.5
1881	86,415	1,923,229	4.5
1891	181,216[1]	2,144,321	8.6
1901	208,040	2,182,947	9.5
1911	376,538	2,523,274	14.9
1921	521,593	2,933,662	17.8

[1] City figure here for 1891 is as revised in 1901.

Source: *Census of Canada*, 1851-1921.

TABLE V
Population Growth in Toronto, 1801-1921[1]

Year	City Population	Numerical Change	Percent Change
1801	681	—	—
1811	1,324	643	94.4
1821[2]	1,559	235	17.7
1831[3]	3,969	2,410	154.6
1841	14,249	10,280	259
1851	30,775	16,526	116
1861	44,821	14,046	45.6
1871	56,092	11,271	25.1
1881	86,415	30,323	54.1
1891	181,216	94,801	109.7
1901	208,040	26,824	14.8
1911	376,538	168,498	80.9
1921	521,893	145,355	38.6

[1] The existent city, not including adjacent suburbs, is covered through this table.
[2] TPL, Minutes of Town Meetings (1801–31 figures).
[3] *Census of Canada*, 1871–1921. *Census of 1871*, vol. 4, substantiates Minutes figures of 1831 and those of 1841–61 in TCA's Statistical Book.

Source: *Census of Canada*, 1851–1921.

TABLE VI
Birthplace of Toronto's Population, 1851-1921

Year	Canadian-Born		British-Born		Foreign-Born		Total
	n	%	n	%	n	%	
1851	10,423	34	18,432	60	1,920	6	30,775
1861	19,385	43	22,788	51	2,648	6	44,821
1871	28,578	51	24,927	44	2,587	5	56,092
1881	51,489	60	30,469	35	4,457	5	86,415
1891	93,162	65	43,039	30	7,831	5	144,023*
1901	113,972	73	33,338	21	8,476	6	155,786*
1911	205,439	63	91,378	28	30,936	9	327,753*
1921	324,768	62	149,184	29	47,941	9	521,893

* The table bases again gave lower city totals than these figures.

Source: *Census of Canada*, 1851–1921.

TABLE VII
Major Religious Affiliations of Toronto's Population, 1841-1921

Religion	1841		1851		1861		1871		1881		1891		1901		1911		1921	
	n	%	n	%	n	%	n	%	n	%	n	%	n	%	n	%	n	%
Church of England	6,754	47	11,577	37	14,125	32	20,668	37	30,913	36	46,084	32	46,442	30	101,856	32	92,328	31
Roman Catholic	2,401	17	7,940	25	12,135	27	11,881	21	15,716	18	21,830	15	23,699	15	43,080	14	41,908	14
Methodist:																		
All Types	1,929	14	4,123	13	6,999	16	9,586	17	16,357	19	32,505	23	35,130	23	63,084	20	43,004	15
Church of Scotland	1,503	11	1,061	3	2,893	6	1,268	2.3	45	.005	27,449	19	30,812	20	65,339	21	58,779	20
Presbyterian	483	3	4,483	14	3,711	8	7,714	14	14,567	17								
Baptist	430	3	948	3	1,288	3	1,953	4	3,667	4	6,909	5	3,148	5	17,548	6	12,734	4
Lutheran	—		40	.13	167	.4	343	.6	494	.6	728	.5	833	.5	2,525	.8	1,008	.3
Jewish	3	.02	57	.18	153	.3	157	.2	534	.6	1,425	.10	3,038	2	6,719	2	31,468	11
Congregational	404	3	646	2	826	2	1,186	2	2,018	2.3	3,102	2.2	2,613	2	3,453	1	1,792	1
Other	342	2	900	3	2,524	6	1,336	2	2,104	2.4	3,991	3	5,383	3	13,249	4	11,882	4
Totals	14,249		30,775		44,821		56,092		86,415		144,023		156,098		316,853		294,903	

Note: Censuses of 1901, 1911 and 1921 show increasing fragmentation of population in religious persuasions, and totals bear no relation to actual population of Toronto but presumably reflect only those who participated in this part of the census. That of 1891 shows the "low" total, later revised to 181,216.

Sources: ICA, Statistical Book of the City of Toronto; *Census of Canada*, 1861–1921.

TABLE VIII
Ethnic Origins of Toronto's Population, 1851–1921

Group	1851 n	1851 %	1861 n	1861 %	1871 n	1871 %	1881[1] n	1881[1] %	1901 n	1901 %	1911 n	1911 %	1921 n	1921 %
Asian	—	—	—	—	—	—	10	.01	219	.1	1,111	.3	2,149	.4
British	29,793	96.8	41,738	93.1	53,603	95.6	80,750	93.4	190,788	91.7	· 325,173	86.4	445,230	85.3
French	467	1.5	501	1.1	572	1	1,230	1.4	3,015	1.5	4,886	1.3	8,350	1.6
German	113	.3	336	.7	985	1.8	2,049	2.4	6,028	3	9,775	2.6	4,689	.9
Netherlanders	—	—			62	.1	163	.19	737	.4	1,639	.4	3,961	.8
Italian	—	—	22	.04	34	.06	104	.12	1,054	.5	4,617	1.2	8,217	1.6
Jewish	—	—	156	.3	11	.01	124	.14	3,090	1.5	18,237	4.8	34,619	6.6
Polish	—	—	23	.05	81	.1	132	.15			700	.2	2,380	.5
Russian	—	—							142	.07	693	.2	1,332	.3
Scandinavian[2]	—	—	7	.01	20	.03	89	.10	253	.12	1,079	.3	1,844	.4
Ukrainian	—	—	—	—	—	—	—	—	—	—	—	—	1,149	.2
Others	402	1.31	2,038	5	724	1.3	1,764	2.1	2,714	1.3	8,628	2.3	7,973	1.5
Totals	30,775	100	44,821	100	56,092	100	86,415	100	208,040	100	376,538	100	521,893	100

[1] 1891 census figures not relevant. Breakdown then gave: natives 32,534; natives with a foreign father 60,628; foreign-born 50,861. Total: 144,023 — the smaller figure again.

[2] Includes Norway, Sweden, Denmark, Finland, Iceland.

Source: *Census of Canada*, 1851–1921.

TABLE IX
Age Composition of Toronto's Population, 1831–1921

Year	Population	Under 16	Over 16
1831	3,969	1,905	2,064
1841	14,249	6,348	7,901

Year	Population	0-15	15-40	40-60	60+	Not Given
1851	30,775	11,885	14,365	3,722	634	169
1861	44,821	16,144	21,072	6,010	1,399	196
1871[1]	56,092	21,478	24,887	7,798	1,911	18

Year	Population	0-14	15-44	45-64	65+	Not Given
1881	86,415	28,339	45,436	10,132	2,387	121
1891	159,288	59,008	78,026	17,597	4,038	619
1901	234,441[2]	55,041	85,592	87,472	6,316	290
1921	521,893	139,757	274,215	86,537	20,482	902

[1] 1871 listed its categories as: 0-16; 16-41; 41-61; 61+.

[2] 1911 did not provide age breakdown for the general population.

Source: *Census of Canada*, 1851–1921. Population totals here do not always correspond to figures in Table V, etc. — again data base variants.

TABLE X
Value of Building Permits Issued in City of Toronto, 1901-14

Year	Value of Permits ($)
1901	3,568,883
1902	3,854,903
1903	4,356,457
1904	5,900,000
1905	10,347,910
1906	13,160,396
1907	14,225,800
1908	11,795,436
1909	18,139,000
1910	21,127,000
1911	24,374,539[1]
1912	27,401,761
1913	27,038,624
1914	20,858,443

[1] In 1906–11 Toronto was the most active of all Canadian cities in building (*Labour Gazette*, May 1910).

Sources: *Canadian Finance, Labour Gazette*, and *Monetary Times Annual Review*.

TABLE XI
Bank Clearings in Toronto, 1895–1918

Year	Value of Clearings ($)
1895	306,239,000
1900	513,629,628
1905	1,047,490,701
1910	1,593,954,254
1914	2,013,055,664
1918	3,379,864,506

Source: *Monetary Times Annual Review*, 1919, vol. 62, p. 54.

TABLE XII
City of Toronto Assessments, 1834–1921

Year	Population	Assessed Totals
1834	9,254	£3,450[1]
1841	14,249	£81,610
1851	30,775	£186,983
1861	44,821	$1,600,000
1871	56,092	$29,600,000
1881	86,415	$53,379,634
1891	181,216	$132,402,383
1901	208,040	$128,271,583[2]
1911	376,538	$309,147,053
1921	521,893	$697,418,435

[1] 1834 includes Statute Labour £1,014.

[2] 1901. There is no explanation in either source as to why figure is lower.

Sources: TCA, Statistical Book of the City of Toronto for 1834–51 especially; TCA, City Council Minutes Appendices for 1861–1921. Where possible, revised totals ascertained after Court of Revision had considered appeals have been used. These figures were often lower than those cited in TCA's Statistical Book, which were before revisions took place.

TABLE XIII
City of Toronto Mayors, 1934–1921

1834	William Lyon Mackenzie
1835	Robert Baldwin Sullivan
1836	Thomas D. Morrison
1837	George Gurnett
1838-40	John Powell
1841	George Monro
1842-44	Henry Sherwood
1845-47	William Henry Boulton
1848-50	George Gurnett
1851-53	John George Bowes
1854	Joshua George Beard
1855	George William Allan
1856	John Beverley Robinson
1857	John Hutchison
1858	William Henry Boulton
1858	David Breakenridge Read
1859-60	Adam Wilson
1861-63	John George Bowes
1864-66	Francis H. Medcalf
1867-68	James E. Smith
1869-70	Samuel Bickerton Harman
1871-72	Joseph Sheard
1873	Alexander Manning
1874-75	Francis H. Medcalf
1876-78	Angus Morrison
1879-80	James Beaty Jr.
1881-82	William B. McMurrich
1883-84	Arthur R. Boswell
1885	Alexander Manning
1886-87	William H. Howland
1888-91	Edward F. Clarke
1892-93	Robert J. Fleming
1894-95	Warring Kennedy
1896-97	Robert J. Fleming
1897-99	John Shaw
1900	Ernest A. Macdonald
1901-2	Oliver Aikin Howland
1903-5	Thomas Urquhart
1906-7	Emerson Coatsworth
1908-9	Joseph Oliver
1910-12	George R. Geary
1912-14	Horatio C. Hocken
1915-21	Thomas Langton Church

Sources: TCA, City of Toronto Municipal Handbook; Victor Russell, *Mayors of Toronto, 1834-99* (Erin, Ont., 1982).

Notes

Abbreviations

CHR   *Canadian Historical Review*
DCB   *Dictionary of Canadian Biography*
OH   *Ontario History*
PAC   Public Archives of Canada
PAO   Public Archives of Ontario
TCA   Toronto City Archives
TPL   Metropolitan Toronto Public Library
UHR   *Urban History Review*

INTRODUCTION

[1] Percy J. Robinson, *Toronto During the French Regime, 1615–1793* (Toronto, 1933; reprinted 1965), pp. 1–3, 6–9, 221–25.
[2] Ibid., pp. 14–42, 46–50.
[3] Ibid., pp. 100–27.
[4] Jacob Spelt, *Toronto* (Toronto, 1973), p. 17. As the purchase terms were too informally drawn, a deed of conveyance was renegotiated in 1805. See Anthony Hall, "The Red Man's Burden: Land, Law and the Lord in Upper Canada" (Ph.D. thesis, University of Toronto, 1984).
[5] Robinson, *Toronto During the French Regime*, pp. 175–76.
[6] E. A. Cruickshank, ed., *The Simcoe Papers*, 5 vols. (Toronto, 1912–31), 1: 339 (Simcoe to Clarke, 1793).
[7] Spelt, *Toronto*, pp. 4–8. See for following environmental aspects.
[8] Ibid., pp. 12–16.
[9] Ibid., pp. 14, 18.
[10] J. M. S. Careless, "Metropolis and Region: The Interplay Between City and Region in Canadian History," *UHR* 78, no. 3 (1979): 108–18.

CHAPTER ONE

[1] M. Q. Innis, ed., *Mrs. Simcoe's Diary* (Toronto, 1965), p. 101.
[2] Ibid., map illustration, following p. 92.
[3] Cruikshank, ed., *Simcoe Papers*, 1: 144 (Simcoe to Dundas, 1792).
[4] E. G. Firth, ed., *The Town of York, 1793–1815* (Toronto, 1962), p.4. (Simcoe to Clarke, 1793).
[5] Cruikshank, *Simcoe Papers*, 2: 57 (Simcoe to Dundas, 1793).
[6] Ibid., 2: 46 (General Order, 26 August 1793).
[7] John André, *William Berczy, Co-Founder of Toronto* (Toronto, 1967), pp. 36–40.
[8] Firth, *1793–1815*, p. 27.
[9] Cruikshank, *Simcoe Papers*, 4: 202 (Circular Letter, 28 February 1796).
[10] Firth, *1793–1815*, p. lxxvii.
[11] Ibid., pp. 114–41.
[12] Ibid., p. lxxvii.
[13] In absence of records, figures are best choices between estimates that range from a clearly low 10,000 for 1791 to a probably high 100,000 for 1812.
[14] Jacob Spelt, *The Urban Development in South-Central Ontario* (Assen, 1955), pp. 27, 29–30.
[15] Firth, *1793–1815*, p. iv.
[16] Ibid., pp. lv–lviii.
[17] Ibid., p. xxxix.
[18] Proclamation of Peter Hunter, 3 November 1803, quoted in Henry Scadding, *Toronto of Old*, ed. F. H. Armstrong (Toronto, 1966), p. 15.
[19] Mary Shortt, "From Douglas to the Black Crook: A History of Toronto Theatre, 1809–1874" (M.A. thesis, Toronto, 1977), pp. 1–4.
[20] John Mitchell, *The Settlement of York County* (n.p., n.d., 1950?), p. 14.
[21] Firth, *1793–1815*, p. lxxvi.
[22] E. W. Hounsom, *Toronto in 1810* (Toronto, 1970), pp. 28–34. See throughout for prewar-built environment.
[23] Firth, *1793–1815*, p. lxxviii.
[24] Ibid.
[25] Ibid., p. xlix.
[26] Ibid., p. lxxxiii.
[27] Ibid., p. xlvi.
[28] Charles W. Humphries, "The Capture of York," *OH* 51, no. 1 (1959): 2–12.
[29] Ibid., pp. 13–21.

[30] Firth, *1793–1815*, p. lxxxviii.

[31] E. G. Firth, *The Town of York, 1815–1834* (Toronto, 1966) p. lxxxii.

[32] T. W. Acheson, "York Commerce in the 1820's," *CHR* 50, no. 4 (1969): 415–16.

[33] Firth, *1815–34*, pp. xxv–xxvi.

[34] G. M. Craig, *Upper Canada: The Formative Years* (Toronto, 1963), pp. 161–62.

[35] Firth, *1815–34*, pp. xxx–xxxi.

[36] G. P. de T. Glazebrook, *The Story of Toronto* (Toronto, 1971), p. 54.

[37] Ibid., p. 59.

[38] E. C. Guillet, *Early Life in Upper Canada* (Toronto, 1933), p. 553.

[39] R. M. Baldwin and J. Baldwin, *The Great Experiment* (Don Mills, 1969), p. 106.

[40] Firth, *1814–34*, p. lxxii.

[41] Ibid., *Census of Canada, 1870–71*, vol. 4 (Ottawa, 1876), p. 86.

[42] Provincial rate is calculated in regression from censuses of 1824 and 1825 (pp. 83–86 in above *Census* volume), weighed with estimates for 1812 and 1820.

[43] See H. I. Cowan, *British Emigration to British North America* (Toronto, 1928; reprinted 1961); Craig, *Upper Canada*, pp. 124–31; and R. L. Jones, *History of Agriculture in Ontario* (Toronto, 1946; reprinted 1977), pp. 50–62.

[44] Firth, *1815–34*, p. lxv.

[45] Ibid., pp. liv–lix.

[46] Scadding, *Toronto of Old*, pp. 221, 279–80.

[47] C. J. Houston and W. J. Smyth, *The Sash Canada Wore* (Toronto, 1980), p. 18.

[48] Firth, *1815–34*, p. xxxvii.

CHAPTER TWO

[1] H. C. Pentland, *Labour and Capital in Canada, 1650–1860* (Toronto, 1981), Table III, p. 82.

[2] Cowan, *British Emigration*, Appendix B, p. 289.

[3] Ibid.

[4] Firth, *1815–34*, p. lxxxii.

[5] G. P. de T. Glazebrook, *History of Transportation in Canada* (Toronto, 1938), p. 142.

[6] Firth, *1815–34*, pp. xxvi–xxvii.

[7] Douglas McCalla, *The Upper Canada Trade, 1834–1872: A Study of the Buchanans' Business* (Toronto, 1979), pp. 20–28.

[8] Firth, *1815–34*, pp. xxvii–xxviii.

[9] *Courier of Upper Canada* (York), 29 September 1832.

[10] Firth, *1815–34*, pp. xxvi–xxvii; F. H. Armstrong, "Toronto in Transition: The Emergence of a City, 1828–1838" (Ph.D. thesis, Toronto 1965), pp. 378–82.

[11] Firth, *1815–34*, pp. xxxii, 66, 80; George Walton, *York Commercial Directory* (York, 1833).

[12] *Colonial Advocate* (York), 4 July 1833.

[13] Armstrong, "Toronto," pp. 418–19.

[14] F. H. Armstrong, "Hugh Richardson," *DCB* (Toronto, 1976), 9: 657.

[15] Armstrong, "Toronto," p. 406.

[16] Firth, *1815–34*, p. xxvii.

[17] Armstrong, "Toronto," p. 482. The firm is now in the Royal Insurance Group.

[18] Ibid., pp. 482–83.

[19] Ibid., p. 455.

[20] Ibid., pp. 458, 468, 471.

[21] Geoffrey Bilson, *A Darkened House: Cholera in Nineteenth Century Canada* (Toronto, 1980), pp. 57, 86.

[22] Firth, *1815–34*, p. lxiv.

[23] Ibid.

[24] Paul Romney, "Voters under the Microscope: A Quantitative Meditation on the Toronto Parliamentary Poll Book of 1836" (Paper given at Canadian Historical Association, 1983), p. 37 and throughout.

[25] Firth, *1815–34*, p. lxx.

[26] Ibid., pp. lxxiv–lxxvii.

[27] Armstrong, "Toronto," pp. 84–97.

[28] Firth, *1815–34*, p. lxxxii.

[29] Armstrong, "Toronto," p. 24. See pages 14–44 for cityscape of 1834.

[30] Eric Arthur, *Toronto, No Mean City* (Toronto, 1964), p. 40.

[31] Firth, *1815–34*, p. xlix.

[32] Arthur, *No Mean City*, p. 248; Graham MacInnes, *Canadian Art* (Toronto, 1950), p. 28.

[33] J. R. Robertson, *Landmarks of Toronto*, 6 vols. (Toronto, 1894–1914), 3: 756; E. C. Guillet, *Toronto from Trading Post to Great City* (Toronto, 1934), pp. 362–63.

[34] Firth, *1815–34*, pp. xxxiii–xxxiv.

[35] Armstrong, "Toronto," pp. 487–89.

[36] Ibid., pp. 106–7.

[37] Ibid., pp. 118–32, 149–56, 171–73. See also P. Romney, "William Lyon Mackenzie as Mayor of Toronto", *CHR* 56, no. 4 (1975): 416–36.

[38] Armstrong, "Toronto," pp. 192–96, 201–6; TCA, Journals of Council, 23 June 1835.

[39] *Courier of Upper Canada*, 14 January 1836.

[40] TCA, Minutes of Council, 19 January 1837; R. B. Splane, *Social Welfare in Ontario, 1791–1893* (Toronto, 1965), pp. 70–73.

[41] Armstrong, "Toronto," pp. 236–37; TCA, Journals of Council, 12 January 1838.

[42] Craig, *Upper Canada*, p. 243.

[43] Ibid., pp. 244–47.

44 Armstrong, "Toronto," pp. 272–73.

45 G. F. G. Stanley, *Canada's Soldiers, 1604–1954* (Toronto, 1954), pp. 202–3.

46 J. M. S. Careless, "James Lesslie," *DCB* (Toronto, 1982), 11: 517.

47 Armstrong, "Toronto," pp. 261, 274–75.

48 Ibid., pp. 276–79.

49 Cowan, *British Emigration,* Appendix B, p. 289.

50 *Patriot* (Toronto), 9 and 12 February 1841; B. D. Dyster, "Toronto 1840–1860" (Ph.D. thesis, Toronto, 1970), pp. 9–12.

51 J. M. S. Careless, *The Union of the Canadas, 1841–1857* (Toronto, 1967), p. 28.

52 J. E. Middleton, *The Municipality of Toronto,* 3 vols. (Toronto, 1923), 1: 228.

53 TCA, Report of the Committee on Fire, Gas and Water, 1847.

54 Arthur, *No Mean City,* p. 79.

55 R. H. Bonnycastle, *The Canadas in 1841,* 2 vols. (London, 1842), 1: 107–8.

56 Quoted in Peter Baskerville, "Donald Bethune's Steamboat Business," *OH* 67, no. 3 (1975): 141.

57 Quoted in Middleton, *Municipality of Toronto,* 2: 679 (Dickens to John Foster, 1842).

58 *Patriot,* 3 April 1841.

59 G. Brown, *Toronto City and Home District Directory* (Toronto, 1846).

60 Cowan, *British Emigration,* Appendix B; Dyster, "Toronto 1840–1860," pp. 36–37.

61 Dyster, "Toronto 1840–1860," pp. 36–37.

62 Spelt, *Urban Development,* pp. 78–79; Dyster, "Toronto 1840–1860," pp. 23–24.

63 M. L. Smith, ed., *Young Mr. Smith in Upper Canada* (Toronto, 1980), pp. 110–11.

CHAPTER THREE

1 Smith, *Young Mr. Smith,* pp. 11–12.

2 Norman Macdonald, *Canada: Immigration and Colonization, 1841–1903* (Toronto, 1966), p. 61.

3 Heather MacDougall, "Health Is Wealth: Development of Public Health Activity in Toronto, 1834–1890" (Ph.D. thesis, Toronto, 1981), pp. 59–64.

4 *British Colonist* (Toronto), 7 September 1847.

5 Ibid., 2 November 1847.

6 Ibid.

7 PAO, Toronto City Council Papers, 1834–96, Jarvis to Boulton, 20 August 1847.

8 *British Colonist,* 31 August 1847.

9 Ibid., 8 February 1848.

10 Ibid., October 23, 1849; Bilson, *Darkened House,* p. 128

11 MacDougall, "Health Is Wealth," p. 74.

12 Cowan, *British Emigration,* Appendix B, p. 289.

13 *Census of the Canadas, 1851–52* (Quebec, 1853), vol. 1, pp. 30–31.

14 Ibid., pp. 66–67.

15 *Census of the Canadas, 1860–61* (Quebec, 1864), vol. 1, pp. 256–57.

16 J. M. S. Careless, *Brown of the Globe* (Toronto, 1959), vol. 1, pp. 123–38; Dyster, "Toronto, 1840–1860," pp. 361–67, 372, 449–59.

17 M. W. Nicolson, "The Other Toronto: Irish Catholics in a Victorian City, 1850–1900," to be published in R. F. Harney, ed., "*Meeting-Place: Peoples and Neighbourhoods of Toronto*" (Toronto, expected 1984).

18 Ibid., pp. 23–26.

19 I. C. Pemberton, "The Anti-Slavery Society of Canada" (M.A. thesis, Toronto, 1967), especially pp. 17–75, 113–39.

20 Nicolson, "The Other Toronto," pp. 24–27.

21 Ibid., pp. 32–38.

22 See Table VI.

23 G. W. Quinn, "Impact of European Immigration Upon the Elementary Schools of Central Toronto 1815–1915" (M.A. thesis, Toronto, 1968), Tables 5, 6.

24 *Census of Canada, 1870–71* (Ottawa, 1873), vol. 1, pp. 350–51.

25 Ibid., pp. 114–17.

26 Dyster, "Toronto, 1840–1860," p. 20.

27 C. C. Taylor, *Toronto "Called Back" from 1886 to 1850* (Toronto, 1886), Tables of Trade, p. 236.

28 *Globe* (Toronto), 5 February 1853.

29 Pentland, *Labour and Capital,* pp. 187–88.

30 *Globe,* 2 July 1853, 6 June 1854. See also S. F. Zerker, *The Rise and Fall of the Toronto Typographical Union* (Toronto, 1982), pp. 31–37, 44–47; and G. S. Kealey, *Toronto Workers Respond to Industrial Capitalism, 1867–1892* (Toronto, 1980), for other skilled trades reactions in the 1850s; e.g., shoemakers (pp. 38–39) and tailors' strike of 1852 (pp. 39–40).

31 Unskilled labour rates rose 40 per cent, e.g., largely due to railway demands: W. T. Easterbrook and H. G. J. Aitken, *Canadian Economic History* (Toronto, 1956), p. 311.

32 Kealey, *Toronto Workers,* pp. 66, 77.

33 Based on examination of shipment notices, market reports and store advertisements in Toronto press for 1850–51, plus hinterland transport services recorded, e.g., in W. H. Smith, *Canada Past, Present and Future,* 2 vols. (Toronto, 1851).

34 *Globe,* 19 March 1860.

35 Spelt, *Toronto,* pp. 24–31.

36 Careless, *Brown,* 1: 229–33.

37 Spelt, *Urban Development,* pp. 121–22.

38 Ibid., pp. 100–1.

39 *Globe*, 21 December 1855.

40 Spelt, *Urban Development*, p. 124. D. McCalla, "The Decline of Hamilton as a Wholesale Centre," *OH* 65, no. 4 (1973): 250–51.

41 Michael Bliss, "John Macdonald," *DCB*, 11: 551–52.

42 D. McCalla, "The Commercial Politics of the Toronto Board of Trade, 1850–1860," *CHR* 50, no. 1, (1969): 51–67.

43 Dyster, "Toronto, 1840–1860," pp. 277–79. See also for insurance and loan companies, pages 280–92.

44 R. D. Smith, "The Northern Railway: Its Origins and Construction," *OH* 48, no. 1 (1956): 26–27.

45 *Globe*, 12 February 1866. Note Gzowski and Macpherson also pushed the abortive cotton mill project: see TCA, Minutes of City Council, 1861, Appendix 27; 1864, Appendix 105.

46 R. D. Smith, "The Northern Railway," pp. 31–32.

47 Gene Allen, "Competition and Consolidation in the Toronto Wholesale Trade" (Research paper, University of Toronto, 1862), pp. 9–11.

48 Province of Canada, *Sessional Papers*, 1860, 1861, Tables of Trade; Dominion of Canada, *Sessional Papers*, 1870, 1871, Tables of Trade.

49 McCalla, "Board of Trade," pp. 58–59.

50 Dyster, "Toronto, 1840–1860," pp. 271–76.

51 D. C. Masters, "Toronto vs. Montreal: The Struggle for Financial Hegemony, 1860–75," *CHR* 12, no. 2 (1944): 133–46.

52 Malcolm Davidson, "The Port of Toronto, 1850–1860" (Research paper, University of Toronto, 1982), pp. 31–36.

53 TCA, Statutes specially relating to the City of Toronto, pp. 243–47.

54 Robertson, *Landmarks*, 3: 322–45.

55 F. H. Armstrong, "The First Great Fire of Toronto," *OH* 53, no. 1 (1961): 201–21.

56 See *Globe*, "Pictorial Supplement," 13 December 1856, for descriptions of these buildings. See also Arthur, *No Mean City*, for buildings named below.

57 L. H. Pursley, *Street Railways in Toronto* (Los Angeles, 1958), pp. 5–7.

58 PAC, Pamphlet 1016, *Esplanade Contract*, Public letter, 1855, pp. 1–8.

59 For the following account of this expansion of the Fifies and Sixties, see ibid., especially pp. 164–69; P. G. Goheen, *Victorian Toronto, 1850–1900* (Chicago, 1970), especially pp. 53–54, 81–90, 115–55. See also Spelt, *Toronto*, pp. 41–47; Robertson, *Landmarks*; and W. C. F. Caverhill, *Toronto City Directory, 1859–60* (Toronto, n.d.).

60 Dyster, "Toronto, 1840–1860," pp. 157, 168–69.

61 Spelt, *Toronto*, pp. 42–43.

62 Goheen, *Victorian Toronto*, pp. 125–27.

63 Quoted in Taylor, *Toronto "Called Back,"* p. 161.

64 Spelt, *Toronto*, p. 47.

65 The city received Crown licence to occupy the land for leasing in 1848, though did not gain complete control and begin letting private lots until 1867.

66 Glazebrook, *Story of Toronto*, p. 120.

67 Ibid., pp. 120–21.

68 Armstrong, "Rebuilding of Toronto," pp. 248–49.

69 J. C. E. Williams, "The Growth of the Toronto Police Force, 1793–1875" (Research paper, University of Toronto, 1981), p. 9.

70 J. Scadding and J. C. Dent, *Toronto, Past and Present* (Toronto, 1884), p. 213.

71 Williams, "Growth," p. 12; TCA, Council Minutes, 2 April 1855.

72 Williams, "Growth," pp. 24–28, 31–34, 38–40.

73 Splane, *Social Welfare*, pp. 72–73, 75, 76–77, 80.

74 Ibid., pp. 223–24, 226–27.

75 *Globe*, 11 December 1851.

76 H. M. Cochrane, ed., *Centennial Story: The Board of Education for the City of Toronto* (Toronto, 1950), pp. 35–38, 42–43, 57–58, 143; Quinn, "Impact," pp. 32–35.

77 MacDougall, "Health Is Wealth," pp. 77–84, 97–106, 120–25.

78 TCA, Proceedings of the Standing Committee on Fire, Water and Gas in Connection with the Supply of Water to the City, 1854.

79 Middleton, *Municipality of Toronto*, 1: 261.

80 TCA, Public Works Department, "Outline History of the Roads in Toronto."

81 Dyster, "Toronto, 1840–1860," pp. 343–44.

82 Ibid., pp. 236–37.

83 Ibid., pp. 345–50.

84 Ibid., throughout, but especially pp. 454–59.

85 Careless, *Brown*, 1: 229, 233, 236–37.

86 Ibid., 1: 177; 2: 5, 41, 68.

87 Ibid., 1: 234–36, 314–22; 2: 247–51.

88 D. C. Masters, *The Rise of Toronto, 1850–1890* (Toronto, 1947), p. 80.

89 *Globe* 1 August 1856.

90 Careless, *Brown*, 2: 161.

91 *Leader* (Toronto), 2 July 1867.

92 C. S. Stacey, "Fenianism and the Rise of National Feeling in Canada at the Time of Confederation," *CHR* 12, no. 3 (1931): 250–52; G. T. Denison, *The Fenian Raid on Fort Erie* (Toronto, 1866), Appendix B.

93 Kane did 100 pictures for Allan by 1856 for $20,000. See *DCB*, 10: 392.

94 Shortt, "From Douglas to the Black Crook."

CHAPTER FOUR

1 Goheen, *Victorian Toronto*, pp. 154–55, 201–6, 219–22. Goheen effectively closes this period of industrialization at 1899. I prefer to end it at 1895, to distinguish a new phase emerging thereafter which brought a

high cycle of world prosperity, the settling of a new western Canadian hinterland, and the rise of financial metropolitanism in Toronto on a scale not witnessed in the phase preceding, stamped as that was much more by industrial developments. Of course the city's industrial growth by no means failed to move onward after 1895, and in this respect the choice of 1899, 1900 or 1914 would equally not mark an end.

2 See Table V. Remember that census records may evince discrepancies. The census of 1891 gives 144,023 for Toronto's total population (1: 370) but the 1891 count was revised in the census of 1901 to 181,216 (1: 22). The revised figure also relates better to the city's own assessment count for 1891, 167,439 (TCA, Statistical Book), and covered annexed areas.

3 See Table I. Again one must warn about discrepancies. Goheen (p. 66) gives 497 industrial units for 1871 (taken from *Census of 1871*, 3: 290–445); Kealey (*Toronto Workers*, p. 32) lists 561. But here both record variants and questions of evaluation arise — e.g., should 8 "painters and glaziers" then employing 36 men and 3 boys in Toronto (*Census of 1871*, 3: 376) be included under manufacturing firms? Accordingly, my total comes best to 530.

4 See Table I.

5 *Globe*, 12 February 1866. See also Michael Bliss, *A Canadian Millionaire ... Sir Joseph Flavelle, Bart, 1858–1938* (Toronto, 1978), p. 52.

6 Kealey, *Toronto Workers*, pp. 25, 27, 30.

7 Ibid., pp. 24–30.

8 *Encyclopedia of Music in Canada* (Toronto, 1981), pp. 423–24.

9 J. M. Gilmour, *Spatial Evolution of Manufacturing: Southern Ontario, 1851–1891* (Toronto, 1972), pp. 32–34, 89–90, 99–100, 110–11; Jane Jacobs, *The Economy of Cities* (Toronto, 1970), pp. 146–62; Taylor, *Toronto "Called Back,"* p. 247.

10 Gene Allen, "Merchants and Manufacturers in Toronto, 1865–1900" (Research paper, York University, 1979), pp. 15–18, 35–36, 40–68, 84–90.

11 Masters, *Rise of Toronto*, p. 63.

12 Ibid., p. 106.

13 *Monetary Times* (Toronto), 2 February 1877.

14 J. E. MacNab, "Toronto's Industrial Growth to 1891," *OH* 47, no. 2 (1955): 74.

15 Ibid., p. 73.

16 Kealey, *Toronto Workers*, pp. 30–31.

17 MacNab, "Toronto's Industrial Growth," p. 73; Masters, *Rise of Toronto*, p. 175.

18 Kealey, *Toronto Workers*, p. 30.

19 Ibid., p. 32.

20 Telephones, too, were stringing wires and poles by then.

21 MacNab, "Toronto's Industrial Growth," p. 75.

22 Carlie Oreskovich, *Sir Henry Pellatt: The King of Casa Loma* (Toronto, 1982), pp. 52–53.

23 Taylor, *Toronto "Called Back,"* pp. 249–53, 402–7.

24 Kealey, *Toronto Workers*, p. 317.

25 Taylor, *Toronto "Called Back,"* pp. 324–25; *Globe*, 16 May 1885.

26 Allen, "Competition and Consolidation," p. 24.

27 Ibid., pp. 35–39, 45.

28 *Toronto Board of Trade, Annual Report, 1886* (Toronto, 1887), p. 10; *Board of Trade Report for 1895* (Toronto, 1896), pp. 10, 45; Taylor, *Toronto "Called Back,"* p. 236.

29 Allen, "Competition and Consolidation," p. 43; *Monetary Times*, 5 September 1890.

30 Allen, "Competition and Consolidation," p. 33.

31 Taylor, *Toronto "Called Back,"* p. 310.

32 Bliss, *Flavelle*, p. 63.

33 Brenda K. Newell, "Toronto's Retail Trade, 1869–1914" (Research paper, University of Toronto, 1981), p. 6.

34 Ibid., pp. 5–8.

35 Bliss, *Flavelle*, p. 63.

36 Newell, "Toronto's Retail Trade," p. 7.

37 Ibid., p. 14.

38 Ibid., p. 16.

39 Bliss, *Flavelle*, pp. 63–64.

40 On banking growth, see R. C. McIvor, *Canadian Banking and Fiscal Development* (Toronto, 1958); E. P. Neufeld, *Money and Banking in Canada* (Toronto, 1964); Victor Ross, *A History of the Canadian Bank of Commerce*, 2 vols. (Toronto, 1920–22).

41 *Monetary Times*, 30 July 1880; 25 July 1890.

42 Masters, *Rise of Toronto*, p. 181.

43 Ibid., pp. 122, 183.

44 Ibid., p. 182.

45 For membership on boards of directors of Toronto banks, finance and insurance companies, see yearly Toronto City Directories for the period.

46 *Globe*, 24 January 1877; 4 May 1885.

47 See chapter 5.

48 T. F. McIlwraith, "George Laidlaw," *DCB* (1972), 10: 481–83.

49 R. M. Stamp, "J. D. Edgar and the Pacific Junction Railway," *OH* 55, no. 3 (1963): 119–30.

50 Masters, *Rise of Toronto*, p. 173.

51 Paul Marsden, "The Development of Toronto Harbour, 1850–1911" (Research paper, University of Toronto, 1982), pp. 22–23, 26.

52 Ibid., pp. 8, 24.

53 Ibid., pp. 28, 30.

54 See F. N. Mellen, "The Development of the Toronto Waterfront during the Railway Expansion Era, 1850–1912" (Ph.D. thesis, Toronto, 1976).

55 Goheen, *Victorian Toronto*, p. 77.

56 See Table VI. *Census of 1891*, 1: 348–49.

[57] Heather MacDougall, "Public Health in Toronto's Municipal Politics, 1883–90," *Bulletin of the History of Medicine* (Baltimore, 1981) 55: 186–202.

[58] Kealey, *Toronto Workers*, p. 115.

[59] Ibid., pp. 116–17.

[60] Houston and Smyth, *Sash Canada Wore*, pp. 157–59; Dyster, "Toronto, 1840–1860."

[61] Masters, *Rise of Toronto*, p. 193.

[62] Note Orangeism was in close support of imperialism: Houston and Smyth, *Sash Canada Wore*, pp. 142–45.

[63] *Globe*, 15 September 1882.

[64] TCA, Report No. 23 of Committee on Water Works, 13 September 1881.

[65] See TCA, "List of Annexations," and "Development of the Ward System."

[66] See Stephen Speisman, "The Development of Annexations in Toronto to the Mid-1920's" (Research paper, University of Toronto, 1969).

[67] Larratt Smith Diaries, TPL.

[68] See Toronto City Directories for the period.

[69] The term is Goldwin Smith's in his letter to Sir J. A. Macdonald, 27 March 1880, quoted in Careless, *Brown*, 2: 367.

[70] Bliss, *Flavelle*, p. 88.

[71] See Kealey, *Toronto Workers*, pp. 128–35; Zerker, *Typographical Union*, pp. 78–88.

[72] "Run down" was the assessment of Sir J. A. Macdonald, who was then engaged in replacing the waning *Leader* with the new *Mail* as the Conservative Toronto organ: D. G. Creighton, *John A. Macdonald* (Toronto, 1955), vol. 2, pp. 116, 124.

[73] Bernard Ostry, "Conservatives, Liberals and Labour in the 1870s," *CHR* 41, no. 2 (1960): 93–120.

[74] Kealey, *Toronto Workers*, p. 177.

[75] Ibid., p. 180.

[76] Ibid., pp. 202–4.

[77] Ibid., pp. 237–51.

[78] Middleton, *Municipality of Toronto*, 2: 562.

[79] Kealey, *Toronto Workers*, pp. 280–88.

[80] Goheen, *Victorian Toronto*, pp. 219–20.

[81] See Arthur, *No Mean City*, and also L. B. Martyn, *The Face of Early Toronto, 1793–1936* (Sutton West, 1982), which is further useful for the detailed maps of streets and buildings it reproduces from Goad's 1884 insurance atlas of Toronto.

[82] Arthur, *No Mean City*, pp. 209–18.

[83] Spelt, *Toronto*, p. 47.

[84] Goheen, *Victorian Toronto*, pp. 199–201.

[85] Electric cars with a between-rail pick-up were used on this Exhibition line of the Toronto Electric Light Company in 1884; but in 1885, overhead *trolley* pick-ups were substituted, thus introducing the effective trolley street-car model to Toronto. See Pursley, *Street Railways of Toronto*, p. 15.

[86] Ibid., p. 7.

[87] Ibid., pp. 7–11.

[88] Goheen, *Victorian Toronto*, pp. 137, 154–55, 179–84.

[89] See Arthur, *No Mean City*, chap. 5.

[90] Toronto's Semi-Centennial of 1884 is recorded in detail in Scadding and Dent, *Toronto, Past and Present*.

[91] Masters, *Rise of Toronto*, pp. 199–200.

[92] Cochrane, *Centennial Story: Board of Education*, pp. 65–89.

[93] *Encyclopedia of Music in Canada*, pp. 604, 917–18, 921.

[94] William Dendy, *Lost Toronto* (Toronto, 1978), p. 100.

[95] TCA, "Statistical Book"; Middleton, *Municipality of Toronto*, 1: 313.

[96] A case in point is Mayor Francis Medcalf. See *DCB*, 10: 504. See also for civic leaders of period, V. L. Russell, *Mayors of Toronto, 1834–1899* (Erin, Ont., 1982).

[97] Desmond Morton, *Mayor Howland: The Citizens' Candidate* (Toronto, 1973), p. 32.

[98] Ibid., p. 34

[99] Ibid., p. 36. See for following account of Howland's mayoralty, pages 40–86.

[100] Christopher Armstrong and H. V. Nelles, *The Revenge of the Methodist Bicycle Company, 1888–1897* (Toronto, 1977), p. 15.

[101] Ibid., pp. 15–18, 20–26.

[102] Ibid., pp. 35–48.

[103] Elwood Jones and Douglas McCalla, "Toronto Waterworks, 1840–77," *CHR* 60, no. 3 (1979): 313–17, 321–22.

[104] Ibid., p. 320.

[105] Ibid.

[106] *Globe*, 18 March 1882.

[107] Middleton, *Municipality of Toronto*, 1: 341, 344.

[108] MacDougall, "Health Is Wealth," chaps. 6, 7, 8.

[109] Ibid., chaps. 9, 10.

[110] Douglas Soga, "Poverty in Toronto, 1870–1901" (Research paper, University of Toronto, 1981), p. 26.

[111] Ibid., p. 17.

[112] Middleton, *Municipality of Toronto*, 2: 638.

[113] Soga, "Poverty," p. 3; James Pitsula, "The Emergence of Social Work in Toronto," *Journal of Canadian Studies* 4, no. 1 (1979): 38–39.

[114] Ibid., p. 14.

[115] Ibid., p. 24.

[116] TCA, *Annual Report of the City Engineer*, 1884.

[117] TCA, "Outline History of the Roads of Toronto."

[118] This term was commonly applied to Toronto at least from the 1880s: e.g., "Canada's rightly named 'Queen City,'" *Toronto Illustrated* (n.a., Toronto, 1893), p. 17.

CHAPTER FIVE

1 See Table V.

2 R.C. Brown and Ramsay Cook, *Canada, 1896–1921* (Toronto, 1974), pp. 91–94; T. W. Acheson, "The Social Origins of Canadian Industrialism" (Ph.D. thesis, Toronto, 1971), pp. 240–48, 252–53, 405–11; Michael Bliss, *A Living Profit* (Toronto, 1974), p. 11.

3 Bliss, *Flavelle*, p. 58.

4 Ross, *Bank of Commerce*, pp. 334–62.

5 *Monetary Times*, vol. 58, *Annual Review*, January 1915.

6 *Canada Year Book for 1915* (Ottawa, 1916), p. 575.

7 See the *Monetary Times Review* for 1915 for the following data on bank branches.

8 Ibid., for 1908–14; see Table XI for the whole era. Bank clearing-house operations began at Toronto in 1891.

9 See Bliss, *Flavelle*, pp. 54–62 for data in this paragraph.

10 Ibid., pp. 65–66, 68–70 for paragraph following.

11 Ibid., pp. 67, 74, 184; Acheson, "Industrialism," pp. 249–51. The car, the Russell, was first offered in 1905.

12 Bliss, *Flavelle*, pp. 50–51.

13 Oreskovich, *King of Casa Loma*, pp. 52–56. On Nicholls, see Acheson, "Industrialism," pp. 228–29

14 Bliss, *Flavelle*, pp. 58, 61.

15 Newell, "Toronto's Retail Trade," pp. 18, 25–26, 31–32.

16 See Mellen, "Toronto Waterfront," p. 238.

17 Acheson, "Industrialism," pp. 317–21, 348–53, 363–64.

18 Newell, "Toronto's Retail Trade," p. 30; *Toronto, Canada's Queen City* (n.a., Toronto, 1912), n.p.

19 Bliss, *Flavelle*, pp. 62–64.

20 See Table I.

21 *Fifth Census of Canada, 1911* (Ottawa, 1913), 3: 353.

22 Ibid., 2: xiii.

23 Ibid. (1915), 6: 262–74. Note this is a tabulation by "occupations," which gives those in *specific* manufacturing pursuits at Toronto just at some 59,000, though the *total* census figure given elsewhere for all those employed in Toronto's manufacturing sector is over 65,000, as stated above.

24 Ibid.

25 Spelt, *Urban Development*, p. 168.

26 Merrill Denison, *The People's Power* (Toronto, 1960), p. 62.

27 Ibid., pp. 27–64.

28 E. M. Ashworth *Toronto Hydro Recollections* (Toronto, 1955), pp. 23–26.

29 Spelt, *Toronto*, p. 74.

30 Marsden, "Toronto Harbour," pp. 26–28.

31 Ibid., pp. 28–29.

32 *Telegram* (Toronto), 31 December 1910.

33 Marsden, "Toronto Harbour," p. 30.

34 *Census of 1901*, 1: 468–69; *Census of 1911*, 2: 403–4. These are tabulations by "birthplaces" which would thus cover older immigrants at Toronto as well as those who entered in the period. But in any case, the English birthplace component shows a strong, consistent lead in all the city's census districts.

35 See Table VIII.

36 *Census of 1911*, 2: 426.

37 See Table VIII.

38 Ibid.

39 Ibid.

40 J. S. Woodsworth, *Strangers Within Our Gates* (Toronto, 1909), p. 256.

41 Janet Evans, "The Toronto Clergy and the Immigrant, 1900–1914" (Research paper, University of Toronto, 1972), pp. 4–20.

42 See Robert Harney and Harold Troper, *Immigrants: A Portrait of the Urban Experience* (Toronto, 1975), for this paragraph, throughout.

43 There was a particularly large 1907 intake of urbanized British immigrants, rousing concern over their potential labour radicalism: Evans, "Toronto Clergy," p. 3 and n. 4.

44 See Table VI.

45 See Table VII.

46 See Table II.

47 *Census of 1911*, 2: 426.

48 See Table V.

49 TCA, Toronto Annexations; Speisman, "Development of Annexations"; see also Map 6.

50 Oreskovich, *King of Casa Loma*, pp. 33–37, 91–96, 107–17.

51 Janet Noel, "Some Aspects of Women's Work in Victorian Toronto" (Research paper, University of Toronto, 1975), pp. 16–45.

52 M. I. Lawrence, ed., *History: The School for Nurses, Toronto General Hospital* (Toronto, 1931), p. 24.

53 Middleton, *Municipality of Toronto*, 2: 575.

54 C. L. Cleverdon, *The Woman Suffrage Movement in Canada* (Toronto, 1974), p. 22.

55 Ibid., p. 26.

56 Ibid., pp. 20–39.

57 *Census of 1891*, 1: 174; *Census of 1911*, 1: 533.

58 Robertson, *Landmarks*, vol. 4.

59 *Census of 1911*, 1: 533.

60 *Centennial Story*, p. 91. See also for this paragraph, pp. 92, 98, 102–4, 149–50.

61 *Annual Report of the Minister of Education, Province of Ontario, 1914* (Toronto, 1914), tables. See also S. E. Houston, "The 'Waifs and Strays' of a Victorian

City," in Joy Parr, *Childhood and Family in Canadian History* (Toronto, 1982), pp. 135–41.

62 Weekly wages calculations for 14 major Toronto industries in Joy Santink, "The Growth of Trade Unions and Manufacturing in Toronto, 1880–1910" (Research paper, University of Toronto, 1977), uses a base of 1901 to reach a Toronto average of between $5 and $6 for a 6-day week then (pp. 43–45). See Ontario Bureau of Labour, *Annual Report*, 1912, which shows weekly rates of $15 and over in 1911–12 for skilled trades (but $6 to $8 for garment workers); yet otherwise "wages for many were abysmally low for nearly the whole period" (Santink, p. 45). Michael Piva asserts that real wages fell from 10% to 15% between 1902 and 1920: *The Condition of the Working Class in Toronto, 1900–1921* (Ottawa, 1979), p. 43.

63 Santink, p. 19.

64 G. H. Homel, "James Simpson and the Origins of Canadian Social Democracy" (Ph.D. thesis, Toronto, 1978), pp. 152–54, 343–51, 587–93.

65 Irving Abella, *The Canadian Labour Movement, 1902–1960* (Ottawa, 1975), pp. 4–5.

66 Middleton, *Municipality of Toronto*, 2: 567. Goldwin Smith, who had donated generously, was guest of honour at the Temple's opening.

67 Homel, "James Simpson."

68 Bureau of Municipal Research, *What Is the Ward Going to Do with Toronto?* (Toronto, 1918), pp. 31–56.

69 Linda Morris, "A Gentleman's Guide to the Sporting Life in Toronto: Prostitution between 1886 and 1910" (Research paper, University of Toronto, 1978), pp. 114–15.

70 Bliss, *Flavelle*, 176–77.

71 K. A. Jordan, *Sir Edmund Walker, Print Collector* (Toronto, 1974), pp. 22.

72 William Colgate, *Canadian Art: Its Origin and Development* (Toronto, 1943), p. 45.

73 *Encyclopedia of Music in Canada*, p. 918.

74 Ibid., pp. 918, 924.

75 Bliss, *Flavelle*, pp. 149–50, 156–58, 171–73, 182.

76 *Canada's Queen City* (1912?), n.p.

77 See Arthur, *No Mean City*, pp. 230–31, and Douglas Richardson, ed., *Beaux Arts Toronto* (Toronto, 1973), pp. 1–23, for design of buildings in following two paragraphs.

78 Middleton, *Municipality of Toronto*, 1: 478–80.

79 *Canada's Queen City*, n.p.

80 J. C. Weaver, "The Modern City Realized: Toronto Civic Affairs, 1880–1915," in A. F. J. Artibise and G. A. Stelter, *The Usable Urban Past* (Toronto, 1979), pp. 39–42.

81 See Table X.

82 Spelt, *Toronto*, p. 102; K. M. Campbell, "Changing Residential Patterns in Toronto, 1880–1910" (M.A. thesis, University of Toronto, 1971).

83 Shirley Spragge, "A Confluence of Interest: Housing Reform in Toronto, 1900–1920," in Artibise and Stelter, *Urban Past*, pp. 248–49.

84 Ibid., pp. 250–51.

85 Ibid., pp. 258–59.

86 Glazebrook, *Story of Toronto*, pp. 181–82; J. F. Due, *The Intercity Electric Railway Industry in Canada* (Toronto, 1966), p. 7.

87 Pursley, *Street Railways of Toronto*, p. 42; Marion Brown, "Toronto Street Railways, 1891–1914" (Research paper, University of Toronto, 1981), p. 36.

88 For this paragraph see Armstrong and Nelles, *Methodist Bicycle Company*, pp. 144–68; Homel, "James Simpson," pp. 34–40.

89 *Mail and Empire* (Toronto), 12 May 1897.

90 Homel, "James Simpson," pp. 571–78.

91 M. J. Doucet, "Mass Transit and the Failure of Public Ownership: The Case of Toronto," *UHR* 77, no. 3 (1978): 6–12.

92 Ibid., pp. 12–14.

93 Brown, "Toronto Street Railways," pp. 29–34, 39, 43.

94 Ibid., p. 46.

95 *Report to the Civic Transportation Committee* (Toronto, 1915), p. 34.

96 For this paragraph, see F. H. Armstrong, "The Second Great Fire of Toronto, 19–20 April, 1904," *OH* 70, no. 1 (1978): 19–32.

97 James Mansergh, *The Water Supply of the City of Toronto* (London, 1896).

98 *Canada's Queen City*, n.p.

99 P. A. Bator, "Saving Lives on the Wholesale Plan: Public Health Reform in the City of Toronto, 1900 to 1930" (Ph.D. thesis, Toronto, 1979).

100 TCA, *Board of Health, Annual Report*, 1896, 1914.

101 *Canada's Queen City*, n.p.

102 Bliss, *Flavelle*, pp. 160–61, 177, 205–7.

103 Soga, "Poverty," pp. 37–38.

104 Piva, *Condition of the Working Class*, p. xii.

105 A. Jones and Leonard Rutman, *In the Children's Aid: J. J. Kelso and Child Welfare in Ontario* (Toronto, 1981).

106 *Fifth Annual Report, Children's Aid Society of Toronto* (Toronto, 1909), p. 5.

107 Ibid., pp. 72–74.

108 *Canada's Queen City*, n.p. The Industrial Exhibition was renamed the Canadian National Exhibition in 1904.

109 Middleton, *Municipality of Toronto*, 1: 339, 357, 373. But $34 million of this debt was "revenue-producing," e.g., in Toronto Hydro System, Exhibition, streetcars, etc.

110 Paul Rutherford, "Tomorrow's Metropolis: The Urban Reform Movement in Canada, 1880–1920," in G. A. Stelter, and A. F. J. Artibise, *The Canadian City* (Toronto, 1977), pp. 368–83. See also J. C. Weaver, "Tomorrow's Metropolis Revisited," in idem, pp. 393–409, which notes

longer-term reform impulses.

111 Rutherford, "Tomorrow's Metropolis," p. 372.

112 Ibid., pp. 369, 382.

113 J. C. Weaver, "The Meaning of Municipal Reform: Toronto, 1895," OH 66, no. 2 (1974): 89–100.

114 TCA, "Growth of the Ward System," typescript.

115 On Beaty's career, see J. C. Weaver, "The Modern City Realized: Toronto Civic Affairs, 1880-1915," in Artibise and Stelter, Usable Urban Past, pp. 46–48.

116 Russell, Mayors of Toronto, pp. 117–35; TCA, information files on mayors. Fleming definitely lost his popular title after becoming general manager of the streetcar company in 1904.

117 Weaver, "Modern City Realized" and "Tomorrow's Metropolis Revisited." See also Christopher Armstrong and H. V. Nelles, "The Great Fight for Clean Government," UHR 77, no. 2 (1976): 50-66.

118 P. W. Moores, "Zoning and Planning: The Toronto Experience, 1904-1970," in Artibise and Stelter, Usable Urban Past, p. 320.

119 Ibid., p. 322.

120 Ibid., pp. 324–25.

121 Ibid., p. 325.

122 Middleton, Municipality of Toronto, 1: 388–89.

123 Katherine Hale, Toronto: Romance of a Great City (Toronto, 1956), p. 192.

124 Ibid. See also H. Groves, Toronto Does Her "Bit" (Toronto, 1918), p. 34.

125 Middleton, Municipality of Toronto, 1: 393.

126 Abella, Canadian Labour Movement, p. 8.

127 Ibid.

128 Middleton, Municipality of Toronto, 1: 397.

129 Canada Year Book, 1919, p. 522.

130 Bliss, Flavelle, p. 318.

131 Ibid., pp. 319–62.

Suggestions for Further Reading and Research

The following outline presents merely a selection from a wide range of sources extant on Toronto to 1918. Much remains to be done on specific topics of research, however, and some valuable material is yet only found in unpublished theses and research papers. Research papers cited in the notes above derived from seminars at the Univerity of Toronto on Ontario regional and urban development, and are accessible for consultation through this author. Otherwise, the sources are available through libraries or particular repositories noted. Each specific item already indicated in the notes is not necessarily included in the selection that follows, but other items not cited are listed, because of their usefulness for further reading.

Bibliographic and Research Materials

General finding aids for published or unpublished sources on Toronto are: Alan Artibise and Gilbert Stelter, *Canada's Urban Past: A Bibliography to 1980 and a Guide to Canadian Urban Studies* (Vancouver, 1981); the Public Archives of Canada (PAC), *Union List of Manuscripts in Canadian Repositories*, 2 vols. (Ottawa, 1975, with supplements, 1976, 1979); and Olga Bishop, *Bibliography of Ontario History, 1867–1976*, 2 vols. (Toronto, 1980). Major documentary holdings on Toronto exist at the Metropolitan Toronto Public Library, the City of Toronto Archives, the Public Archives of Ontario and the PAC. And special holdings are also found in Toronto at repositories that range from the Harbour Commission and Transit Commission to the Consumers' Gas Company, the Educational Centre Archives to the United Church Archives, or those of the Anglican and Roman Catholic dioceses. See also: J. Lemon and J. Simmons, "A Guide to Data on 19th Century Toronto," xeroxed typescript (Department of Geography, University of Toronto, n.d.).

Research materials further include reports of the Board of Trade, of police authorities or social and health agencies; the official censuses; statistical returns in appendices to parliamentary journals (sessional papers); city directories; land and legal documents; company or union records; and still more. Newspapers particularly must be added — Toronto had a wealth of these to 1918. Apart from the early papers like the *Colonial Advocate, Gazette* or *Patriot*, the *Globe* bulks large from the mid-1840s; soon followed by the *Leader* (1852–78), then by the *Mail* or *Telegram* in the Seventies, and by the *World* or *Star* later in the century. Such a sampling of Toronto's popular journals also omits its special-interest literary, religious or social publications, labour or business papers, in which last category the *Monetary Times* (from 1867) can be singled out. For finding aids to this abundant source, see National Library of Canada, *Union List of Canadian Newspapers Held by Canadian Libraries* (Ottawa, 1977), and Edith Firth, *Early Toronto Newspapers, 1793–1867* (Toronto, 1961).

General Works

While there are numerous anecdotal, amateur or journalistic accounts dealing with Toronto before 1918, some of which have lasting worth, the following professional studies that cover all or part of the period merit particular attention: F. H. Armstrong, *Toronto: The Place of Meeting* (Toronto, 1983); G. P. de T. Glazebrook, *The Story of Toronto* (Toronto, 1971); Peter Goheen, *Victorian Toronto, 1850-1900* (Chicago, 1970); Donald Kerr and Jacob Spelt, *The Changing Face of Toronto* (Toronto, 1965); Donald Masters, *The Rise of Toronto 1850-1890* (Toronto, 1947); Jesse Middleton, *The Municipality of Toronto, a History*, 3 vols. (Toronto, 1923); and Jacob Spelt, *Toronto* (Toronto, 1973). In addition, Percy Robinson, *Toronto during the French Regime 1715-1793* (Toronto, 1933, reprinted 1965), remains important for the pre-settlement era, while Edith Firth, *The Town of York, 1793-1834*, 2 vols. (Toronto, 1962 and 1966), is indispensable for the pre-city years. Still further, *The Dictionary of Canadian Biography* provides considerable biographical and related data on Toronto's development (Toronto, 1972-82).

Older books still of significance include: G. M. Adam, *Toronto Old and New* (Toronto, 1891, reprinted 1972); Edwin Guillet, *Toronto from Trading Post to Great City* (Toronto,1934); C. P. Mulvany, *Toronto: Past and Present* (Toronto, 1884, reprinted 1970); William Pearson, *Recollections of Toronto of Old* (Toronto, 1914); Henry Scadding, *Toronto of Old* (Toronto, 1873, abridgement by F. H. Armstrong, 1966); C. C. Taylor, *Toronto "Called Back" from 1886 to 1850* (Toronto, 6 editions 1886-97); and *The Illustrated Historical Atlas of the County of York* (Toronto, 1878, reprinted 1969). The closely illustrated series, *Landmarks of Toronto*, edited by John Ross Robertson in six volumes (Toronto, 1894-1914), is important both for its coverage of streets and structures and its historical accounts (not to be taken unquestioned).

Economic Growth and Metropolitan Development

Some works already referred to should again be named for this category: at least those of Firth, Goheen, Kerr and Spelt, and Masters. Also, Jacob Spelt's seminal study, *The Urban Development in South Central Ontario* (Assen, 1955, reprinted 1972), is important, while J. M. Gilmour, *Spatial Evolution of Manufacturing: Southern Ontario, 1851-1891* (Toronto, 1971), has background value. Other substantial background works are: George Nader, *Cities of Canada*, 2 vols. (Toronto, 1975-76); G. P. de T. Glazebrook, *History of Transportation in Canada* (Toronto, 1938, reprinted in 2 vols., 1964); Douglas McCalla, *The Upper Canada Trade, 1834-1872* (Toronto, 1979); T. Naylor, *The History of Canadian Business, 1867-1914*, 2 vols. (Toronto, 1975); and R. C. McIvor, *Canadian Monetary, Banking and Fiscal Development* (Toronto, 1982).

For closer examinations of business aspects see: T. W. Acheson, "York Commerce in the 1820's," *CHR* 50 (1969), and his "John Baldwin, Colonial Entrepreneur," *OH* 61 (1969); Douglas McCalla, "The Commercial Politics of the Toronto Board of Trade, 1850-1860," *CHR* 50 (1969); G. H. Stanford, *To Serve the Community: The Story of Toronto's Board of Trade* (Toronto, 1974), and *Annual Reports* of the Board; S. D. Clark, *The Canadian Manufacturers' Association* (Toronto, 1939); Victor Ross, *A History of the Canadian Bank of Commerce*, 2 vols. (Toronto, 1920-22); G. R. Stevens, *The Canada Permanent Story* (Toronto, 1955); Hugh Johnson, *A Merchant Prince: Life of the Hon. Senator John Macdonald* (Toronto, 1893); Mollie Gillen, *The Masseys, Founding Family* (Toronto, 1966); William Stephenson, *The Store that Timothy Built* (Toronto, 1965); and Michael Bliss, *A Canadian Millionaire: The Life and Business Times of Sir Joseph Flavelle, Bart., 1858-1939* (Toronto, 1978).

On land transport, see also: G. R. Stevens, *The Canadian National Railways*, vol. 1, *1836-1896*, vol. 2, *1896-1922* (Toronto, 1960 and 1962); T. D. Regehr, *The Canadian Northern Railway* (Toronto, 1976); R. D. Smith, "The Northern Railway, Its Origins and Construction, 1834-1855," *OH* 48 (1956); and R. M. Stamp, "J. D. Edgar and the Pacific Junction Railway," *OH* 55 (1963). Water transport offers less, the best source being scattered articles in *Inland Seas*, the quarterly of the Great Lakes Historical Society. On early industrial growth, the two-volume *History of Toronto and the County of York* (no author, Toronto, 1885) is useful for its accounts of major current city firms, as is J. Timperlake's *Illustrated Toronto, Past and Present* (Toronto, 1877). See also John MacNab, "Toronto's Industrial Growth to 1891," *OH* 47 (1955); and part 1 of Gregory Kealey, *Toronto Workers Respond to Industrial Capitalism, 1867-1892* (Toronto, 1980). The last named is obviously significant as well for labour and union development, as is Sally Zerker, *The Rise and Fall of the Toronto Typographical Union, 1832-1972* (Toronto, 1982).

Unpublished theses fill in gaps and add much to the urban economic record. They include: F. H. Armstrong, "Toronto in Transition: The Emergence of a City, 1828-1838" (Ph.D., Toronto, 1965); Barrie Dyster, "Toronto, 1840-1860: Making It in a British Protestant Town" (Ph.D., Toronto, 1970); and for later years, Brenda Newell, "From Cloth to Clothing: The Emergence of Department Stores in Late 19th Century Toronto" (M.A., Trent, 1983); T. W. Acheson, "The Social Origins of Canadian Industrialism" (Ph.D., Toronto, 1971); Francis Mellen, "The Development of the Toronto Waterfront in the Railway Expansion Era, 1850-1912" (Ph.D., Toronto, 1974). Census statistics, civic assessments, and banking, company and trade returns in sessional papers and the commercial press (or compiled in the *Canada Year Book* by the early twentieth century) provide other sources of economic data.

Population and Ethnicity

While minutes of York town meetings, assessment rolls and even poll books assist in reconstructing demographic profiles for the early Toronto community, the first very scanty Upper Canada census did not appear until

1824, the first, more substantial, decennial census not till 1842, and the first of much real value for Toronto only in 1851-52. Thereafter, the published decennial *Censuses of Canada* from 1861 down to 1921 still present difficulties through omissions, errors and recurrently altered categories, yet remain basic on the city's population to 1918. Other than this, assessment records, directories, or church and charity registers offer supplementing and modifying data, as do immigration reports, which grow fuller from about mid-century. Vital statistics, infirmity and morbidity returns do likewise; but transiency, in- and out-migration yet require extensive, computer study in regard to Toronto.

Early British or American immigration into the town and district are dealt with by Firth, Spelt (*Urban Development*) and Leo Johnson, "Land Policy, Population Growth and Social Structure," in J. K. Johnson, ed., *Historical Essays in Upper Canada* (Toronto, 1975). On subsequent British immigration and ethnicity, see Dyster, Masters, Goheen, and generally Norman Macdonald, *Canada, Immigration and Colonization: 1841-1903* (Toronto, 1966). For the mid-century Irish migration and its ethnic influences, see Murray Nicholson, "The Catholic Church and the Irish in Victorian Toronto" (Ph.D. thesis, Guelph, 1980); D. S. Shea, "The Irish Immigrant Adjustment to Toronto, 1840-1860," *Canadian Catholic Historical Association*, Study Sessions, 1972; and for the Ulster Protestant side, Dyster, the writings of Hereward Senior on Canadian Orangeism, and Cecil Houston and William Smyth, *The Sash Canada Wore* (Toronto, 1980). Other immigrant communities of the later nineteenth and earlier twentieth centuries are now receiving attention through the archival and publishing activities of the Multicultural History Society of Ontario (as in its journals, *Polyphony*); but see also "Immigrants in the City," studies of some of these elements in Toronto in *UHR* 78, no. 2 (1978). In addition, see Robert Harney and Harold Troper, *Immigrants: A Portrait of the Urban Experience, 1890-1930* (Toronto, 1975); Stephen Speisman, *The Jews of Toronto: A History to 1937* (Toronto, 1979); John Zucchi, "The Italians in Toronto, 1885-1930" (Ph.D., Toronto, 1983); and D. G. Hill, "Negroes in Toronto, 1793-1865," *OH* 55 (1963).

Social History

Social patterns in the urban collectivity are treated in Firth, Armstrong (thesis), Dyster, Goheen, Masters and Acheson (thesis). On the elite and established upper ranks more especially, see: David Gagan, *The Denison Family of Toronto, 1792-1925* (Toronto, 1973); David Flint, *John Strachan: Pastor and Politician* (Toronto, 1971); John Lownsborough, *The Privileged Few* (Boultons, Smiths and The Grange) (Toronto, 1980); R. Burns, "God's Chosen People: The Origins of Toronto Society, 1793-1818," Canadian Historical Association, *Historical Papers* (Ottawa, 1973); M. L. Smith, ed., *Young Mr. Smith in Upper Canada* (Toronto, 1980); Elizabeth Wallace, *Goldwin Smith,*

Victorian Liberal (Toronto, 1957); A. S. Thompson, *Spadina: A Story of Old Toronto* (Toronto, 1975), and *Jarvis Street* (Toronto, 1980); Lucy Martyn, *Aristocratic Toronto* (Toronto, 1978); Michael Bliss, *A Canadian Millionaire* (Flavelle) (Toronto, 1978); and Carlie Oreskovich, *Sir Henry Pellatt: The King of Casa Loma* (Toronto, 1982).

On contesting elements, working classes and the poor, see: E. J. Hathaway, *Jesse Ketchum and His Times* (Toronto, 1929); William Kilbourn, *The Firebrand* (William Lyon Mackenzie) (Toronto, 1956); Charles Clark, *Sixty Years in Upper Canada* (Toronto, 1908); J. M. S. Careless, *Brown of the Globe*, 2 vols. (Toronto, 1959 and 1963); Gregory Kealey, *Toronto's Workers* (listed above), and *The Working Class in Toronto at the Turn of the Century* (Toronto, 1973); Michael Piva, *The Condition of the Working Class in Toronto, 1900-1921* (Ottawa, 1979); Gene Homel, "James Simpson and the Origins of Canadian Social Democracy" (Ph.D., Toronto, 1978); Wayne Roberts, "Studies in the Toronto Labour Movement, 1896-1914" (Ph.D., Toronto, 1978); C. S. Clark, *Of Toronto the Good: A Social Study* (Montreal 1898, reprinted 1970); J. J. Kelso, *Can Slums Be Abolished?* (Toronto, 1907); and Susan Houston, "The Impetus to Reform: Crime, Poverty and Ignorance in Ontario, 1850-1875" (Ph.D., Toronto, 1974).

Further on social problems and social responses, see: James Jones, *Pioneer Crimes and Punishments in Toronto and the Home District* (Toronto, 1924); Lucy Brooking, "Prostitution in Toronto," in Ramsay Cook and Wendy Mitchinson, eds., *The Proper Sphere* (Toronto, 1976); Richard Splane, *Social Welfare in Ontario, 1791-1893* (Toronto, 1965); Stephen Speisman, "Munificent Parsons and Municipal Parsimony: Voluntary versus Public Poor Relief in 19th Century Toronto," *OH* 65 (1973); and generally, the published reports of welfare agencies in the city (chiefly from the 1860s), together with those of provincial inspectors (see sessional papers). Religious bodies, missions and related moral reform movements like temperance in Toronto offer a host of references, including Jean Burnet, "The Urban Community and Changing Moral Standards," in S. D. Clark, ed., *Urbanism and the Changing Canadian Society* (Toronto, 1961); Robertson's *Landmarks*, vol. 3, on city churches; T. C. Champion, *The Methodist Churches of Toronto* (Toronto, 1899); and denominational press, such as the Anglican *Church* or Roman Catholic *Mirror*.

Women's activities and roles in Toronto are at length receiving more treatment, but again one may only note as follows: Mary Innis, *The Clear Spirit* (Toronto, 1966); Catharine Cleverdon, *The Woman Suffrage Movement in Canada* (Toronto, 1950, reprinted 1974); Linda Kealey, *A Not Unreasonable Claim: Women and Reform in Canada, 1880-1920* (Toronto, 1979); and Linda Kealey et al, *Women at Work in Ontario, 1850-1930* (Toronto, 1974). For the city of the period, children's life, other than in "care" institutions or in the school system, still receives less emphasis, but broadly useful are Alison Prentice and Susan Houston, eds., *Family, School and Society in Nineteenth Century Canada* (Toronto, 1975); Neil Sutherland, *Children in English Canadian*

Society, 1880–1920 (Toronto, 1976); and Joy Parr, ed., *Childhood and Family in Canadian History* (Toronto, 1982), in which particularly see Susan Houston, "The 'Waifs and Strays' of a Victorian City."

The Built and Cultural Environments

The development of Toronto's urban landscape over the last century is well described in works on buildings, of which the most distinguished is Eric Arthur, *Toronto, No Mean City* (Toronto, 1964), an authoritative, if not faultless, architectural study, and superbly illustrated. Others of note are: William Dendy, *Lost Toronto* (Toronto, 1978); Charles De Volpi, *Toronto, a Pictorial Record, 1813–1882* (Montreal, 1965); Michael Filey, *A Toronto Album: Glimpses of a City That Was* (Toronto, 1970); Lucy Martyn, *Toronto, A Hundred Years of Grandeur: The Inside Story of Toronto's Great Homes* (Toronto, 1978), and *The Face of Early Toronto: An Architectural Record, 1797–1936* (Sutton West, 1982). The last-named reprints the Charles Goad insurance maps of Toronto, 1884, as a key to streets and structures covered; Goad atlases detailing individual buildings for insurance purposes (published in Toronto, e.g., for 1880, 1890, 1902, etc.) are of high value for tracing changes in the built environment.

The early town setting and associated lifestyles are dealt with in Firth; Armstrong (thesis); John André, *William Berczy, Co-Founder of Toronto* (Toronto, 1967); Eric Hounsom, *Toronto in 1810* (Toronto, 1970); and in Robertson's *Landmarks* or Scadding's *Toronto of Old*. Other older works that treat the Victorian cityscape include: G. M. Adam and J. Timperlake (both listed above); Alfred Sylvester, *Sketches of Toronto* (Toronto, 1858); H. F. Walling, ed., *Toronto in the Camera* (Toronto, 1868); and *Toronto Illustrated* (n.a., Toronto, 1893). The early twentieth-century street scene is well within the range of photographs, as witnessed in the excellent (and much used) James Collection at the City Archives. *Toronto of Today* (n.a., Toronto, 1913) might be added, along with Douglas Richardson, ed., *Beaux Arts Toronto* (Toronto, 1973). Useful, too, for ambience are James Lorimer, *The Ex: A Picture History of the Canadian National Exhibition* (Toronto, 1973); and G. P. de T. Glazebrook, *A Shopper's View of Canada's Past: Pages from Eaton's Catalogues, 1886–1930* (Toronto, 1969).

Land use, spatial development and housing patterns may be approached through Kerr and Spelt, *Changing Face of Toronto*, Goheen, *Victorian Toronto*, and Spelt, *Toronto* (each previously noted); through the Goad atlases, maps and plans at the major city repositories named; or through directories and assessment records. Much subsequent work is to be found in theses and research papers — for instance, Isobel Ganton, "Development between Parliament Street and the Don River, 1793–1884," and "Development of the Military Reserve, 1792–1862" (research papers, Toronto, 1974, 1975); G. H. K. Gad, "Toronto's Central Office Complex: Growth, Structure and Linkages" (Ph.D., Toronto, 1975); K. Campbell, "Residential Mobility in Toronto, 1880–1910" (M.A., Toronto, 1971), and Frances Mellen, "Development of the Toronto Waterfront" (cited above). See also, in Alan Artibise and Gilbert Stelter, ed., *The Usable Urban Past* (Toronto, 1979), Shirley Spragge, "A Confluence of Interests: Housing Reform in Toronto, 1900–1920," and Peter Moore, "Zoning and Planning: The Toronto Experience, 1904–1970."

For the cultural environment, a number of the foregoing treatments of the man-made physical setting are also applicable (e.g., Arthur, Dendy, Firth, Hounsom, Martyn), and some more-general sources deserve attention: Carl Klinck et al, *The Literary History of Canada*, vol. 1 (Toronto, 1976); Wilfred Kesterton, *A History of Journalism in Canada* (Toronto, 1967); Paul Rutherford, *A Victorian Authority: The Daily Press in Late Nineteenth-Century Canada* (Toronto, 1982); J. R. Harper, *Painting in Canada: A History* (Toronto, 1977); T. H. Levere and R. A. Jarrell, eds., *A Curious Field Book: Science and Society in Canadian History* (Toronto, 1974); W. B. Howell, *Medicine in Canada* (New York, 1933); and W. S. Wallace, *A History of the University of Toronto* (Toronto, 1927). On public schooling in Toronto, see particularly, H. M. Cochrane, ed., *Centennial Story: The Board of Education for the City of Toronto, 1850–1950* (Toronto, 1950); on library growth, Toronto Public Library, *75 Years of the Toronto Public Libraries: 53 Years as the Mechanics Institute* (Toronto, 1958); and on sports, S. F. Wise and Douglas Fisher, *Canada's Sporting Heroes* (Don Mills, 1974).

Urban Politics and Services

Early background for emerging municipal institutions lies in J. H. Aitcheson's old but important study, "The Development of Local Government in Upper Canada, 1793–1850" (Ph.D., Toronto, 1954). Middleton (cited above) provides material on civic affairs throughout, and for our late period, the publications of S. Morley Wickett — e.g., *Municipal Government in Canada* (Toronto, 1907) — remain significant. Firth, and the Armstrong and Dyster theses (all cited) span political aspects from pre-incorporation days down to the 1860s, while Eric Jarvis carries onward in "Mid-Victorian Toronto: A Social and Administrative History, 1857–1873" (Ph.D., Western Ontario, 1978). Then Desmond Morton, *Mayor Howland: The Citizens' Candidate* (Toronto, 1973), deals admirably with city politics in the 1880s; a topic brightly forwarded in Christopher Armstrong and H. V. Nelles, *The Revenge of the Methodist Bicycle Company: Sunday Streetcars and Municipal Reform in Toronto 1888–1897* (Toronto, 1977). Political concerns in the early twentieth-century city are traced in Gene Homel's thesis "James Simpson... Canadian Social Democracy" (cited), and in a number of valuable articles on current urban reform drives. These include: Paul Rutherford, "Tomorrow's Metropolis: The Urban Reform Movement in Canada, 1880–1920," and "Tomorrow's Metropolis Revisited" by J. C. Weaver, both in Gilbert Stelter and Alan Artibise, *The Canadian City* (Toronto, 1977); and further by Weaver: "The Meaning of Municipal Reform: Toronto 1895," *OH* 66 (1974), and "The Modern City Realized: Toronto Civic Affairs, 1880–1915," in Artibise and Stelter, *The Usable Urban Past* (Toronto, 1979).

Apart from Howland's, Toronto mayoralties have not received much specific study, but Victor Russell, *Mayors of Toronto, 1834–1899* (Erin, Ont., 1982), gives brief accounts of their regimes. A successor volume is in preparation. *The Dictionary of Canadian Biography* is helpful, too. On territorial annexations and ward divisions, the Toronto City Archives provide maps and documents, such as the "Growth and Development of the Wards of the City of Toronto," or *Statutes Specially Relating to the City of Toronto* (Toronto, 1894). On issues raised by urban expansion and congestion, see Gene Homel, "Business, Labour and the Reform of Housing and Street Railways in Toronto, 1900–1914," paper presented at Canadian Historical Association annual meeting, 1980; and see also Toronto Housing Company, *Better Housing in Canada* (Toronto, 1913); Bureau of Municipal Research, *What Is the Ward Going to Do with Toronto?* (Toronto, 1918). On streetcar service, the following are suggested: L. H. Pursley, *Street Railways of Toronto, 1861–1921* (Los Angeles, 1958); Toronto Transit Commission, *Transit in Toronto, 1849–1967* (Toronto, 1973, reprinted 1982); Michael Doucet, "Mass Transport and the Failure of Private Ownership: The Case of Toronto," *UHR* 77, no. 3 (1978); and Donald Davis, "Mass Transit and Private Ownership: An Alternative Perspective on the Case of Toronto," *UHR* 78, no. 3 (1979). For water service and views on public or private operation, see Elwood Jones and Douglas McCalla, "Toronto Waterworks, 1840–1877: Continuity and Change in Nineteenth-Century Toronto Politics," *CHR* 60 (1979). On fires and fire service see F. H. Armstrong, "The First Great Fire of Toronto, 1849," *OH* 53 (1961), and "The Second Great Fire of Toronto, 1904," *OH* 70 (1978).

Municipal finance over the period is still largely under research. The development of a civic electrical utility is presented in E. M. Ashworth, *Toronto Hydro Recollections* (Toronto, 1955). Urban roads are a topic for Toronto City Archives records; dock and waterfront supervision for the Archives of the Harbour Commission. Matters of public health and hospitals are treated in two major theses: Heather MacDougall, "Health Is Wealth: Development of Public Health Activity in Toronto 1834–1890" (Ph.D., Toronto, 1981); and Paul Bator, "Saving Lives on the Wholesale Plan: Public Health Reform in the City of Toronto, 1900–1930" (Ph.D., Toronto, 1979). These are also better than most books, so far, dealing with hospitals; but one may name Charles Clarke, *A History of the Toronto General Hospital* (Toronto, 1913). On social services of an increasing public character, see James Pitsula, "The Emergence of Social Work in Toronto," *Journal of Canadian Studies* 4, no. 1 (1979); also his thesis, "The Relief of Poverty in Toronto, 1880–1930" (Ph.D., York, 1979). Note as well, Andrew Jones and Leonard Rutman, *In the Children's Aid: J. J. Kelso and Child Welfare in Ontario* (Toronto, 1981). On police and the tending of public peace and property,

much remains in primary documents, but one may mention G. T. Denison's *Recollections of a Police Magistrate* (Toronto, 1920), an anecdotal yet revealing memoir by a Proper Torontonian of the period, at times prejudiced or dogmatic, but conveying also a concern with responsibility and rectitude that many would still ascribe to the Victorian and post-Victorian city.

Index

Abell, John, 112
Act of Union (1841), 62
Adelaide Street, 86, 89
Albany Club, 128
"Algonquin School," 173
Allan, George William, 96, 97, 101, 107
Allan, William, 31, 33, 35, 50, 96
Allan family, 124
Allan Gardens, 97, 183
American Civil War, 104
American Federation of Labor, 169
American immigrants, 25, 73, 76
American Revolution, 10-11
Ames, Alfred Ernest, 118, 152, 154
Anglicanism, 30, 39, 73, 128
Annex, 124, 138, 161, 179
Architectural styles, 27, 86, 89, 133, 175, 179
Argonaut Club, 141
Armouries, 194
Art Gallery of Toronto, 172, 173
Ashbridges Bay, 124, 144
Associated Charities, 172
Association for the Promotion of Canadian
    Industry, 111
Austin, James, 96, 117
Avenue Road, 89, 161, 179

Bain, James, 172
Baldwin, Robert, 51, 54, 60, 62, 73, 96
Baldwin, William Warren, 29, 38, 41, 50, 51, 56, 60
Balmy Beach, 161
Bank of British Columbia, 150
Bank of British North America, 50, 64
Bank of Commerce, 86, 117, 118, 150, 152, 154,
    194
Banking Act (1871), 117
Bank of Montreal, 46, 83, 96, 118, 150, 194

Bank of Montreal building (Front and Yonge), 136
Bank of Nova Scotia, 150
Bank of the People, 50
Bank of Toronto, 81, 117, 150
Bank of Toronto building, 175
Bank of Upper Canada, 35, 46, 50, 56, 59, 83, 150
Barry, Thomas, 25
Bathurst Street, 54, 89
Battle of Ridgeway, 104
Bay of Quinte, 11, 25
Bay Street, 97
Beaty, James, 111, 130
Bedford Estate, 161
Bell Electric Light Company, 112
Bengough, J.S., 139
Berczy, William, 21, 23, 27, 29
Berkeley Street, 21
Berthon, George Thomas, 107
Bethune, Donald, 64
Bishop Strachan School, 163, 194
Black immigrants, 74, 76
Blake, Edward, 124, 138
Bloor, Joseph, 56
Bloor Street, 21, 54, 56, 94, 96, 97
Bloor Street Church, 166
Board of Control, 190
Board of Health, 59, 71, 73
Board of Police Commissioners, 100
Board of Trade, 64, 81, 83, 86, 102, 111, 112, 115,
    128, 154, 155, 193
Board of Trade building (1889), 136
Borden, Robert, 193
Boswell, A.R., 143
Boulton, D'Arcy, 38
Boulton, Henry John, 54, 56
Boulton, William Henry, 64, 67, 73, 101, 124
Boulton family, 29, 96, 124

Bowes, John George, 102
Boys' Home, 100, 145
Bracondale, 161
Branksome Hall, 163
Brantford, 83
British Amalgamated Society of Engineers, 77
British American Fire and Life Assurance
    Company, 48, 50
British immigrants, 64, 73, 76
Brock, Isaac, 31
Brockton, 124
Brown, George, 67, 74, 77, 102, 104, 111, 128, 130
Brulé, Étienne, 9
Buchanan, Isaac, 46, 50, 102
Buildings and landmarks. *See* under Toronto
Built environment and urban landscape. *See* under
    Toronto
Bystander, 139

Cabbagetown, 96
Calgary, 117
Campbell, William, 38
Canada Cycle and Motor Company (CCM), 152
Canada First Movement, 104, 107, 138, 139
Canada Life Assurance Company, 150, 152
Canada Permanent Building and Savings Society,
    81
Canada Permanent Mortgage Corporation, 118
Canadian Correspondent, 51
Canadian Freeman, 39, 41, 51
Canadian Institute, 107, 128
Canadian Manufacturers' Association, 154, 193
Canadian Monthly, 139
Canadian Northern Railway, 152, 155, 194
Canadian Pacific Railway, 81, 112, 115, 118, 155
Canadian Pacific Railway Building, 175
Canniff, William, 145

Capreol, Frederick, 81
Carlton Street, 97
Caroline (Sherbourne) Street, 54
Cartier, George Étienne, 102
Casa Loma, 163, 179
Castle Frank, 21
Catholicism. *See* Roman Catholicism
Cawthra, Joseph, 33, 56
Cawthra family, 163
Censuses:
  1851, 73
  1871, 76
  1911, 157, 158, 161
Central Canada Savings and Loan Company, 152
Central Technical School, 169
Champlain Society, 172
Chewett, J.G., 81
Chewett, William, 27, 29
Chewett Block, 89
Chicago, 81, 117
Chicago Exhibition (1893), 175
Children's Aid Society, 187, 190
Cholera epidemics, 51, 59, 73
Christian Guardian, 51
Christie Brown Ltd., 112
Church, Tommy, 194
Church Street, 54, 64, 86, 89, 97
City Hall, 54, 64, 136
City and Suburbs Act (1912), 193
City Surveyor's Office, 193
Civic Car Lines, 183
Civic Improvement Committee, 193
Clark, C.S., 172
Clarke, E.F. (Ned), 133, 143
Cobourg, 89
Colborne, John, 56
College (University) Avenue, 56, 64, 84, 96, 97
Collins, Francis, 39, 51
Colonial Advocate, 41, 50, 51
Commercial Bank of Kingston, 50
Commercial growth. *See* under Toronto
Confederation, 104, 107
Confederation Life, 118, 150, 152
Confederation Life Building, 136
Conservatism, 41, 51, 54, 58, 59, 60, 64, 67, 102, 133, 141, 143
Consumers' Gas Company, 101

Copp Clark publishing company, 111, 139
Courier, 51
Cox, Edward, 152
Cox, Frederick, 152
Cox, George Albertus, 117, 150, 152
Cox, Herbert, 152
Credit Valley, 118
Croft, H.H., 107
Crystal Palace, 96
Cultural life. *See* under Toronto
Cumberland, Frederic W., 81, 86, 89

Dalton, Thomas, 51
Danforth Avenue, 161, 179
Darling, Frank, 136
Darling and Pearson (architect firm), 175, 187
Davies, William, 109
Deer Park estate, 161
Demographic changes. *See* under Toronto
Denison, Flora McDonald, 166
Denison, George T., 58, 138, 139, 147
Denison family, 30, 96, 163
Dickens, Charles, 64
Doel, John, 58
Dominion Bank, 117, 150
Dominion Securities, 152
Don Jail, 96
Don River, 13, 21, 27, 38, 96
Don Viaduct, 179
Dorchester, Lord, 11, 19, 21, 23
Dovercourt, 161
Draper, William, 39, 50, 59, 67
Dufferin Street, 54
Duggan, George, 41
Duke Street, 21
Dundas Street, 25
Durham, Lord, 62
Durham County, 77
Durham Report (1839), 62, 67

Earlscourt, 161
East Toronto, 161
Eastern Gap, 120
Eastern Townships Bank, 150
Eaton, John Craig, 154, 193
Eaton, Timothy, 115, 117, 154
Eaton family, 128, 163, 187

Eaton's department store, 136, 154
Eaton's catalogue, 117
Education. *See* under Toronto
Eglinton Avenue, 60
Electric Development Company, 155
Elite class, 27, 29, 30, 41, 81, 124, 128, 133, 138, 152, 158, 161, 163, 172
Empire, 139
Erie Canal, 48, 69, 76, 81, 83, 120
Esplanade, 94, 96, 102
Ethnic composition. *See* under Toronto
Evening Telegram, 139
Examiner, 62
Exhibition Grounds, 97, 112, 138, 194
Exhibitions. *See* under Toronto
Expansion and annexation. *See* under Toronto

Falconer, Robert, 172
Family Compact, 35, 39, 41, 48, 50, 51, 60, 62, 67
Farmers Bank, 50
Fenian raids, 104
Financial growth. *See* under Toronto
Fires, 1849, 97; 1904, 183
First World War, 194, 198
FitzGibbon, James, 60
Flavelle, Joseph, 152, 154, 172, 175, 179, 187, 198
Fleming, Robert, 193
Fleming, Sandford, 81, 96, 107
Fort Niagara. *See* Niagara
Fort Rouillé, 10
Foster, William, 138
Fraser, John, 139
Freehold Loan and Savings, 118
Front Street, 21, 35, 56, 77, 89, 94, 97
Fugitive Slave Law, 74
Furniss, Albert, 64

Gage publishing company, 139
Garrison centre, 19, 21, 23, 24, 27
Garrison Creek, 21, 27, 56, 96
Garrison Reserve, 94, 112
General Hospital, 51, 73, 89, 96, 166, 187, 193, 194
George Street, 21, 86
Gerrard Street, 89, 179
Gibraltar Point, 21, 25
Girls' Home, 100, 145

Globe, 67, 77, 101, 102, 104, 107, 111, 130, 139, 175
Glockling, Robert, 169
Good, James, 83
Gooderham, George, 150
Gooderham, William, 48, 81, 109, 111, 112, 117, 118, 139, 150
Gooderham distillery, 83, 109, 111, 112
Gooderham family, 128, 163, 187
Gore, Francis, 29, 31
Gouinlock, F.M., 136
Gould Street, 86
Government House, 56, 89, 97
Grand Opera House, 133, 136, 141, 173
Grand Trunk Pacific Railway, 152, 155
Grand Trunk Railway (GTR), 77, 81, 83, 86, 94, 102, 118
The Grange, 38, 173
Grasett, George, 73
Great Western Railway (GWR), 77, 81, 94, 118
Grip, 139
Group of Seven, 173
Guild of Civic Art, 190, 193
Gurnett, George, 51, 58, 59, 64, 73
Gurney stove foundry, 111
Gzowski, Casimir, 81, 83, 89, 94

Halifax, 19
Halifax Banking Company, 150
Hallam, John, 139
Hamilton, 46, 77, 81, 83
Hanlan, Ned, 141
Hanlan's Point, 175
Harbour, 13, 35, 48, 64, 86, 94, 120, 155
Harris, Lawren, 173
Hart House, 172
Hastings, Charles, 179, 187
Havergal school, 163
Hay, William, 89
Head, Francis Bond, 59, 60
Heintzman, Theodore, 111
Hewitt, John, 130
High Park, 147
Hincks, Francis, 46, 50, 62, 86, 102
"Hogtown," 109
Holland House, 56
Holland Landing, 43, 46

Holland River, 9, 21
Holman, George, 107
Holwood House, 179
Holy Trinity Church, 64
Home District Mutual Fire Insurance Company, 50
Hopkins, Castell, 172
Horticultural Society of Canada, 97
Hospital for Sick Children, 145, 175
House of Industry, 59, 100, 145, 187
House of Providence, 100, 145
Housing Commission, 179
Howard, John, 54, 58, 64, 100, 147
Howland, H.S., 86, 115, 117, 118
Howland, W.H., 115, 143, 144, 145, 147
Howland family, 128
Hudson's Bay Company, 46, 77
Humber River, 9, 10, 11, 13, 21, 38
Hunter, Peter, 27, 29
Hunter Rose publishing company, 139
Huron Indians, 9

Immigration, 25, 29, 33, 39, 43, 51, 62, 64, 67, 71, 73-74, 76, 120, 149, 157, 194
Imperial Bank, 117, 150
Imperial Life, 152
Imperial Munitions Board, 198
Import and export trade. *See* under Toronto
Industrial Exhibition, 112, 117, 133
Industrial growth. *See* under Toronto
Inglis, John, 112
Intercolonial Railway, 111
Irish immigrants, 71, 73, 74, 76
Iron Moulders, 77
Iroquois Confederacy, 9

Jackson, A.Y., 173
Jacques and Hay furniture company, 109
Jarvis, William, 27, 29, 30, 51, 54, 56, 60, 73
Jarvis family, 96, 124, 163
Jarvis Street, 35, 89, 97, 179
Jefferys, Charles, 141, 173
Jubilee Riots, 122, 147

Kane, Paul, 107
Kauffman, William, 89
Kelso, J.J., 187, 190

Ketchum, Jesse, 30, 33, 41, 53
King Edward Hotel, 175
King's College, 56, 64, 89
Kingston, 11, 19, 21, 23, 25, 29, 31, 35, 43, 62, 69, 77, 83, 89
Kingston Road, 38, 183
King Street, 21, 35, 38, 54, 58, 59, 64, 86, 89, 94, 97, 104, 107, 112, 115
Knights of Labor, 130, 133, 143
Knox College, 136, 139

Labour force, 109, 111, 122, 154
Labour Temple, 169
Lachine Canal, 48
Laidlaw, George, 118
Lake Erie, 11
Lake Huron, 9
Lake Iroquois, 13
Lake Ontario, 9
Lake Ontario-St. Lawrence transport system, 15
Lake Simcoe, 9, 13, 21
Lane, Henry, 64
Langley, Henry, 133
Lash, Zebulon, 152, 187, 193
Laurier, Wilfrid, 193
Lawrence Park, 161
Law Society of Upper Canada, 56, 89
Leader, 102, 107, 111, 130, 139
Lennon, E.J., 136, 175, 179
Lesslie, James, 39, 41, 50, 58, 60
Liberalism, 77, 102, 104
Lind, Jenny, 86
Lismer, Arthur, 173
Literary and Philosophical Society, 58
Little Trinity Church, 64
Lombard Street, 58
London (Ontario), 19, 81, 83
Lot (Queen) Street, 21, 27, 54, 56
Loudon, James, 172
Lount, Samuel, 60
Loyalists, 11, 25, 29
Lyle, John P., 175

Macallum, A.B., 172
McCaul, John, 107
Macaulay, James, 29
Macaulaytown, 29, 56, 94, 96, 136, 138

MacDonald, J.E.H., 173
Macdonald, John, 81, 86, 89, 102, 115
Macdonald, John A., 102, 130
Mackay, Gordon, 111, 115
Mackenzie, William, 152, 154, 183
Mackenzie, William Lyon, 41, 50-51, 53, 54, 58-59, 60
Maclean's Magazine, 175
McLennan, John, 172
McMaster, A.R., 111, 115
McMaster, Mrs. Samuel, 145
McMaster, William, 67, 86, 89, 117, 118, 139
McMaster family, 128
McMaster Hall, 139
McMurrich, John, 111
McMurrich family, 128
Macpherson, D.L., 83
Mail, 139
Mail and Empire, 175
Maitland, Peregrine, 35
Mann, Donald, 152, 155
Mann, Gother, 11, 96
Manning, Alexander, 143
Manning Arcade, 136
Manufacturers Life, 118, 152
Martin, Clara Brett, 166
Martin, T. Mower, 139, 141
Massey, Hart, 112, 141
Massey family, 128, 152, 163, 187
Massey Hall, 141
Massey-Harris, 112
Masonic Hall, 35, 58, 89
Matthews, Peter, 60
Mavor, James, 172
Mechanics Institute, 58, 86, 89, 128, 139
Medcalf, Francis, 102
Medical College for Women, 166
Mendelssohn Choir, 141, 173
Methodism, 25, 30, 39, 41, 73
Methodist Publishing Company, 139
Metropolitan Church, 133, 166
Metropolitan development, 17
Middle class, 39, 58, 128, 133, 138, 158, 163, 166
Midway, 161
Mirror, 86
Mississauga Indians, 9, 11
Monetary Times, 107

Monro, George, 58, 59, 64
Montgomery's Tavern, 60
Montreal, 15, 17, 46, 69, 77, 81, 83, 89, 94, 115, 117, 118, 149
Moore Park, 161, 179
Morang, G.N., 172
Morrison, T.D., 51, 53, 58, 59, 60
Moss Park, 96, 97
Mowat, Oliver, 128
Municipal and social services. *See* under Toronto
Music Hall, 107

Nation, 138
National Club, 128
National Policy, 112, 141, 193
National Transcontinental Railway, 155
National Trust, 152
Necropolis, 96
Nesbitt, Beatty, 193
New (Jarvis) Street, 35
New York City, 81, 83, 100, 117
News, 139, 175
Newspapers, 30, 39, 41, 50-51, 139, 173, 175
Niagara, 10, 21, 23, 25, 43, 46
Niagara Peninsula, 11
Niagara River, 77
Nicholls, Frederic, 152, 155
Nickinson, John, 107
Nine Hours Movement, 130
Normal School, 86
North American Hotel, 54, 56
North American Life, 152
Northern Railway, 77, 81, 83, 86, 94, 102, 118
North Toronto, 161, 179
North West Campaign, 102, 104
North West Company, 10, 11, 46
North West Rebellion, 122

O'Brien, Lucius, 139
O'Donoghue, Daniel, 133
O'Grady, William, 51
Oliver, Joseph, 193
Ontario Bolt Company, 112
Ontario Hydro-Electric Power Commission, 155
Ontario, Simcoe and Huron Railway. *See* Northern Railway
Ontario Society of Artists (OSA), 139, 141

Ontario Workman, 130
Orange-Green clashes, 73, 76, 100, 120
Orange Order, 41, 64, 67, 73, 100, 102, 122
Orphans' Home and Female Aid Society, 100
Osgoode Hall, 56, 89, 107
Osler, Edmund Boyd, 118, 150, 152, 163, 187
Ottawa, 89
Ottawa Valley, 83
Owen Sound, 115, 118

Pacific Scandal, 118
Palace Street, 35
Parkdale, 124, 138, 179
Parliament Buildings, 89, 97, 104, 136
Parliament Street, 54, 96, 101
Patriot, 51, 86
Patti, Adelina, 86
Pellatt, Henry, 118, 152, 155, 163
Peter Street, 27, 101
Pike, Zebulon, 31
Planning and development, 27, 94, 96
Politics and government. *See* under Toronto
Polson Iron Works, 112, 115
Population changes. *See* under Toronto
Post office, 136
Powell, John, 60, 64
Powell, William Dummer, 27
Power, Michael, 73
Presbyterianism, 39, 41, 73
Press, 30, 39, 41, 50-51, 139, 173, 175
Prince, William, 100
Princess Theatre, 173
Prohibition, 194
Protestantism, 41, 73, 74
Province of Ontario, 104
Provincial Asylum, 64, 96
Provincial capital, 21, 23, 62, 89, 104
Public health. *See* under Toronto
Public Library, 58, 139
Public market, 27, 35
Public School Board, 101

Quality of life, 31, 97, 147, 187
Quebec City, 19, 77, 89
Queen's Hotel, 89, 133
Queen's Own Rifles, 163
Queen's Park, 97, 104

Queen's Plate, 141
Queen's Rangers, 19, 21, 29
Queen Street, 21, 64, 89, 94, 96, 97, 115, 117, 138, 161. *See also* Lot Street
Queen's Wharf, 86

Railway system, 71, 77, 81, 83, 94, 118-20, 155
Rebellion of 1837, 59, 60, 62
Reciprocity Treaty, 76, 83, 104
Red Lion Hotel, 94
Red River Rising, 122
Reform movements, 50, 51, 53, 54, 58, 59, 60, 62, 64, 101-102, 143, 144, 190
Religious census, 73, 76
Religious composition and differences. *See* under Toronto
Residential building and districts. *See* under Toronto
Richardson, Hugh, 48, 64, 86, 136
Richmond Street, 64
Ridout, George Percival, 46, 50, 54
Ridout, Joseph, 46
Ridout, Thomas, 27, 29, 30, 86
Ridout family, 124, 163
Riel, Louis, 122
Riverdale, 124, 179
Riverdale Park, 147
Robertson, John Ross, 139, 145, 175, 190
Robinson, Christopher, 29
Robinson, John Beverley, 29, 32-33, 35, 41, 51, 56, 67, 73
Robinson, John Beverley, Jr., 101, 102
Robinson family, 96, 124
Rogers, Elias, 120, 143
Rolph, John, 53, 54, 60, 107
Roman Catholicism, 41, 73, 74, 122
Rosedale, 56, 96, 124, 138, 161, 179
Rossin House, 89
Rousseau, Jean Baptiste, 10, 11, 19, 25
Royal Alexandra Theatre, 173
Royal Canadian Academy, 139, 141
Royal Canadian Yacht Club, 128, 163
Royal Conservatory of Music, 141
Royal Lyceum, 107, 141
Royal Ontario Museum, 172, 175
Royal York Hotel, 89
Russell, Elizabeth, 29, 31

Russell, Peter, 27, 29, 96
Russell, William, 97
Ryerson, Egerton, 86, 89, 101, 128

Sabbatarianism, 183
St. Alban's Church, 166
St. Alban's Ward, 124
St. Andrew's Presbyterian Church, 54, 136, 166
St. Andrew's Ward, 94
St. Clair Avenue, 13, 161
St. David's Ward, 94
St. George, Laurent Quetton de, 25, 33, 35
St. George Street, 138
St. George's Ward, 94
St. James's Cathedral, 54, 86, 96, 166
St. James's Ward, 94
St. John's Ward, 94, 138
St. Lawrence Hall, 86
St. Lawrence Market, 86, 94
St. Lawrence's Ward, 94
St. Mark's Ward, 124
St. Matthew's Ward, 124
St. Michael's Cathedral, 64, 166
St. Michael's College, 89, 139
St. Michael's Hospital, 145
St. Patrick's Ward, 94
St. Paul's Church, 41, 166
St. Paul's Ward, 124
St. Stephen's Ward, 122
St. Thomas (Ontario), 118
St. Thomas's Ward, 94
Salvation Army, 147, 172
Sarnia (Ontario), 77, 81
Saturday Night, 175
Scadding, Henry, 139
Scarborough, 11, 179
Scarborough Beach, 183
Scarborough Bluffs, 13
School of Practical Science, 139, 172
Schreiber, Charlotte, 141
Seaton Village, 124
Seneca Indians, 9, 10
Sheard, Charles, 145
Shea's Vaudeville, 173
Sherbourne Street, 54, 96
Sherbourne Street Church, 128, 166
Sherwood, Henry, 64

Shore Plain area, 13, 21, 54, 94
Simcoe, Elizabeth, 19, 31
Simcoe, John Graves, 11, 19, 21, 23, 24, 27, 29, 31, 43
Simcoe County, 77
Simpson, James, 169, 172, 183
Simpson, Robert, 115, 117
Simpson's catalogue, 117
Simpson's department store, 136, 154
Site and development of Toronto. *See* under Toronto
Skinner, Isaiah, 21
Small, James, 51, 54
Small, John, 29
Smith, A.M., 102
Smith, Frank, 128, 133
Smith, Goldwin, 124, 138, 139, 147, 163, 173
Smith, Larratt, 69, 71
Snively, Mary, 166
Social life. *See* under Toronto
Society of Artists and Amateurs, 58
Society for the Relief of Strangers, 39
Spadina Avenue, 56, 96
Spadina House, 96
Sports and popular culture. *See* under Toronto
Standard Stock and Mining Exchange, 149
Stanley Barracks, 96
Star, 139, 175
Storm, W.G., 86, 89
Stowe, Emily (Jennings), 166
Stowe-Gullen, Augusta, 166
Strachan, John, 29, 31, 33, 35, 38, 41, 56, 67, 73, 89
Streetcars, 138, 143, 147, 183
Sullivan, Robert Baldwin, 59
Sunnyside, 124, 183
Swansea, 161

Taylor safe works, 111
Teiaiagon, 9
Telegram, 139, 175
Temiskaming and Northern Ontario Railway (TNO), 155
Temple Building, 136
"Ten Thousand Pounds Job" scandal, 102
Theatre Royal, 58
Thomas, William, 64, 86, 96
Thompson, Phillips, 133, 169

Thompson, Thomas, 115
Thomson, Poulett, 62
Thomson, Tom, 173
Toronto:
  architectural styles, 27, 86, 89, 133, 136, 175, 179
  Board of Control, 190
  Board of Health, 59, 71, 73
  Board of Police Commissioners, 100
  Board of Trade, 64, 81, 83, 86, 102, 111, 112, 115, 128, 154, 155, 193
  buildings and landmarks, 27, 35, 38, 54, 56, 64, 86, 96, 133, 136, 175, 179
  built environment and urban landscape, 27, 35, 38, 39, 54, 56, 64, 76, 89, 94, 96, 133, 138, 149, 175, 179
  census, 73, 76, 157, 158, 161
  commercial growth, 17, 24, 25, 27, 33, 34, 43, 46, 48, 62, 64, 67, 69, 76, 81, 104, 115, 117, 154, 194
  Conservatism, 51, 54, 58, 59, 60, 64, 67, 102, 133, 141, 143
  cultural life, 17, 29, 30, 56, 58, 104, 107, 138-39, 141, 172-73
  demographic changes, 73, 76, 120, 122, 158, 161
  education, 30, 56, 58, 89, 100-1, 133, 139, 141, 166, 169
  elite class, 27, 29, 30, 41, 81, 124, 128, 133, 138, 152, 158, 161, 163, 172
  ethnic composition, 29, 30, 73, 74, 76, 157-58
  Exhibitions, 112, 117, 133, 136, 138, 190
  expansion and annexation, 25, 56, 94, 96, 109, 120, 122, 124, 138, 149, 161, 179
  financial growth, 17, 35, 48, 50, 62, 77, 83, 86, 117-18, 149-50, 152, 194
  garrison centre, 19, 21, 23, 24, 27
  General Hospital, 51, 73, 89, 96, 166, 187, 193, 194
  harbour, 13, 35, 48, 64, 86, 94, 120, 155
  immigration, 25, 29, 33, 39, 43, 51, 62, 64, 67, 71, 73-74, 76, 120, 149, 157, 194
  import and export trade, 33, 35, 48, 69, 76, 81, 83, 104, 111, 112, 115, 149
  incorporation act, 54
  industrial growth, 17, 46, 48, 81, 109, 111, 112, 115, 120, 149, 154, 194, 198
  labour force, 109, 111, 122, 154

Liberalism, 77, 102, 104
middle class, 39, 58, 128, 133, 138, 158, 163, 166
municipal and social services, 53-54, 59, 64, 73, 100, 101, 144, 145, 147, 154, 185, 187, 190
planning and development, 27, 94, 96
politics and government, 27, 29, 30-31, 41, 53, 54, 58-59, 60, 62, 64, 67, 101-2, 104, 141, 143, 190, 193
population changes, 24, 39, 43, 54, 73, 76, 109, 120, 122, 149, 158, 161
press, 30, 39, 41, 50-51, 139, 173, 175
provincial capital, 21, 23, 62, 89, 104
public health, 51, 59, 71, 73, 101, 144-45, 187
public market, 27, 35
public space, 97, 147
quality of life, 31, 97, 147, 187
Rebellion of 1837, 59, 60, 62
Reform movements, 50, 51, 53, 54, 58, 59, 60, 62, 64, 101-2, 143, 144, 190
religious composition and differences, 30, 39, 41, 73, 74, 76, 100, 120, 122
residential building and districts, 35, 76, 89, 94, 96, 133, 138, 179
site and settlement, 9-11, 13, 15, 19, 21, 27
social life, 17, 27, 29, 31, 128, 172
sports and popular culture, 141, 175
streetcar service, 138, 143, 147, 183
suffrage movement, 166
technological change, 109, 136, 155
trade unionism, 58, 77, 130, 133, 169
transportation and traffic, 15, 17, 25, 43, 46, 48, 62, 64, 69, 76, 77, 81, 83, 86, 94, 109, 118, 120, 138, 155, 179, 183, 194
urban economy, 24-25, 27, 33, 35, 76-77, 109, 111, 149, 194
utilities, 101, 144, 154, 185, 187
War of 1812, 31-33
working class, 89, 94, 128, 130, 133, 138, 158, 166, 169
Toronto Anti-Slavery Society, 74, 86
Toronto Art Students League, 141
Toronto Bay, 13, 24, 77, 101
Toronto Choral Society, 141
Toronto Club, 128
Toronto Cricket Club, 128
Toronto Destitute Widow and Orphan's Society, 73

"Toronto Eighteen," 193
Toronto Electric Light Company, 112
Toronto Employers' Association, 169
Toronto General Trust, 118
Toronto Golf Club, 128
"Toronto the Good," 122
Toronto, Grey and Bruce Railway, 118
Toronto Harbour Commission, 155
Toronto Harbour Trust, 86, 120
Toronto Housing Company, 179
Toronto Hydro-Electric System, 155
Toronto Island, 13, 97, 120
Toronto Lawn Tennis Club, 128
Toronto Light Company, 147
Toronto Mower and Reaper Company, 112
Toronto and Nipissing Railway, 118
Toronto Passage, 10, 11, 15, 43, 77, 104
Toronto Philharmonic Society, 141
Toronto Railway Company (TRC), 147, 152, 183
Toronto Relief Society, 147
Toronto Rolling Mills, 83, 109
Toronto School of Medicine, 107
Toronto Stock Exchange, 81, 118, 149
Toronto Street Railway Company, 133, 143
Toronto Symphony Orchestra, 173
Toronto Trades Assembly (TTA), 130
Toronto Trail, 9, 10, 21
Torrington, F.H., 141
Trades and Labour Congress (TLC), 130, 169
Trade unionism, 58, 77, 130, 133, 169
Transportation and traffic. See under Toronto
Trinity College, 89, 96, 107, 172
Tully, Kivas, 89
Typhus epidemic, 71, 73
Typographical Union, 130

Underground Railroad, 74
Union Station, 133, 175, 194
University Avenue, 193. See also College Avenue
University College, 89
University of Toronto, 89, 97, 107, 139, 166, 172, 193
Upper Canada, 11, 17, 23, 24, 25, 33, 62
Upper Canada College (UCC), 56, 58, 97, 139, 163
Upper Canada Gazette, 30, 51
Upper class. See Elite class
Urban development. See Planning and development

Urban economy. *See* under Toronto
Urban planning. *See* Planning and development
Utilities, 101, 144, 154, 185, 187

Vancouver, 149
Van Horne, William, 152
Varley, Frederick, 173
Verner, Frederick, 107, 139
Victoria College, 89, 107, 136, 139

Walker, Byron Edmund, 117, 150, 152, 163, 172,
    173, 187, 193
The Ward, 157, 172, 193
Ward system, 94, 124
Ward Three, 193
War of 1812, 31-32, 33, 43, 46
Water Works Commission, 144
Week, 139
Welland Canal, 48, 120
Wellington Street, 97
Western Channel, 120
West Toronto, 161
White, W.T., 193
Whitney government, 193
Wickett, S. Morley, 190
Willcocks, William, 30
Williams, J.S., 130
Willison, John, 175
Wilson, Adam, 102
Wilson, Daniel, 124, 128
Windsor (Ontario), 81
Winnipeg, 117, 149
Winter Garden, 173
Withrow, J.J., 143
Women's Christian Temperance Union, 166
Women's Enfranchisement Association, 166
Wood, Alexander, 25, 29, 30, 33, 35
Wood, E.R., 152, 193
Woodbine racetrack, 138, 141
Woodstock (Ontario), 81
Woodsworth, J.S., 157
Working class, 89, 94, 128, 130, 133, 138, 158, 166,
    169
World, 139, 175, 190
Worts, James, 48, 81, 109, 111, 112
Worts family, 128
Wrong, G.M., 172

Wychwood, 161
Wycliffe College, 139

YMCA, 139
Yonge Street, 21, 25, 43, 46, 48, 56, 59, 60, 64, 94,
    96, 97, 147. *See also* Toronto Trail
York. *See* Toronto
York Street, 89
Yorkville, 56, 94, 124, 138, 161